Essays on Criminal Law in Japan

Shin Matsuzawa

Waseda University Comparative Law Study Series 52

Essays on Criminal Law in Japan
ISBN978-4-7923-5428-2 C3032
Published by
The Institute of Comparative Law, Waseda University
1-6-1, Nishi-waseda, Shinjuku-ku, Tokyo 169-8050, Japan
ⓒ2024　by Authors & Editor All rights reserved. Printed in Japan.

Seibundo Publishing Co., LTD.
1-9-38 Nishi-Waseda, Shinjuku-ku, Tokyo 169-0051, Japan

Preface

This book is a collection of articles on criminal law that I have published in English, together with some new articles.

There are very few books/articles written in English that explain Japanese criminal law. When I have spoken with foreign scholars, they have occasionally asked me such a book exists. I would be happy if this book could be the answer to such a request.

The articles in this book were written on different occasions and for different purposes. The reader is therefore asked to bear in mind that the tone of the articles is not uniform. However, the series of articles in this book touch on general criminal law, criminal law, criminal procedure, economic criminal law, international criminal law and criminal law methodology, and I believe that the book has a relatively balanced structure. Therefore, the book is worthwhile as a quick reference for readers interested in Japanese criminal law. In some cases, the book can also be used as course material for lectures on Japanese criminal law.

Due to its historical conditions and geographical environment, Japan has been influenced by both Anglo-American and continental law. It both shares the liberal values of Western Europe and has an Asian legal tradition in its background. Japanese criminal law should be an interesting subject of study for the European countries that were the originators of modern legal culture, for the Asian countries which have inherited it, and for other countries as well. I hope that an increasing number of people will develop an interest in Japanese criminal law.

Because it is intended for a foreign audience, this book is mainly an overview. Although some of the articles in this book are being published in

English for the first time, they were originally written with a foreign audience or reader in mind. However, many of these papers reflect the individuality of the authors. While the methodological papers are the obvious choice, many of the other papers are concerned with empirical rather than normative considerations.

To some readers it may seem that only the normative is being developed, as in German law, while to others the normative and theoretical pursuits may seem inadequate. If such differences arise, they may be due to differences in the legal culture to which the reader belongs. For my part, I look forward to receiving such different impressions from readers.

This book is published by the Institute of Comparative Law of Waseda University. The Institute of Comparative Law was established at Waseda University more than 60 years ago. The Institute fulfils the important role of disseminating information on Japanese law internationally, and I would be happy if this book could contribute towards this goal.

March 2024, Tokyo –
Awaiting the cherry blossoms,

Shin Matsuzawa

About the articles in this book

The following indicates whether each article in this book is published or unpublished and, in the case of published articles, the journal/book in which it was originally published. As the articles have been published in different media, variations exist in citation styles, the inclusion or exclusion of notes, and, to a lesser extent, the complexity of the descriptions. Although the content has been kept as it was at the time of writing, slight changes have been made to expressions etc. where necessary.

Chapter 1   Previously published as: *Shin Matsuzawa*, A Study of Omission Crimes involving Children as Victims in Japan, in Yearbook Human Rights Protection, Ombudsman of Republic of Serbia (5), 2022.

Chapter 2   Unpublished. Written for this book in 2023.

Chapter 3   Previously published as: *Shin Matsuzawa*, Accomplice criminal liability to masterminds – What is the most appropriate legislation? in Kriminalistiske Pejlinger: Festskrift til Flleming Balvig, *Britta Kyvsgaard etl.* ed., 2013. DJØF Forlag.

Chapter 4   Unpublished. Written to discuss this topic with *Prof. Andreas von Hirsch* and *Prof. Thomas Elholm* in 2018.

Chapter 5   Previously published in Danish as: *Shin Matsuzawa*, Om japansk strafferet: træk af den japanske strafferets historie og udvikling, Kriminalistiske Årbog 1996, Københavns universitet.

Chapter 6   Unpublished. English translation of a manuscript presented in Japanese at the symposium titled "International Forum on Judicial Control of Death Penalty", held at Jilin University PRC on 25 February 2012.

Chapter 7   Unpublished. Written in 2018 in response to a request for publication in an anthology on low-level penalties, but that project was subsequently shelved.

Chapter 8   Previously published as: *Shin Matsuzawa*, Using Equity Reasons to evaluate Mitigating Circumstances - An Explanation of Sentencing Principles, Waseda Bulletin of Comparative Law (36), 2018.

Chapter 9   Previously published as: *Shin Matsuzawa,* Judicial Persons as Victims: An Introduction from a Japanese Perspective, Waseda Bulletin of Comparative Law (28), 2010.

Chapter 10   Previously published as: *Shin Matsuzawa*, Specialized Frauds in Japan, in Yearbook Human Rights Protection, Ombudsman of Republic of Serbia (6), 2024.

Chapter 11   Previously published as: *Shin Matsuzawa*, Anti-Corruption and Human Rights —An Analysis of Japan's Foreign Public Official Anti-Bribery Act, in Yearbook Human Rights Protection, Ombudsman of Republic of Serbia (4), 2021.

Chapter 12   Unpublished. Written for this book in 2023.

Chapter 13   Unpublished. English translation of the online report in Japanese from the symposium titled "The Northeast Asia Forum and Seminar on Criminal Legislation and Criminal Policy under the COVID-19 Pandemic", held at Liaoning University, PRC on September 24, 2022.

Chapter 14 Previously published as: *Shin Matsuzawa*, Protection of Victims of Crime - The Case of Japan – in Yearbook Human Rights Protection, Ombudsman of Republic of Serbia (3), 2020.

Chapter 15 Previously published in Danish as: *Shin Matsuzawa*, Nyt Lægdommersystem i Japan, in Ikke kun straf: Festskrift til Vagn Greve, *Thomas Elholm etl.* ed., 2008. DJØF Forlag.

Chapter 16 Previously published as: *Shin Matsuzawa*, An analysis of the seven Mutual Legal Assistance (MLA) agreements concluded by Japan and the uniqueness of the EU-Japan MLA Agreement, in Europe and Japan Cooperation in the Fight against Cross-border Crime: Challenges and Perspectives, *Shin Matsuzawa, Anne Weyembergh and Irene Wieczorek* ed., 2022. Routledge.

Last Chapter Previously published as: *Shin Matsuzawa*, The Methods of Legal Dogmatics of Criminal Law: From a Realistic Perspective, in Methodology of Criminal Law Theory: Art, Politics, or Science? *Shin Matsuzawa and Kimmo Nuotio* ed., 2021. Nomos/Hart Publishing.

TABLE OF CONTENTS

Preface i
Abaot the articles in this book iii

Chapter 1
Scope of Omission Crimes in Japan
I.	Introduction	1
II.	Theoretical issues of omission	2
III.	Abandonment causing death or injury: neglect by parents	5
IV.	Homicide by omission	9
V.	Omission crime and complicity	11
VI.	Last remarks	13

Chapter 2
Moral Luck and Criminal Law Theory
I.	Introduction	15
II.	Subjective attempt theory and moral luck	17
III.	Outcome of a crime and moral luck	22
IV.	"The control principle" and moral luck	24
V.	"The control principle" and the *Schuldprinzip*	27
VI.	Final remarks	28

Chapter 3
Accomplice Criminal Liability to Masterminds
—— What is the most appropriate Legislation? ——
I.	Agenda	31

II.	General Theories on Punishment of Masterminds ·············	34
III.	The Mastermind's Complicity Object ························	42
IV.	What is the Most Appropriate Legislation for Accomplices? ··········	46

Chapter 4
A Contribution to the Development of Criminal Theory based on the Desert Theory ························ 49

Chapter 5
Traces the History and Development of Japanese Criminal Law

I.	Introduction ···	59
II.	From the Meiji Restoration to the beginning of World War II ···	60
III.	The period immediately following Japan's defeat in World War II and the development of the 'formal responsibility doctrine' ·····	64
IV.	The influence of Anglo-American law and empirical criminal jurisprudence ······························	66
V.	Failure of the Criminal Code Revision ························	68
VI.	The present situation and future of Japanese criminal law ·······	69

Chapter 6
Death Penalty in Japan
──In light of the introduction of the mixed-panel system and recent developments in the criteria for applying the death penalty──

I.	Introduction ···	73
II.	Provisions in the Penal Code and Current Status of Execution of the Death Penalty ······························	74
III.	Criteria for death penalty selection under the mixed-panel system ··	76
IV.	Effects of the death penalty and its use ························	80

V. Conclusion 82

Chapter 7
Low-level Penalties in Japan: Fines and Petty Fines

　　I. Introduction 83
　　II. General Knowledge of Sentencing in Japan 84
　　III. History of the Punishment System in Japan 86
　　IV. Current Fines in Japan 87
　　V. The Daily Fine System: A discussion of
　　　　legislation or legal policy 97
　　VI. Detailed Analysis of Fines 100

Chapter 8
Using Equity Reasons to evaluate Mitigating Circumstances
——An Explanation of Sentencing Principles——

　　I. Preface 105
　　II. Which factors are important in sentencing? 107
　　III. Humanity —— a fundamental viewpoint 108
　　IV. Existing criminal records 109
　　V. The defendant's degree of remorse or admission 111
　　VI. When the defendant is largely disadvantaged by his or
　　　　her own doings 113
　　VII. The defendant's age, health, and occupation 115
　　VIII. When the defendant is already subject to
　　　　 other societal punishments 115
　　IX. When some time has already passed from
　　　　the date of the criminal act 116
　　X. Conclusion 117

Chapter 9
Judicial Persons as Victims: An Introduction from a Japanese Perspective
I.	Introduction	119
II.	Legal dogmatic analyses	120
III.	Empirical research	123
IV.	Conclusion	130

Chapter 10
Specialized Frauds in Japan
I.	What are "Specialized Frauds"?	133
II.	Consideration of Attempted Crime of Specialized Fraud	136
III.	Consideration of Complicity of Specialized Fraud	139
IV.	Consideration of Intent of Specialized Fraud	142
V.	Final Remarks	144

Chapter 11
An analysis of Japan's Foreign Public Official Anti-Bribery Act
I.	Introduction	147
II.	The Enactment of the Foreign Public Officials Anti-Bribery Act	148
III.	The Foreign Public Officials Anti-Bribery Act and its Application	149
IV.	Theoretical Analysis —— Dogmatics/Doctrine	150
V.	Evaluation from a Criminal Policy Perspective —— The Function of Criminal Law	154
VI.	Conclusion	155

Chapter 12
A consideration of the protection of trade secrets in Japan

I. Introduction 159
II. International situation regarding confidential information 160
III. The situation in Japan regarding confidential information 161
IV. What is meant by protection of confidential information? 162
V. What is the offence of trade secret infringement? 163
VI. The concept of trade secrets 164
VII. Three objective requirements 165
VIII. Subjective requirement - "the intent to gain an unfair advantage or to cause damage to the holder of the trade secret" 166
IX. What constitutes trade secret infringement? 167
X. How can trade secret infringement be detected? 167
XI. How can companies defend themselves against trade secret infringement? 168
XII. Conclusion 169

Chapter 13
The Case of Criminal Regulation as a Strategy to Control the Covid-19 Pandemic in Japan

I. Introduction 171
II. Criminal Regulation as a Strategy to Control the Covid-19 Pandemic —— The Situation in Japan 172
III. Under what circumstances are criminal penalties permissible? —— An Examination from the Perspective of Punishment Theory 174
IV. Again, under what circumstances are criminal penalties permissible? 178

V. Evaluation of Criminal Regulation as a Strategy to Control the Covid-19 Pandemic in Japan ·· 181

Chapter 14
Protection of Victims of Crime──The case of Japan──
I. Introduction ··· 183
II. The development process of victim protection ···················· 184
III. The development of victim protection in criminal proceedings ·· 189
IV. The development of basic rights protection for victims of crime ·· 191
V. Conclusion ··· 194

Chapter 15
New Lay Judge System in Japan
Presentation of the topic ·· 197
I. History and general principles of Japanese criminal procedure ·· 198
II. The background to the introduction of a lay judge system in Japan ·· 199
III. Participation of lay judges at first instance ···························· 201
IV. Appointment of lay judges and their rights and duties ············ 203
V. New rules on the preparatory meeting of the court ·············· 204
VI. Form and content of the judgment ·· 204
VII. Assessment and analysis of the new system ························ 205
Conclusion ··· 207

Chapter 16
An analysis of the seven Mutual Legal Assistance (MLA) agreements concluded by Japan and the uniqueness of the EU-Japan MLA Agreement
I. Introduction ··· 209
II. Concept and history of international MLA in criminal matters:

	The case of Japan ···	211
III.	The contents of the MLA treaties that Japan has concluded ·····	215
IV.	The EU-Japan MLA Agreement: Background and its 'uniqueness' or 'novelty' ··	222
V.	The role for values and legal culture in shaping the text of international agreements ··································	225
VI.	Conclusion ··	232

Last Chapter
The Methods of Legal Dogmatics of Criminal Law
——From a Realistic Perspective——

I.	Foreword ···	235
II.	What is Legal Dogmatics of Criminal Law? ····················	236
III.	Methodologies for Scientific Dogmatic of Criminal Law ········	240
IV.	Criticism of the Methodology/Issues and Review ··············	252
V.	Method for Dogmatic of Criminal Law: Methodology for extraction and structuring of theories ··························	258
VI.	Methods of Criminal Law Policies: Preliminary Observation ····	261
VII.	Conclusion ··	267

Chapter 1
Scope of Omission Crimes in Japan

I. Introduction

1.1. This article discusses the issue of omission crimes in Japan, focusing on cases in which children are the victims.

1.2. Omission crimes are often committed by the dominant person in the power relationship, such as guardians, supervisors and parents. As a result of power imbalance, children are often the victims. When considering the protection of children under criminal law, consideration of omission crimes cannot be avoided. A number of theoretical problems exist with omission crimes.

First, in omission crimes, the stillness of the body is the offence. In the case of commission crimes, it is, to a large extent, clear whether his or her action is, or is not, a criminal offence if the physical movement of the offender's body is observed. In the case of omission crimes, however, there is no physical movement that has to be observed, which raises difficult questions as to whether his or her attitude can be assessed as a crime.

Second, as omission is, physically, non-existent, the question arises as to how to construct a theory of causality. Some have suggested that because omission is nothing, there is no causal relationship. The statement that "nothing comes from nothing" is persuasive. Consider, however, the case of a child who is victimized by the neglect of his or her parents. In a case where those in a position to protect, e.g. the parents, put the child's life in danger and ultimately caused his death by failing to protect him, can we say that there is no causal relationship between the parents' omission and the child's death? We need to consider the theory in this case.

Third, there is the difficult question of what type of offence it is when a person causes the death of a victim, such as a child, without providing the protection necessary for survival. Normally, it would seem that if the perpetrator had the intent to kill, the offence would be homicide by omission. However, the Japanese Penal Code contains a crime category called 'Abandonment Causing Death or Injury', which is punished much less severely than homicide. On the other hand, in Japanese judicial practice, even in cases where there is an intention to kill, the offence may be considered to fall within this crime category.

Fourth, in Japan, there are cases where one of the parents (typically the father) physically abuse the child and the other parent (typically the mother) stands idle. In this case, the question arises as to whether complicity in assault by omission is established in respect of the other parent who stood idle (i.e. did not prevent it). This issue provides a difficult problem, as it is a compounded question of omission crime and complicity.

In this article, I introduce the Japanese debate on the above-mentioned issues, which I hope will be of reference to many people.

II. Theoretical issues of omission

2.1. Some criminal law theorists said that omissions are not actions, because they constitute nothing. It has also been said (in one German criminal law theory) that omissions without a purpose are not acts because human action is the performance of a purposeful activity.

These ideas, while understandable in theory, are not realistic. If a parent fails to feed his or her child and causes the child to starve to death, the child is considered to have starved to death as a result of the parent's actions, and such a parental attitude is, in any event, an attitude that should be criminalized.

Therefore, omissions, as well as commissions, must be punished in certain cases. Such a value judgement would be unmovable.

However, the above theory is significant in that it argues that the existential structure of omission is different from that of commission, and makes it clear that a precise theory is required to justify punishing omission. This paper addresses that issue first.

2.2. Acts can be either commissions or omissions. If we look at the facts as they are, commission is the movement of the body and omission is the stillness of the body. Defined in this way, acts of commission and omissions are both acts, and are therefore considered punishable.

It should be noted, however, that omission is not pure bodily stillness. Omission is, more precisely, the absence of an expected commission. In relation to that expected commission, a person may be doing some activity at the same time, even if the body is stationary. Consider, for example, the case of a parent chatting in a café without feeding his or her child. Even though chatting in the café involves physical movement of the body, in relation to the expected commission (feeding the child), the person's act would be assessed as an omission.

Thus, inaction is always understood as 'omission of an expected commission'.

2.3. The next question is: what is the causal relationship of omission? In some criminal law theory (in Germany) it was once said that no consequences can result from doing nothing. Indeed, nothingness cannot be the cause of an outcome. However, as noted above, omission is not mere nothingness. An omission is the failure to fulfil an expected commission. Current Japanese criminal law theory therefore sees the causal relationship of omission in the form of 'if the expected commission had taken place, this result could have been avoided'.

Causal relationships in ordinary cases are determined using the cwonditio-sine-qua-non formula. This is "if the act P had not taken place, the result Q would not have occurred". It is then not possible to apply this formula to omissions that do not exist in the first place (there is no P, so the assumption that if there had been no P is itself impossible). Therefore, we are forced to add a condition for the causal relationship of omission in the form of 'if the expected commission had taken place'. This is known as the hypothetical causal relationship formula.

2.4. Thus, the causal relationship of omission is whether 'there was a possibility to avoid the result by performing the commission'. If so, the next question is the level of the possibility. What level of probability is needed to assess that there is a possibility? On this, we shall refer to the Japanese case-law (1989(A)551).

The case involved a 13-year-old girl who was the victim. The victim girl became delirious and died as a result of the injection of methamphetamine by the accused. If she had been given immediate emergency medical care at this point, she would have been able to save her life "in eight or nine out of ten cases". The Supreme Court held in this case that a causal relationship could be established between the omissions of the accused and the outcome of the girl's death.

The Supreme Court used the expression "in eight or nine out of ten cases", which does not literally mean 80% to 90%. This is understood in the sense of probability bordering on certainty, i.e. certainty beyond reasonable doubt.

2.5. In parallel with the crime of commission, if the causal relationship of omission is lacking, an attempted crime is also concluded for the omission crime, since the perpetrator has commenced the execution of the crime. However, if there is no objective possibility of avoiding the result, then the expected commission cannot be conceived in the first place, and therefore the omission itself is absent (there is no possibility of committing the act). In fact, there is an example of a District Court case-law in which omission per se was rejected and the offence of attempted homicide was rejected.

The question at issue here is whether the commission is possible. If the expected commission is impossible, the omission cannot be conceived. This is because the law does not force a person to do the impossible. For example, if a person who cannot swim fails to rescue a drowning person, he cannot be assessed as having killed the person by omission.

However, there can be a debate on how to determine this possibility. Let us make a slight variation to the case of the case-law of the Supreme Court referred to earlier. Suppose that even if the girl had been taken to an emergency hospital, from an ex post facto and objective point of view it would have been impossible to save her life. However, suppose that at the time the girl was in a state of confusion, it looked to the general public as if she might be saved if she had been taken to an emergency hospital. In this case, ex post facto and objectively, there was no possibility of saving her life, however, the accused could have taken her to the emergency hospital. If that is the case, then, although it was indeed impossible to save her life, the attempted offence could be established. This is because at the point when the girl was delirious, the general public would not have known whether or not there was a chance of saving her life, and therefore it would be necessary to oblige the parent to take part in a life-saving act. Without this consideration, the victim cannot be adequately protected.

III. Abandonment causing death or injury: neglect by parents

3.1. A classic example of omission crime against children is what is known as 'neglect'. "Neglect" is a term used in Japan to describe the neglect of a child by the parents who have to take care of the child's needs, neglecting the child, putting the child in danger, causing the most life-threatening conditions and ultimately causing the child's death. In this case, the Japanese Penal Code provides for the crimes of unprotected offences and unprotected manslaughter. The following are the provisions:

Article 218 (Abandonment by a Person Responsible for Protection)
When a person who is responsible for protection of a senile, immature, physically disabled or sick person, abandons, or fails to give necessary protection to such person, the person shall be punished by imprisonment with work for not less than 3 months but not more than 5 years.

Article 219 (Abandonment Causing Death or Injury)
A person who commits a crime prescribed under the preceding two Articles and thereby causes the death or injury of another, shall be dealt with by the punishment prescribed for either the crimes of injury or the preceding Articles, whichever is greater.

As can be seen from the text of the articles, this crime applies not only to cases where children are victims, but also to cases where the elderly, the sick and other vulnerable persons are victims. However, this paper will focus on cases where children are the victims.
In Japan, incidents of parents leaving their children unattended and causing their deaths are often reported. A typical example is a case in which a parent took his or her child to a so-called pachinko parlor and left the child in a private car while he or she played, where the hot summer temperatures made the inside of the car extremely hot and the child died of heat stroke. In such cases, a crime of Abandonment (failing to give the protection) Causing Death is

concluded.

3.2. Recently, the Japanese Supreme Court issued a new decision (2003(A) 1468) on the interpretation of 'failing to give protection':

> "The act of committing abandonment by a person responsible for protection by failing to give the protection referred to in Article 218 of the Penal Code is based on the premise of a situation where a senile, immature, physically disabled or sick person requires a specific protection act for his/her survival (a protection requiring situation) and means not conducting the specific act that is expected to be conducted under the Penal Code as the act of protection necessary for the survival of such person."

According to this case law, simply not taking care of the necessities of daily life does not constitute 'failing to give protection'. The Supreme Court is considered to have interpreted the phrase 'failing to give protection' in Article 218 of the Japanese Penal Code as protection which, if not provided, would result in a danger to life.

So, a crime of abandonment (failing to give the protection) is a crime where a parent's failure to protect their child (e.g. by not feeding them, keeping them clean, not taking care of their illness or health, etc.) results in a risk to the child's life.

3.3. If this is interpreted in this way, the next issue is the distinction between Abandonment Causing Death and Homicide by omission.

In Japanese criminal law, there are two types of omission crimes punishable as omission crimes: genuine omission crimes and non-genuine omission crimes. This concept derives from German criminal law theory.

A crime of abandonment (failing to give the protection) under Article 218 of the Japanese Penal Code is provided for in the form of punishment for the omission (i.e. 'failing') of the perpetrator. This is referred to as a 'genuine omission crime'. And if the failure to protect caused the death of a person, then this is punishable as a crime of Abandonment Causing Death or Injury under Article 219 of the Japanese Penal Code. 'Genuine omission crimes' pose virtually no theoretical problems, since it is simply a matter of applying the case to the article.

On the other hand, the homicide is provided for in a form that punishes the perpetrator's commission of the act (i.e. 'kill'). The provision of the homicide is as follows:

Article 199 (Homicide)
A person who kills another shall be punished by the death penalty or imprisonment with work for life or for a definite term of not less than 5 years.

Such a case where a crime originally prescribed in the form of a commission is committed by omission is called an 'omission crime by omission'. The term 'omission crime by omission' applies the case to the text of the article in a way that is somewhat remote from the wording of the article. This leads to various interpretative problems. This will be discussed in the next chapter.

The question is how to distinguish between A Crime of Abandonment (failing to give protection) Causing Death and Homicide. To begin with, the former has a much lighter statutory penalty. Is it appropriate to punish a parent as A Crime of Abandonment (failing to give protection) Causing Death if he or she fails to protect the child with the intent to kill?

However, the distinction in Japanese case law and in academic theory is based not on whether there is an intent to kill, but on whether the omission poses tremendous risks to a person's life which can result in death. It is not reasonable to treat an act as Homicide simply because it has the intent to kill, nor is it reasonable to impose a punishment on par with that of Homicide where an act poses a low risk to life. From this perspective, only cases where a guardian (parents) kills a person by omission with a high risk to life, based on the natural assumption that there is an intention to kill, are punishable as a Homicide omission crime by omission, and other cases are punishable as A Crime of Abandonment (failing to give protection) Causing Death.

IV. Homicide by omission

4.1. Let us now look at the cases in which the homicide by omission can be committed. With regard to the homicide by omission, there is no typical case-law for cases where a child is the victim. Therefore, we shall look at the debate in Japanese law, focusing on theories.

Since the homicide by omission is the realization by omission of a crime that is prescribed in the form of an act of commission, the first question is whether it violates the principle of legality. In response to this question, Japanese academic theory answers that, since the norms of criminal law include prohibitive norms as well as imperative norms to a certain extent, the same article may be used to punish a violation of an order to 'do an act' by doing nothing.

4.2. The question is: to which persons is such a imperative norm directed? Consider, for example, the following case study.

[**Case study**]
A child was drowning in a park pond. Mr. A, who had nothing to do with the child and was passing by, left without helping the child, hoping the child would die (with intent to homicide). The child subsequently drowned. In this case, is Mr. A guilty of homicide by omission?

Conclusion first. Under Japanese law, Mr. A is not guilty of any crime (even if his act is morally condemnable, it cannot be punished as a criminal offence under the Criminal Code). This is because Japanese criminal law does not impose a duty on Mr. A to rescue the child.

According to Japanese criminal law theory, for an 'omission crime by omission' to be concluded, the perpetrator must have a duty to perform a commission. The obligation to perform a commission arises from several grounds. (1) The first is a statutory duty, (2) the second is a contractual duty/duty from benevolent intervention in another's affairs and (3) the third is a duty arising from the perpetrator's own prior acts. In the case study, none of these grounds exist.

Suppose, for example, in the case study, the person passing by was a parent. In this case, the parent has a statutory duty to rescue the child (see Article 820 of the Japanese Civil Code). In addition, if the perpetrator accidentally pushes a child into a pond, the perpetrator has a duty to rescue based on his or her own act.

4.3. The Supreme Court has only issued one case-law on omission crimes for homicide. This case was like the following: The leader of a religious organization had attracted followers who claimed to have the power to cure illness through his religious acts. On one occasion, his followers asked him to treat a seriously ill patient, so he had the patient brought to the hotel where he was staying, disregarding the instructions of the doctor in charge. However, when he failed to treat the patient properly, he left the patient to die, with the intent to kill him.

The Supreme Court stated the duty to rescue the accused as follows:

> "the defendant caused a concrete threat to the patient's life due to reasons within his control, despite the fact that in the hotel into which the patient was taken, the defendant was fully entrusted by the patient's relatives, who were believers of the defendant, to perform treatment for the patient suffering from a serious illness.

Considering that at that time, the defendant was aware of the patient's serious condition and had no reason to believe that he was able to save the patient's life, the defendant was responsible for having the patient immediately receive necessary medical treatment for keeping him alive."

The Supreme Court refers to the fact that the risk was caused by reasons attributable to the accused (requirement (3) above). It then states that the accused is in a position of full entrustment of the allowance, i.e. the accused has control over the entire treatment of the patient.

This element of 'control' is something that has been argued for in Japanese academic theory in recent years. In this case, since the perpetrator has control over the entire event, it can be said that the perpetrator's omission can be assessed as equivalent to an commission, even if it did not cause the result. From this perspective, it is reasonable to require 'control' of the event for the conclusion of an 'non-genuine omission crime'.

V. Omission crime and complicity

5.1. Incidents may occur where one of the parents (typically the father) is predominantly violent towards the child and the other parent (typically the mother) lets it happen. In this case, the question arises as to whether the other parent, who has left the assault or injury of one parent unattended (i.e. not prevented it), is guilty of complicity in the crime of assault or injury by omission.

Before we jump into the discussion of this issue, let me explain a little about the Japanese complicity provisions. The Japanese Penal Code distinguishes between co-principals and accessory:

Article 60 (Co-Principals)
Two or more persons who commit a crime in joint action are all principals.

Article 62 (Accessoryship)
(1) A person who aids a principal is an accessory.

Article 63 (Reduced Punishment for Accessories)
The punishment of an accessory shall be reduced from the punishment for the principal.

If two parents, through their will, decide to assault a child together, they are co-principals under Article 60 of the Criminal Code. And in practice, this is often the case. The problem is when there are no such circumstances and only one of them commits the assault and the other stands idle.

In this regard, there is a case-law that provides an important decision. A, the mother of her own stepchild, the victim child V (3 years old), knew that her husband B was assaulting V and did not stop the violence. As a result, V died as a result of B's assault. In this case, B is the perpetrator of the crime of injury causing death. On the other hand, as regards A considered an accessory by omission to the crime of injury causing death. The key question here is how to distinguish between a co-principal by omission and an accessory by omission. In Japanese criminal law theory, the general view on the distinction between co-principal by omission and accessory by omission is that, as starting point, the participation by omission is an accessory.

In Japan, when more than one person is involved in a crime, most participants are assessed as co-principals (approximately 97%). In contrast, only about 3% are assessed as accessory. In this light, it seems reasonable to assume that the above cases are also assessed as co-principals. However, in the case we now have in question, it is B who controls the crime; A does not control this crime, nor does she play a significant role in it. In such a case, A, who was a bystander to the crime, can only be guilty of an accessory.

5.2. In addition, in recent times, the Supreme Court has issued the following case-law. The accused persistently encouraged the mother of a diabetic child (7 years old) not to administer insulin to the child. As a result, the child died. In this case, the Supreme Court found the accused guilty of homicide for taking advantage of the mother's omissions.

In this case, directly the child died because the mother did not administer insulin to the child. However, the mother was mentally dominated by the accused and was in a psychological state of blind faith in what she was saying. The accused therefore took advantage of the mother's omissions to perform the crime.

The problem in this case was that the mother had a blind religious belief in the accused. In the case-law reviewed earlier, a case in which the victim died because of blind faith in the leader of a religious organization was also discussed. There have been many cases where a parent or guardian's blind faith in a cult has led to the death of a child or sick person due to the fact that the victims did not receive medical treatment that they needed.

VI. Last remarks

This article examines theoretical issues related to omission crimes in Japan, focusing on cases where children are the victims. The victimization of children by parents' failure to protect their children is a major problem in contemporary society and appears to be prevalent in many countries around the world. The legal issues examined in this paper are probably also being debated in many other countries.

From a comparative legal perspective, I would be happy if the Japanese discussion can be of some help.

Chapter 2
Moral Luck and Criminal Law Theory

"I believe in luck: how else can you explain the success of those you dislike?"

Jean Cocteau

I. Introduction

1.1. Consider the following situation. X punches V1 and Y punches V2 with equivalent force and with the intention of bruising the victim's face. While X's punch causes a bruise around V1's eye, V2 dodges Y's punch and runs away. It would seem that X is guilty of injury and Y is guilty of assault, but it could also be understood that "in this case, whether or not an injury occurred is entirely a matter of chance". However, it could also be said that "in this case, it is a matter of luck that V2 did not suffer an injury", and that based on such an understanding, X and Y committed the same act with the same intention, but the fact that V2 did not suffer an injury is merely a matter of luck. In this case, the question may arise as to whether the element of "luck", which is a coincidental element, should be taken into consideration and whether moral blame should be placed on X and Y with regard to their criminal liability and punishment.

From the viewpoint of Japanese criminal law scholarship, whether or not a consequence occurs is a decisive circumstance in establishing unlawfulness. It is thought that X is treated as a crime of injury and Y as a crime of assault without much consideration of the issue. However, in the British theory of attempted crime, this issue is actively debated. The reason for this is that there is a very active discussion of moral luck in Anglo-American ethics.

1.2. The consequences of this argument can be formulated in terms of the idea that a perpetrator cannot be held liable for circumstances beyond his control, and that his criminal liability must therefore be considered without taking into account moral luck. It can also be stated that moral luck should be excluded in order to define the appropriate scope of criminal liability for the perpetrator in question.

The issue of moral luck was originally brought to the attention of ethicists Thomas Nagel and Bernard Williams in the early 1980s when they wrote articles on moral luck and raised the issue, respectively. This is a topic which has been the subject of debate in Anglo-American ethics and has become highly referenced and highly controversial in discussions of Anglo-American criminal jurisprudence.

It is in attempted crime theory that arguments about the exclusion of moral luck most typically appear. Due to the British theory of attempted crime, which has been influenced by this argument, we see a strong subjectivist tendency where the exclusion of moral luck has come to be used as support for its theoretical basis.

1.3. In Scandinavia as well, an important article exists on the exclusion of moral luck in criminal law theory. It is by Nils Jareborg, Professor Emeritus at the Faculty of Law, Uppsala University, who is a Swedish criminal law scholar. Swedish criminal law studies draw inspiration from both German and Anglo-American criminal law scholarship, organizing them and integrating them with original Nordic criminal law scholarship to form a new theory. The theory of attempted crime in Swedish criminal law, as in Japan, is founded on the objective theory of attempt. In the above paper, Jareborg addresses the issue of moral luck from a different perspective than that of the British, who adopt the subjective attempt theory, and an interesting discussion ensues.

1.4. The following is an outline of this paper. First, we will look at Andrew

Ashworth's view, which is considered to be the prevailing view of subjective attempt theory in the United Kingdom, to see how he treats moral luck. We then refer to Jareborg's analysis. Jareborg rejects the introduction of moral luck exclusion in the theory of attempted crime, and we will examine his argument. In doing so, we will also refer to Joel Feinberg's view as an analysis which points in essentially the same direction as Jareborg's analysis (II). Next, as a discussion related to the elimination of moral luck, we will examine the meaning of the criminal law theory of crime outcomes (III). As a conclusion to the above summary, it will be shown that the issue of moral luck is not limited to a discussion of attempted crime, but is a discussion which relates to various parts of criminal law. Furthermore, the theoretical implications of the idea of eliminating moral luck will be discussed (IV). Finally, we briefly summarize the results obtained by this paper (V).

II. Subjective attempt theory and moral luck

2.1. First, let us review the meaning of the claim that moral luck is precluded in attempted crimes. To begin, a crime is an attempted crime if no consequence has occurred, or if a consequence occurs but has no causal relationship to the act. The occurrence of a consequence, however, is an accidental result unrelated to the perpetrator's act. In order to eliminate accidental consequences, or moral luck, from criminal liability it is necessary to make criminal liability and punishment the same for both attempted and committed crimes. -this is the basic idea.

This consequence is consistent with the idea of subjectivist criminal jurisprudence since it considers criminal liability and punishment for attempted and already attempted crimes to be the same, and as a theory of attempt, it is consistent with the idea of the so-called subjective attempt theory.

2.2. In the United Kingdom it was Oxford University professor Andrew Ashworth [1] who developed the subjective attempt theory, taking into account the exclusion of moral luck. Ashworth states the following:

> "Since fairness is an integral element..., it would be wrong to allow random or chance factors to determine the threshold of criminal liability or the quantum of punishment. In criminal endeavours, as in other spheres of life, things do not always turn out as one expects. The emphasis in criminal liability should be upon what D was trying to do, intended to do and believed he was doing, rather than upon the actual consequences of his conduct. The point may be restated in terms of the "intent principle" and the "belief principle": the intent principle is that individuals should be held criminally liable for what they intended to do, and not according to what actually did or did not occur; the belief principle is that individuals should be judged on the basis of what they believed they were doing, not on the basis of actual facts and circumstances which were not known to them at the time.
>
> ......
>
> A rational system for judging human behaviour should pay attention to choice, not chance. The fully subjective principle should be the foundation of criminal liability (subject to derogation by other appropriate principles), and the element of chance in resulting harm means that it should have only a secondary role."

2.3. Jareborg critically examines the above view of Ashworth. As the premise for this, he divides the various problems of the attempted crime theory into four categories. [2] Let us follow them precisely. The four issues are:

1. At what point does an attempt begin? What is merely preparing a deed, and what is beginning to perform the deed?
2. What kind of mens rea is required? Is intention required, or is mere belief

---

(1) Andrew Ashworth, 'Criminal Attempts and the Role of Resulting Harm under the Code, and in the Common Law' (1988) 19 Rutgers LJ 725.
(2) Nils Jareborg, 'Criminal Attempts and Moral Luck' (1993) 27 Isr L Rev 213.

concerning the outcome sufficient?

3. Is the attempt basically constituted by the mental (fault) element or the physical (conduct) element of the deed? Should attempts to do the impossible be criminalized?

4. Should the punishment be the same for an attempt and a completed (consummated) crime, or should the punishment be less severe for an attempt?

According to Jareborg, the first two are policy issues, while the latter two are ideological/theoretical issues. Jareborg then addresses the fourth issue as one that is directly related to moral luck.

Jareborg first examines this as a matter of punishment ideologies. Jareborg's analysis on this is very interesting, but we will skip it here because it has little direct relevance to moral luck. Even as a consequence of Jareborg, it is shown that this analysis, even as an important guide to interpretation, does not function in a theoretically binding way. Rather, what is theoretically binding is the (metaphysical) discussion of "morality" that follows.

As a groundwork for his argument, Jareborg discusses the importance of the metaphysical argument, linking it to aspects of science and fact. He states, "A transcendental, structuring element has been added as soon as the world is seen through a language, a system of concepts. All science has a metaphysical aspect." [3]

Thus, Jaheborg begins his discussion with metaphysical ethics. First, he points out that there are two types of ethics: mentality ethics (Gesinnungsehik) and conduct ethics (Handlungsethik). He then presents moral judgments by mentality ethics as follows. That is, every human being should have the potential to act in a morally acceptable manner; that factors beyond his/her control should therefore be irrelevant to moral judgment; that moral judgment should not be influenced by chance or luck; that the subject of moral judgment should

---

(3) *Jareborg* (fn2) 219.

be limited to a person's intentions, beliefs and inner world and that the subject matter of moral judgment is limited to what happens in a person's will, beliefs, and inner world. As a result, the idea of mentality ethics precludes moral luck. [4]

After formulating the ethics of the mind in this way, Jareborg states that in the theory of attempted crime, it is appropriate to make judgments by the ethics of conduct ethic. The conduct ethic is a way of thinking that makes moral judgments about acts that involve harmful consequences. This conception is consistent with our usual moral practice and it leads to common-sense thinking. For example, exam results, Olympic rankings, Nobel prizes, and so on. According to Jareborg, we do not deny the significance of moral judgments based on emotional ethics, but we deny that they are appropriate for building a criminal justice system [5]—especially here to determine the punishment for attempted crimes. The question is to be answered from the perspective of whether or not it is appropriate for the establishment of a criminal justice system. [6]

2.4. A somewhat similar perspective to Jareborg's can be found in the views of Joel Feinberg. In his article 'Problematic Responsibility in Law and Morals', [7] Feinberg contrasts moral responsibility with legal responsibility. He says, "Moral responsibility is conceived as being similar to legal responsibility in some respects and radically dissimilar in others". He clarifies the characteristics of both (moral responsibility here means the same as moral judgements in Jareborg's argument).

---

(4) *Jareborg* (n2) 219.
(5) *Jareborg* (n2) 223.
(6) Jareborg also argues that negligence liability in practice cannot be based on a mentality ethics. *Jareborg* (n2) 223.
(7) Joel Feinberg, 'Problematic Responsibility in Law and Morals' in *Doing and Deserving*, (Princeton University Press 1970) 25.

According to Feinberg, moral responsibility is "of judgments which are superior in rationality and perfectly precise, imputing an absolute responsibility wholly within the power of the agent". [8]

He lists four characteristics of moral responsibility. It is the fourth characteristic that is important in relation to moral luck. Namely, "Moral responsibility must be regular and predictable; nothing can be left to chance or to unforeseeable contingencies. Above all, it cannot be a matter of luck, as responsibility so often is in law." [9] In other words, moral responsibility excludes moral luck.

Feinberg positions such moral responsibility as distinct from legal responsibility. Furthermore, he refuses to apply moral responsibility in situations where a legal solution is required, as "in those cases where legal responsibility is problematic, moral responsibility would be absolutely undecidable in principle and therefore inapplicable since, in respect to moral responsibility as here understood we are not allowed to purposes and policies". [10]

Thus, Feinberg's view is similar to Jareborg's view and may be said to be identical in its basic conception. In short, ethical moral judgement/moral responsibility is different from legal judgement/legal responsibility. This should not be taken directly into the theory of attempted crime. This would seem to be persuasive. [11]

---

(8) *Feinberg* (n2) 30.
(9) *Feinberg* (n2) 31.
(10) *Feinberg* (n2) 32.
(11) However, Feinberg wrote a much later article on attempted offenses, in which he argued for the elimination of moral luck, that consequences have no meaning in criminal liability, and that the punishment for attempted and completed crimes should be the same. Joel Feinberg 'Criminal Attempts: Equal Punishments for Failed Attempts' in *Problems at the Roots of Law* (OUP 2003) 77). I believe that his article listed in fn (7) is superior, both in the logic of the argument and in the conclusion.

III. Outcome of a crime and moral luck

3.1. The problem here is the following: the structure of criminal law norms indicate that only acts can be the object of prohibition, not results. In other words, since norms regulate human attitudes, they include and end with the description of acts and the imperatives to those acts. Advancing this forward leads to the conclusion that the outcome is not an important factor with respect to the crime committed by an offender.

The issue here is as follows: the structure of criminal law norms indicates that only acts can be the object of prohibition, not consequences. In other words, since norms can regulate only human attitudes, they contain and end up describing acts and the imperatives for those acts. Advancing this forward, we can conclude that the consequences of a crime are not an important element with respect to the crime committed by the offender.

Certainly, the object of a norm may be an act, and it may be the only act that a human being can control simultaneously and directly by the force of his will. However, the scope of "possible" control of an object is not limited to simultaneous and direct control. If we take into account the "possibility" of control, then not only acts but also consequences may be included in the scope of regulation. In other words, direct control can only be exercised over acts, but it is also "possible" to control the consequences of crimes. From this perspective, since the purpose of criminal law is to deter (prevent) crime, the important question for criminal law is "what do we want to deter (prevent)"? What the criminal law wants to deter are acts that create a risk of infringement of legal interests and acts that cause consequences. Conversely, there is no need to prohibit acts that do not pose a risk of causing consequences. In the first place, an act that has a "risk" of consequence is an act that carries a "possibility" of consequences, which logically presupposes that the act includes a "possibility" of controlling the consequences. In this way of thinking, the occurrence of a consequence is not completely coincidental. There are degrees of chance.

3.2. Although moral luck has been developed exclusively in the theory of attempted offenses, as discussed above, it can also be an issue in other situations. Feinberg, for example, discusses this issue in a case familiar to Japanese criminal law scholars.

"There is a famous case in criminal law in which the defendant was found guilty of manslaughter when his victim, an unsuspected hemophiliac, died from uncontrollable bleeding resulting from a small cut in his mouth caused by the defendant's slapping him in the face. The slapper of the hemophiliac was held responsible for a death because of an unsuspected abnormal susceptibility in his victim, whereas a thousand persons are wrongfully slapped every day with no resultant criminal responsibility." [12]

This is also a case that has traditionally appeared in Japanese criminal law lectures and textbooks for a long time. Ask a student just beginning to study criminal law about this case, and many will say that the criminal should not be held liable for the consequences of the victim's death.

This conclusion has been the dominant theory in Japan for a long time because it is consistent with our common sense - as many students would support.

On the other hand, the case law and, moreover, prevailing theory in Japan does not exclude moral luck at this level. The current Japanese common law generally accepts the conclusion that where there are special circumstances at the time of the act concerning the victim, the consequences of the occurrence are attributable to the perpetrator even if these are not known to the

---

(12) *Feinberg* (n7) 32.

general public. If we now ask students who are advanced in their study of criminal law, most will probably answer that the consequence of death can be attributed to the perpetrator in the above cases.

Let us leave aside for the moment the question of which of these answers is more appropriate. What should be at issue is that, if we proceed in this way of thinking, the issue of the exclusion of moral luck is not limited to the issue of attempted crimes. Furthermore, it must also be considered in relation to causal relationships and negligent offenses (foreseeability). Based on this understanding, the following discussion will expand the issue of moral luck to the entirety of criminal law.

IV. "The control principle" and moral luck

4.1. The question is as follows. There are multiple situations in criminal law where the exclusion of moral luck should be discussed, but how do we categorize each of these situations in light of the system of criminal theory (Verbrechenslehre)?

In answering this question, it is important to note that Japanese criminal theory, like German theory, distinguishes between illegality (Rechtswidrigkeit) and guilt (Schuld). This means that it is important to first categorize each situation in which moral luck seems to be an issue and which category in the theory of crime it relates to. Next, let us consider the following issues.

4.2. First, let us consider the categorization of moral luck with respect to illegality. In Japanese criminal law, illegality (Rechtswidrigkeit) means that an act causes an infringement of legal interests or a danger thereof. The danger of infringement of legal interests or the occurrence of infringement of legal interests arises after the act of the perpetrator is carried out and a certain causal process has been followed. Therefore, it is affected by various events which occur in this process, and the chances of its occurrence cannot be completely discounted. However, even so, it can be said that there exists "controllability" by the perpetrator with regard to its occurrence in the first place. After the perpetrator gives this up, so to speak, there is no simultaneous control, but until then, there is control, i.e., there is a prior controllability. Therefore, even if there was the possibility of chance intervening, it is acceptable to attribute the resulting consequences to the perpetrator. Jareborg states the following in regard to this; "Chance, luck, is thus of some importance for whether, and if so how, someone should be punished. This is, however, unavoidable if more than dolus (a criminal intention or belief) is required for liability. It is often a matter of chance whether the border of the criminalized area is passed at all." [13] Thus, in situations that are categorized as illegal, moral luck cannot be ruled out.

Of course, it is possible to limit the scope of moral luck by some value judgment. This theoretical possibility is not excluded. However, it can be said to be the result of thinking based on a different concept than that of eliminating "chance" in criminal law. In other words, in this case, it goes beyond the theoretical and metaphysical issue of simply not being able to attribute accidental consequences to the perpetrator, and becomes a matter of policy (politics): "What does the state want to deter by means of criminal law"?

4.3. By itself, the above conclusion might appear harsh, even if it is the consequence of proper thinking. However, criminal law provides a device to control the overextension of the scope of punishment. This is the concept of blameworthiness, and the concept of capacity for criminal responsibility.

Let us refer again to Jareborg's words. "The criminal law is primarily designed for preventing different sorts of harm. This makes a conduct ethics

---

(13) *Jareborg* (n2) 226.

approach "natural". The important thing is to see to that no one is punished for something which lies outside of his or her control or possibilities of control. This is done by making culpability a prerequisite for liability, by making lack of culpability exculpatory. This ensures that punishment implies blame, but it does not ensure that equal culpability always renders equal punishment, or punishment at all." [14]

What Jareborg is probably stating here is the following. Moral luck is not excluded at the level of determining illegality. However, at the level of judging guilt, it is necessary to limit punishment by taking the view that blameworthiness can only be imposed to the extent that it is within one's control.

Certainly, moral luck should not be excluded from criminal law in practice, since - as Jareborg states - criminal responsibility does not consist solely of inner evil will. Moreover, moral luck cannot logically be eliminated from criminal law since - as Feinberg states - the influence of the perpetrator's natural ability and unavoidable environment is also an element of moral luck.

At the same time, however, one should not be punished due to circumstances beyond one's control. And this control requires that the act be controllable at the time of the act. By doing so, the principle of not holding the perpetrator responsible for uncontrollable contingencies is satisfied.

4.4. The above principle is often referred to as the "control principle" (the principle that "blame can only be placed on events over which the perpetrator exerted control"). And this "control principle" and the exclusion of moral luck are often discussed on the same plane. However, as noted above, I believe that they are issues of different phases.

It is important to note that there is an aspect of "luck" in determining what acts are punishable under criminal law, consistent with the fact that

---

(14) *Jareborg* (n2) 226.

blame can only be placed on events over which the perpetrator had control, i.e., events over which the perpetrator has no control cannot be punished (the control principle).

This presumably corresponds (approximately) to the distinction between illegality (Rechtswidrigkeit) and guilt (Schuld) in Japanese/German theoretical criminal law studies. The exclusion of moral luck is a matter of illegality, while the control principle belongs to the category of guilt.

On the other hand, in ethical/moral philosophical discussions, there is no strict distinction between illegality and guilt as there is in criminal law theory. Therefore, the elimination of moral luck and the principle of control may have been discussed on the same plane. In other words, the distinction between illegality and responsibility, which can lead to the above conclusion, is understood to be critically important in criminal law theory.

In my opinion, this also seems to be the reason for why the subjective attempt theory is insisted upon in discussions of Anglo-American criminal law studies by Ashworth and others. Anglo-American criminal law scholarship is considered to be extremely highly developed in its theory of punishment, and the theory of criminalization is elaborately constructed to reflect this. However, there is little awareness of the theoretical distinction between illegality and guilt. [15] This is probably why even Ashworth, the leading Anglo-American theoretical criminal law scholar, is unable to escape from the subjective attempt theory (which has already been overcome as a past theory in Japan).

V. "The control principle" and the *Schuldprinzip*

In recent years, through the study of moral luck, a German scholar has

---

(15) The discussion developed in Andrew Simester & Andreas von Hirsch *Crimes Harms and Wrongs* (Hart 2011) is the pinnacle of Anglo-American jurisprudence and is meticulous, but even so, there is little awareness of the distinction between *Rechtswidrigkeit* and *Schuld*.

argued for replacing the "control principle" with the *Schuldprinzip* (principle of the guilty party, which states that an illegal act which could not have been avoided by the perpetrator, assuming his/her personal physiological capacity and knowledge, is not punishable). [16] B. Burchhardt opposes the use of the concept of "guilt" (Schuld) and tries to replace the *Schuldprinzip* with the control principle – according to Burchhardt, it means that normative valuations of an action can only be correlated with facts which are within the control of the actor. [17]

In Burckhardt's view, the use of the concept of "guilt" leads to the claim that it is legitimate to impose punishment because a crime has been committed, [18] but this is based on the old-fashioned concept of retribution. Therefore, the concept of guilt must be abandoned.

It is true that the Guilt concept is a somewhat worn-out concept and may not be entirely sophisticated. However, it still seems questionable to replace all *Schuldprinzip* with the control principle. The premise of Burchhardt's argument, i.e., the criticism of the use of the Guilt concept in criminal law, is also questionable in itself. [19] In this respect, it seems that one must still be cautious in following Burchhardt's argument. However, it is also true that there are similar aspects to *Schuldprinzip* and the control principle. The differences between them are not easy to define. Therefore, it seems to me that the relationship between the two principles and the contrast in their content still warrant further detailed study.

VI. Final remarks

Finally, let us briefly summarize the results obtained in this paper, as

---

(**16**) Boris Burghardt *Zufall und Kontrolle* (Mohr Siebeck 2018).
(**17**) Burghardt (n16) 325.
(**18**) Burghardt (n16) 214.
(**19**) Claus Roxin/ Luís Greco *Strafrecht Allgemeiner Teil Band I* (2020 C.H.Beck) 996.

well as the consequences that can be derived from them.

(1) First, as mentioned at the end of the previous section, it is important to note that there is an element of "luck" in determining what acts deserve punishment (moral luck cannot be eliminated in criminal law liability), which is not inconsistent with the fact that blame can only be placed on events over which the perpetrator had control. Namely, this means that there is no contradiction in the fact that an actor cannot be punished for events over which he or she had no control (the control principle).

(2) Second, that mentality ethics (Gesinnungsehik) and conduct ethics (Handlungsethik) are different, and that in criminal law, the latter must be determinative.

As Jareborg puts it, insofar as objective requirements beyond the perpetrator's subjectivity are required to conclude criminal responsibility, the intervention of chance is inevitable; according to Jareborg, "Chance is not completely neutralized appears strange only from a metaphysical position that presupposes that it should be neutralized".[20]

(3) If the above consequences are applied to the attempt theory, the consequences obtained there are consistent with the objective attempt theory. In other words, if we believe that it is necessary to take the position of conduct ethics in criminal law decisions, then the objective attempt theory is attributed. If this is the case, there is no room for an attempt to commit an act for which the possibility of harmful consequences does not exist. Moreover, the consequences (harm) caused by the act are an important subject for criminal law judgments, which leads to the conclusion that a reduction of the penalty for attempted crimes is desirable.

(4) Finally, it should be noted that although there is a close relationship between criminal law studies and ethics and moral philosophy, we should be cautious about bringing philosophical arguments directly into criminal law. Often,

---

(20) *Jareborg* (n2) 226.

discussions of criminal law studies and ethics do not connect in a straight line. When we use arguments from moral philosophy, we need to take into account the purpose of criminal law and take care to be consistent with criminal jurisprudence.

Chapter 3
Accomplice Criminal Liability to Masterminds
―― What is the most appropriate Legislation?――*

> "*Making the simple complicated is commonplace; making the complicated simple, awesomely simple, that's creativity.*"
>
> Charles Mingus

I. Agenda

1.1. Criminal law scholar Hermann Kantorowitcz once made the following statement: "The accessory liability theory is the darkest and most complicated chapter in German criminal law (Die Teilnahmelehre ist das dunkelste und verworrenste Kapitel der Deutschen Strafrechtwissenschaft)." [1]

He wrote this in the late nineteenth century; however, the "darkest chapter" in German criminal law studies still exists, even in the 21st century. Indeed, it seems to have become even darker. The situation is the same in Japan.

1.2. In Japan and Germany, penalties for criminal acts involving multiple persons are determined systematically, by identifying the form of involvement of each offender, and applying the penalty requirement corresponding to the form of involvement. Firstly, "co-principals", which refer to offenders that actually carry out the defined criminal acts, are distinguished from other offenders (the accomplices) falling under the definition of "complicity" who are also involved in a criminal act. In turn, the accomplices are separated into "instigators" who incite criminal will and "accessories" who provide psychological/

---

* Many thanks to Prof. Andrew P. Simester for valuable comments.
(1) Kantorowicz, H. *Aschaffenburgs Monatsschrift*, 7. Jahrg., 1910, p.306.

physical support to the "principal."

In what follows, this system of categorisation will be referred to as the "Complicity System."

1.3. Various confusions exist over the interpretation of regulations concerning complicity in countries that have adopted the Complicity System. Of particular concern is the issue of penalizing a person who does not actually carry out the criminal act, but who controls the overall crime as the mastermind behind the perpetrators.

The sarin gas attack on the Tokyo subway in 1995 is a typical example. In that case, the cult leader X ordered several followers to scatter highly poisonous chemical weapon sarin on the Tokyo subway, causing twelve civilian deaths and physically injuring more than a thousand others.

A country with Complicity System would generally treat a case like this by applying the "instigator" provisions. Japan and Germany fall under this category:

> Japanese Criminal Code Article 61, Paragraph 1: A person who induces another to commit a crime shall be dealt with in sentencing as a principal.
> German Criminal Code Section 26: Whoever intentionally induces another to intentionally commit an unlawful act, shall, as an inciter, be punished the same as a perpetrator.

Under such legal systems, the mastermind will be treated as an instigator —that is to say, as an accomplice rather than the principal. (The reference to the "same" penalty being applied indicates the mastermind is not deemed to be the principal, which in turn suggests that he or she must be an accomplice.)

1.4. In Complicity System countries, an accomplice is a regarded as a less serious criminal category than the principal, often being described as a form of "secondary liability".

However, looking at the example above, common sense would suggest that X brought about the deaths of those people who were killed by the sarin, and that indeed he, the mastermind played the key criminal role. Is it enough, then, to punish X only as an instigator, i.e. as an accomplice?

1.5. Under both Japanese and German Criminal Codes, at the sentencing stage, a principal and an accomplice (instigator) can be punished with the same penalty. However, the determination as principal or accomplice reflects the social assessment of the criminal act committed. A principal is a "person who is murderer," whereas an accomplice is a "person who incited murder." These are totally different assessments. In the sarin gas case, is not X a "murderer"? At the very least, he is the moral equivalent of that person.

In addressing this issue, Japanese criminal law scholar Ryuichi Hirano rightly questioned whether it was appropriate to regard the person who actually dropped the atomic bomb or the person who gave the order as responsible for the atomic bombing.[2] Does the Complicity System offer sufficient answer to this question?

1.6. This leads to the issue of punishment for the perpetrator who was responsible for carrying out the defined criminal act, but whose role is not significant in reality, with the mastermind playing the key role. In such a case, can we always say that the perpetrator is the principal because he or she carried out the act? There may be cases where the perpetrator should be treated in law as "the person who assisted the crime" rather than as "the person who carried out the crime."

---

[2] Cf. Hirano, R. "Seihan to Jikko" in *Hanzairon no Shomondai* (*1*), 1981, p.132f. Hirano suggests the right answer would be both of them.

1.7. Many countries with the Complicity System face similar problems. How can we resolve this issue? This paper will examine the penalties imposed and propose a theory for appropriate punishment of accessories. The paper proceeds as follows:

Following is the outline of the paper.

> (1) Firstly, the general theory on punishment of masterminds will be reviewed. If the mastermind is playing a significant role in the overall criminal scheme, is it appropriate to apply a lighter punishment to such person as the instigator rather than as the principal? The issues are classification as accomplice (instigator), and application of legislative theory.
>
> (2) Next, we review the effect on the mastermind where the act of the perpetrator is prima facie a defined crime but the act happened to be justified. Under the German criminal law, the perpetrator must meet certain prerequisites for the crime in order to punish the mastermind as an accomplice. That is to say, the perpetrator must have carried out a defined crime that is not justified. This is a leading theory in Japan as well as Sweden. The appropriateness of this theory will be examined.

I urge readers to consider how penalties will be applied to these cases under your own country's legal system and taking a step back from those laws, what the appropriate punishment is from a legal policy perspective, and what sort of legislation would present the least contradiction as criminal law theory.

II. General Theories on Punishment of Masterminds

2.1. Case Study and Existing Methods of Resolution

2.1.1. Case Study: Cult leader X ordered several followers including Y to scatter highly poisonous chemical weapon sarin on the Tokyo subway. As a result, twelve civilians were killed, and more than a thousand were physically injured.

2.1.2. What is the crime committed by X? "Murder" would be the obvious answer (regardless of various degrees of the crime). For a crime of murder, the perpetrator must be deemed to have committed the act of "killing."

In this case, X did not personally scatter the sarin. Y and others did. If the focus is on the physical act, X has not committed the crime. He simply incited Y and others to do so. In other words, X is not the perpetrator, but the instigator of the murder.

This would be the basic interpretation under the Complicity System. As we have seen, if the provisions of the Criminal Code in Japan or Germany are applied literally, X's crime would be punished as that of an instigator.
However, such a result seems morally questionable. Isn't the mastermind the paradigm criminal subject?

2.2. Theoretical Development
2.2.1. Japan
2.2.1.1. In Japan, the courts have long recognized this question. Even in the era of the former Criminal Code of 1882, case law treated multiple conspirators as co-principals where the crime was carried out by just one of them. The same treatment continued after implementation of the present Criminal Code in 1908. Leading criminal scholars were strongly against this practical treatment, [3] but the courts never took their criticism into account. This indicial categorization as co-principals was initially applied only to intellectual crimes such as extortion. However, it was eventually expanded to arson, murder and robbery, and established as a rule of general application in 1936. [4]

Co-principals are defined as follows:

---

(3) About scholarly opinion, see, Dando, S. *The Criminal Law of Japan: The General Part*, 1997, p239.
(4) Keishu Vol. 15, at 715. Date of the judgment ((pre-war) Supreme Court decision): 1936.05.28.

Japanese Criminal Code, Article 60:
Two or more persons who commit a crime in joint action are all principals.

If taken literally, this seems to require each perpetrator to carry out the murder. In practice, however, the expanded case-law doctrine has been applied to cases like the sarin example in Japan.

2.2.1.2. Many theories have been proposed as the rationale. Until the World War II era, the mainstream theory [5] was to borrow from the union theory in the Japanese Civil Code that the "conspiracy" created an inseparable agent of joint intention, whereupon participants become fully liable for the acts of the agent. However, as this theory was supportive of collective responsibility, it lost persuasiveness under the democratic and liberal constitution introduced after WWII. The theory that took its place focused on the point that the mastermind suppressed objection from the perpetrator by engaging in the "conspiracy" and made all of the co-perpetrators act as his/her tools. It argued that the person who only participated in the "conspiracy" can be held liable as co-principal. It is understood that this theory is being adopted in practice since the Supreme Court decision in 1958. [6]

2.2.1.3. More recently, a theory has appeared that a principal should not be considered as synonymous to a perpetrator, and a person who has not acted as a perpetrator of a crime can be a principal. [7] Under this theory, a principal is a "person who played a significant role" in the crime.

---

(5) Represented by Hyoichiro Kusano, so-called "the theory of a body having a common intent". About Kusano's theory, see, Dando, S. op.cit.fn.3. p.238.
(6) Keishu Vol. 12, No. 8, at 1718. Case number: 1954(A) 1056, Date of the judgment (Supreme Court decision): 1958.05.28. English translation is findable on the following web-site; http://www.courts.go.jp/app/hanrei_en/search
(7) Cf. Hirano, R. op.cit.fn.2. p.132ff., Nishida, N. *Kyohanriron no Tenkai*, 2010, p.51ff.

By developing this theory further, "conspiracy," which was necessary for punishing the mastermind as co-principal, will no longer be a prerequisite. "Conspiracy" can be deemed as a factor for judging the significance of the role.

This more recent theory provides a rationale for punishment of a person involved in a joint crime who plays a significant role as a co-principal (the author believes the Supreme Court decision in 2003 [8] indicates such directionality).

2.2.2. Germany

2.2.2.1. Germany has the following provision for co-principals.

German Criminal Code Section 25:
Article 1: Whoever commits the crime himself or through another shall be punished as a perpetrator.
Article 2: If more than one person commits the crime jointly, each shall be punished as a perpetrator (co-perpetrator).

Cult leader X in the case above incited murder, but did not carry out the crime himself or perform a criminal act jointly with Y. If the letter of the law is followed, Section 25 will not be applicable to X, and he would be deemed to be an instigator in Germany.

2.2.2.2. However, there is an interesting theory in Germany that treats such person as "indirect principal," seen as having committed the crime "through another" in Section 25 Article 1. An indirect principal is subject to punishment as a principal rather than an instigator, despite not having actually committed the crime.

---

(8) Keishu Vol.57, No. 5 at 507. Case Number: 2002 (A) 164, Date of the judgment (Supreme Court decision): 2003.05.01. English translation is findable on the following web-site; http://www.courts.go.jp/app/hanrei_en/search

2.2.2.3. Why is an indirect principal treated as a principal rather than accomplice even though the crime is carried out by another person, and no criminal act is performed by the indirect principal?

The general explanation in Germany is as follows. With an indirect principal, the perpetrator is used as a tool by the mastermind, and cannot be held liable as the principal. Therefore, the mastermind will be treated as the principal. Typically, it applies where the perpetrator does not have capacity to assume liability. Such person lacks mens rea, and will not be punished. Therefore, the liability will be traced back to the mastermind, who will be treated as the principal. (This principle is referred to as the "Responsibility Principle (Verantwortlichkeitsprinzip)" or "Autonomy Principle (Autonomieprinzip)." On the other hand, if the perpetrator is the principal, regression is prohibited (referred to as the "Principle of Non-Regression (Prinzip der Regreßverbot)"). The theory should hold that if the perpetrator is punished as the principal, the mastermind can only be held as accomplice leaving no room to be recognized as an indirect principal.

2.2.2.4. However, this interesting theory assumes that it is possible for the mastermind to actually control the crime. The sarin case would be the most typical example. Because the mastermind controls the act of the perpetrator, the mastermind as well as the perpetrator is the principal under the theory. This is referred to as the "principal behind the principal" (Täter hinter dem Täter).

2.2.2.5. The concept of "principal behind the principal" was created by Richard Lange, [9] and developed by Friedrich-Christian Schröder. [10] Claus Roxin further developed the theory, [11] and German case laws now partially

---

(9) Cf. Kohlrausch, E. & Lange, R., *StGB Kommentar*, 39-40.Aufl., 1950, Vorb.I.B.1 vor§47, p.95.
(10) Cf. Schröder, H. *Der Täter hinter dem Täter*, 1965, p.107ff.

adopt this. (12)

Roxin states that in an organized power structure, the mastermind can be punished as the "principal behind the principal." (13) In the sarin case, an autocratic leader of an organized religious cult instructed his devotees. This would be considered as an example of such power structure. A principal behind the principal is recognized as an exception to the principles of responsibility and autonomy, and as Y and others who committed the act is punished for murder, X will also be punished as the principal for the murder. The principle of non-regression (Regreßverbot) is not applied in such an exception.

2.3. Appropriateness of Punishment as Principal

2.3.1. In the end, for justice to be served, the mastermind ought to be punished as the principal. There are countries other than Japan and Germany that share the idea that the mastermind should be treated as the principal from a practical point of view.

2.3.2. Sweden is one example. Swedish criminal code has the Complicity System similar to Japan and Germany, and distinguishes between the co-principal, instigator and accessory. There are different requirements for each, and whoever satisfies the given requirement will be deemed to be the co-principal, instigator, or accessory. Swedish law distinguishes between principal and accomplice, with co-principal bearing the primary liability, instigator and accessory positioned as bearing secondary liabilities.

However, what makes Sweden unique is that after the classification, facts are observed again, and where necessary, it is permissible to re-classify the principal as an accomplice, and vice versa. A paper by Petter Asp and

---

(11) Cf. Roxin,C. "Bemerkungen zum Täter hinter dem Täter": in *Lange-Festschrift*, 1976, p.173ff.
(12) Cf. BGHSt.40, 218.
(13) Cf. Roxin, *LK* 11.Aufl. §25 Rn.128ff.

Magnus Ulväng provides the following explanation. [14]

> "Swedish law, however, also allows for a re-labeling which could be described as an adjustment made at the very end of the process. Under this procedure persons who are principals (i.e. who actually fulfill the requirements of a specific offence), may in the end be designated as instigators or aiders (depending on whether one or the other fits best) and persons who are "only" instigators or aiders (i.e. persons who do not fulfill the requirements of a specific offence, but is held responsible under Chapter 23 section 4) may in the end be designated as principals. A court can in this way extend (designate and aider or instigator as principal), reduce (designate a principal as an aider or instigator) or convert the role (do both things at the same time) of the parties."

Under a legislative policy that allows such re-labeling, a mastermind that has not actually committed the crime can be punished as the principal.

2.4. Observations

2.4.1. What is clear from the practical development in Japan is that by eliminating the formal standard which allows only those who carried out the criminal act to be co-principals, the difference between principal and accomplice (instigator) immediately becomes vague, and ultimately becomes indistinguishable. In Japanese practice, the instigator category was gradually absorbed into co-principal, and has virtually disappeared except for particular crimes where the principal cannot be punished, such as instigation of suppression of evidence.

2.4.2. On the other hand, if the formal standard such as the one in Germany that requires co-principals to have committed the criminal act is pursued, the distinction between principal and accessory (instigator) may be clear but the decisions will become unjust. Germany is bound by the formal standard due to

---

(14) Asp, P. & Ulväng, M. "Sweden": in A. Reed & M. Bohlander (Eds.), *Participation in Crime*, 2013, p.438.

the Section 25 definition that a person who commits the crime himself shall be the principal, and the consequent requirement that the mastermind must be found to be the principal in order to apply proper punishment. The theory of "principal behind the principal" was a desperate measure created by the Germans to apply justice. The theory is a device invented to solve a problem created only by the formal structures of German complicity law.

2.4.3. Perhaps one may say that provided the instigator is punished with the same penalty as the principal, and that should be enough. Under the Japanese and German criminal laws, the punishment is the same as the principal, so that is sufficient.

However, if the instigator is treated as an accomplice, the instigator cannot be punished with a heavier penalty than the principal, due to its secondary liability categorization. It would be difficult to explain why a penalty heavier than the perpetrator (principal) should be imposed in actual cases. But in reality, the mastermind may well deserve to be punished more than the perpetrator. So, again the formal classification can impede justice.

2.4.4. Another method may be to accept re-labeling like Sweden. However, re-labeling lacks any clear rationale and is inconsistent with rule of law principles. Such process cannot avoid criticism for being opportunistic and ad hoc, and even Swedish scholars are very critical of this provision.

2.4.5. Ultimately, it would be most practical and theoretically consistent to eliminate the concept of instigator, and consolidate it to co-principal, leaving the treatment of individual circumstances to sentencing.

2.4.6. One concern over such legislation is the risk that an act of instigation may be automatically punished as act of a principal, even in cases of criminal attempt. German criminal scholar Roxin has made such argument. [15]

Certainly, if an extremely subjective approach to criminal attempts law is taken, as in Denmark, [16] there could be such a risk. German case law also applies subjective approach to criminal attempts law, so such a criticism could be understandable. [17]

However, the risk can be avoided by requiring "negative value inherent in results (Erfolgsunwert)" in order to punish as criminal attempts. In other words, under an objective approach, punishment for criminal attempt will require a criminal act as well as the emergence of risk of legal interests infringement, i.e., the need for "negative value inherent in results (Erfolgsunwert)."

In short, it is not enough that the perpetrator carries out some act, for the criminal attempts law to be applied. This is also a product of the liberal view of the state, which interprets illegality not as a breach of obligations set by the state, but an infringement of interests protected by the law. Also, the occurrence of "negative value inherent in results (Erfolgsunwert)" is the occurrence of actual harm, which in turn is a requirement for imposing retributive penalty. If the essence of penalties is understood to be retribution, such limits must be set.

III. The Mastermind's Complicity Object

3.1. Case Study and Existing Methods of Resolution

3.1.1. Case Study: B was resentful of the manager of a restaurant, and decided to murder him. B aggressively persuaded A, who was hesitant to accompany B. In the taxi, with the intent that killing the manager may not be avoided, B

---

(15) Cf. Roxin, C. *Strafrecht, Allgemeiner Teil. Bd.2*, 2003,§25 Rn.3.
(16) Cf. Langsted, L.B., Garde, P. & Greve, V. *Criminal Law in Denmark* 3. ed., 2007, p.74.
(17) Cf. Roxin, C. op.cit. fn.15,§29 II , Rn.32, (RGSt.1,439; BGHSt.11, 324.); Jakobs, G. *Strafrecht Allgemeiner Teil*. 2.Aufl, 1991,§25 Rn.17.

persuaded A by instructing him to "use the knife if you get hit," and to wait near the exit of the restaurant. A was waiting for further instruction from B near the exit of the restaurant when the manager unexpectedly came out and mistook A for B. A was beaten, and to defend his life and body, A hit the manager and inflicted minor injuries. How should B be penalized?

3.1.2. In the above case, A committed acts that prima facie constitute a crime of causing bodily injury. However, A acted in self-defense, and was justified. On the other hand, B had positive will to cause harm, and it would be inappropriate to allow B to claim self-defense (at least the established Supreme Court case law in Japan [18] holds that self-defense will not apply as the infringement is not imminent in such a case). Therefore, B will be recognized as the instigator of crime of bodily injury (or, following the debates of the previous chapter, co-principal for the crime of bodily injury).

Seen purely from the appropriateness of the result, there is no practical reason to allow the mastermind whose actions result in harm to the victim to claim self-defense and be left unpunished. More generally, if the justification is personal to the perpetrator, there is no reason why that justification should be available to the mastermind, so the punishment shall naturally apply. [19]

3.2. Theoretical Review

3.2.1. Responsibility for complicity presupposes something in which the accomplice can participate. It could be referred to as a "complicity object". The controlling theory in Germany, Japan and Sweden require that the mastermind

---

(**18**) Keishu Vol.31, No. 4 at 747. Case Number: 1977 (A) 671, Date of the judgment (Supreme Court decision): 1977.07.21.

(**19**) In the case of excessive self-defense, Japanese Supreme Court decided like this. Keishu Vol.46, No. 4 at 245. Case Number: 1992 (A) 788, Date of the judgment (Supreme Court decision): 1992.06.05.

of crime must have a complicity object for the accomplice to be punished.

The act of the principal must be a defined crime, and such act must be illegal and not justified. This is referred to as "limited accessory (limitierte Akzessorietät) " requirement in Germany. A mechanical application of this to the above case would result in the mastermind being unpunished, as the act of the principal is justified.

(None that the indirect principal theory is not applicable, as the perpetrator is neither controlled by the mastermind, nor is his tool.)

3.2.2. Why is there a requirement for complicity object? The background to this theory is the theory that the reason for punishment of the mastermind is for bringing about the criminal act by the principal, or entrapping the principal into a crime. This is referred to as the "Shared Liability Theory (Schuldteilnahmetheorie)" or "Illegal Accomplice Theory (Unrechtsteilnahmetheorie)." If this is the case, the reason for punishment of accomplice will depend on the penalty of the principal, which requires complicity object.

However, the accomplice has not infringed on interests to be protected by law just by entrapping the principal into an illegal act. He only created a criminal. However, as discussed above (see 2. 3. 6.), criminal law can only be applied where the legal interest is infringed upon. Creating a criminal cannot be the reason for punishment as an accomplice.

3.2.3. A more rational explanation would be as follows. The mastermind/accomplice urges the principal through his or her act as accomplice (inciting, aiding, etc.), and causes the resulting infringement of legal interests through the principal. Whether or not the act of the principal is a crime or illegal is irrelevant. What is significant is whether or not there is "Unrecht," that is, "a situation where the legal profit is infringed upon as a matter of fact." This is the most thorough application of the German "Provocation Theory (Verursachungstheorie)."

It argues that thorough application of individual liability in modern society will require that each actor be punished according to his/her act and its results. Even if the act of the perpetrator/principal is justified, the mastermind could be punished if "a situation where the legal profit is infringed upon as a matter of fact" is elicited. If the mastermind is causing "negative value inherent in results (Erfolgsunwert)" by his/her act, i.e., "causing infringement of legal profits by willful act of breach of obligations," he/she meets the requirement for criminal punishment (Note that even if the act of the principal is justified as self-defense, i.e., deemed not to be illegal, "a situation where the legal profit is infringed upon as a matter of fact (Unrecht)" exists if the victim suffers bodily injury).

3.2.4. Thorough application of individual liability would require that the punishment be determined independently for each actor. Whether or not other actors' conducts are defined crimes, or that illegality exists, should be irrelevant. It should be enough that the conduct of the actor and The infringement of legal interests has a causal relationship. Hence, the argument about the complicity object itself is unnecessary.

3.2.5. The conclusion from these reviews is that the rationale for punishment of accomplice should be the same as for the principal. This approach can be called the "Monistic System (Einheitstätersystem)" as opposed to the Complicity System. It is a legislative form that would punish anyone involved in a joint-crime as the principal.

This is not an extraordinary format. In Europe, it is adopted in the criminal codes of Italy, Denmark, Norway, and Austria, and Administrative Offenses Act in Germany. (In practice, similar process is applied to negligence in Germany.) It is also the standard approach in the common law.

IV. What is the Most Appropriate Legislation for Accomplices?

4.1. The above review suggests that, when accommodating legal responses to the realities of crimes, establishing instigator provisions as a legislative theory would not be the best way. A Monistic System is more appropriate.

4.2. Would a dichotomy distinguishing principals and accessories work? This may be possible as legislative theory. However, it is inappropriate to distinguish the two by whether or not a criminal act has been carried out personally; on the other hand, eliminating the distinction based on acts will make the distinction between principals and accessories extremely vague.

In Japan, application of the practical standard, in which the person who plays the significant role is the principal, is already unstable in practice. There are examples where a person who committed the criminal act was punished as an accessory as a result of considering the overall structure of the crime (for example, giving, using and/or smuggling illegal drugs and/or firearms). [20] Even a person who played the significant role of carrying out the crime is treated as an accessory in such cases.

4.3. Trying to distinguish principals and accomplices requires comprehensive determination of vast number of factors; abandoning such distinction and considering the issue as part of sentencing would be the more practical approach. The Monistic System seems superior in actual problem solving.

We have already seen that if individual liability in criminal law is pursued

---

(20) Giving : Hanreijiho No.842 p.127. Date of the judgement (Yokohama district court Kawasaki branch decision): 1976.11.25.
Using : Hanreijiho No.924 p.145. Date of the judgement (Otsu district court): 1978.12.26.
Smuggling: Hanreijiho No.1300 p.153. Date of the judgement (Tokyo district decision): 1988.07.27.

thoroughly, Provocation Theory should be adopted, which leads to the Monistic System. The Monistic System is a necessary outcome as a development stage of modern criminal law.

4.4. There are various criticisms against the Monistic System. In particular, the loss of legal stability (security of rule of law) has been raised over and over again.

However, the important thing in the punishment of participants of a crime is whether or not an infringement of legal interests have occurred as a result of such person's act, and it is essential to ensure its confirmation. If it is confirmed, criminal liability of each person should be determined according to the specifics of each case. [21]

4.5. Furthermore, legal stability cannot be secured by making distinctions between principals and accomplices based on merely superficial form of involvement such as inciting or aiding, without taking account of the importance of the role actually played. The distinction can certainly be made, but unless we recognize the purpose, it would be meaningless. "Clear standards" and "appropriate punishment" is definitely not synonymous.

4.6. Legal security can be maintained by reviewing various factors in sentencing, and clarifying how and why each factor was reflected on the sentence.

4.7. Ultimately, what is important is the visibility of decision-making factors. If some factors are not handled properly, they should be reviewed and criticized. Abolishing the Complicity System and utilizing sentencing does not mean locking up the issue of complicity in a black box.

---

[21] Cf. Matsuzawa, S. "Seihan to Kyohan no Kubetsu ni tsuite" : in *Sone-Taguchi-Festschrift*, 2013, p.827f.

4.8. By adopting the Monistic System, almost all of the difficult issues surrounding accomplices can be resolved. The Complicity System was the source of the darkness that created the confusion described by Kantorowitcz in the nineteenth century, and it continues to haunt complicity theory in many countries today. By eliminating it, the darkness can be lifted, and a clear vision can be gained.

4.9. The legislative formats of Italy, Austria, Denmark and Norway supply examples of what is possible in this respect. However, there seems to be little academic exchange between the Scandinavian nations, Italy and Austria, and not enough comparison is being made with the Brazilian criminal law and US Model Penal Code, which are said to have adopted the same kind of legislative format.

It is important to review practical standards to determine how certain acts should be punished, and what the appropriate level of sentencing is, by referencing the development of practical concept of Monistic System in Japan, and actual operations of re-labeling in Sweden. There is a need for an international joint study from this perspective.

Chapter 4
A Contribution to the Development of Criminal Theory based on the Desert Theory

1. Desert theory is neither too close nor too remote from the criminal theory (Verbrechenslehre). Criminalization of an act is deemed justifiable by the fact that such act is reproachable and can be generally prevented by criminalization. Such grounds for justification form the foundation of the punitive sanctions system itself. On the other hand, punishment based on the desert theory must correctly correspond to the degree of punishment recognized under the criminal theory; therefore, the conclusion drawn under the desert theory is significantly affected by the underlying criminal theory.

This paper attempts to compose a criminal theory suited for the desert theory. That is, to propose a desirable criminal theory not only for one country, but for (1) countries that have adopted, or are in the process of adopting, the desert theory; and (2) criminal scholars who are interested in such theory.

2. Many legal systems recognize that a crime is comprised of both the objective element of an illegal act and the subjective element of liability. Examples include actus reus and mens rea under the common law, and illegality and liability under civil law. Let us first discuss the former element (*actus reus* or illegality).

What is an illegal act? In case of the common law, its origin is believed to lie in the Harm Principle formulated by J.S. Mill. Under civil law, Karl Binding and Franz von Liszt established the Rechtsgüterschutz (protection of legal goods) Theory. Both developments took place in the early 20th century.

Both the Harm Theory and Rechtsgüterschutz Theory have liberal tendencies. This became apparent though arguments on non-criminalization that took place in various countries around the world between the 1960s and 1970s. Both the Harm Principle (through arguments between its proponent H.L.A. Hart and Lord Devlin, who asserted that the mission of criminal laws is to protect morality) and Rechtsgüterschutz Theory (through argument with the conflicting Schutzzweck der Norm / protective scope of the norm Theory) reached the same conclusion. That is, unless there is actual harm, criminal law should not interfere with social life, and that criminal law should not penalize crimes without victims for the mere purpose of protecting morals and order. This suggests that both are based on the principle of liberalism, which prizes the determination of value by citizens, rather than legal moralism, which supports enforcement of morals and ethics by the state. The significance of Harm Principle and Rechtsgüterschutz Theory were recognized as a bulwark against the enforcement of moralism by the state.

More recently, however, the concept of legal goods has become markedly spiritualized. Interests that are extremely vague and ambiguous are now recognized as legal goods, and many laws which impose penalties by capturing the acts long before actual harm occurs are being enacted. Typical examples include laws that penalize the development of human cloning technologies, or organ trading. The Rechtsgüterschutz Theory is being questioned for its lack of substance, and the theory is in a critical situation. There has been significant argument for about fifteen years on what to make of the situation where its function on legislative regulation (i.e., the control function against legislation, in that criminalization is not possible without harm or risk of harm to legal goods) has been lost.

3. On this point, we could refer to the arguments based on the common law tradition. For example, Andreas von Hirsch and A.P. Simester have built on the Harm Principle, which has played a central role in existing criminalization theories by taking hints from Joel Feinberg, by performing detailed analysis

and systemizing the offence theory to use it as the basis of criminalization. Their criminalization theory is based on dual-element account of "harm" and "wrongfulness."

While this dual-element theory is clear to scholars of common law, it is somewhat difficult to understand for civil law academics. In particular, under the German legal concept, the theory of criminalization belongs to the same field as the theory on grounds for penalizing criminal acts, and how it is captured is directly linked with the understanding of the nature of illegality. As such, it is understandable that there would be some resistance to the introduction of dual-element accounts. Namely, Wolfgang Wohlers argues that the dual-element theory is certainly useful and superior to the German theory, but that we need more fundamental principle to unite the Harm and Offence Principles.

However, integration of a dual-element theory into a unitary theory, methodologically speaking, is not easily done (if a monistic theory could have been designed to begin with, dualism would not have been necessary). Thus, what is required here is a basic idea that loosely controls the concept, rather than a unifying theory. A common idea shared between the two theories should be consolidated and presented as a higher-level principle that controls the existing "legal goods theory."

4. The legal goods theory and the Harm Principle originally developed from the utilitarianism concept. J.S. Mill, who was instrumental to the establishment of the Harm Principle, is a utilitarian, and the criminal law itself was based on utilitarianism. This can be seen from the emergency provisions under the civil laws (which require a strict balance of interests for justification). On the other hand, Andreas von Hirsch appears to have been affected by the theory of justice proposed by John Rawls and Amartya Sen. That is, capturing legal goods based on fairness rather than efficiency. On this point, his theory can be

deemed to have propelled the antiquated criminal laws to the level of modern value philosophy and political philosophy.

Let us further develop this theory. While the concept of goods and resources presented by John Rawls stopped at reviewing the allocation of interest, Amartya Sen took it one step further to focus on the functions and nature of the allocated resources, or how they can be utilized. This is referred to as the 'capability approach'.

According to Sen, capability is "a combination of functionings that are feasible for a person to achieve." Under the capability approach, availability, in addition to the conventional resources, can be harmed. For example, a conclusion may be drawn, overall, that an act of destroying potential availability, even if the harm to the resource itself is small or null, can be prohibited strictly, or is punishable.

It may also be applied as a basis of justification for punishment under the offence theory. That is, even offences that do not actually cause harm may have a negative effect on latent pacifistic emotion or psyche of the people. An offence against potential availability may be deemed punishable, even if it does not cause harm to the actual resource.

5.   The effectiveness of the capability approach is also apparent when resources are put under a different light. That is, taking an approach to consider how much latent risk is involved in permitting an unjust act. Sen's theory is said to be better at highlighting injustice rather than justice. If so, it should be useful in measuring latent risks involved in unjust acts.

Let us consider the human cloning technology previously mentioned. If development of human cloning technology was to be punished, the legal goods to be protected can only be assumed to be "human dignity." In Japan, this is the explanation offered by the legislators, which has received some support among scholars. However, this is too ambiguous as the legal goods. Acceptance of such ambiguous legal goods indicates that the concept of legal goods lacks substance in its current form.

On the other hand, the capability approach can capture the risks inherent in the development of human cloning technology. Not only is the outcome of development of human cloning technology unpredictable, but there may be dangerous capabilities that could undermine the existence of the human race. Such acts would provide grounds for restriction.

These dangerous capabilities are comparable to what has been referred to as 'secondary damages'. Secondary damages are not directly caused by an act, and to incorporate them into the determination of illegality is not appropriate for assessment of an act committed by a person, as it would include harm to legal goods which has not actually occurred in the equation. However, it should be possible to add the likelihood of occurrence of a secondary damage as an indicator for assessment of risks and offences from the perspective of capability. In fact, an assessment reflecting capability becomes appropriate for the act.

6. Furthermore, let us consider the issue of remote harm. Is it possible to penalize an act with an abstract risk at a stage considerably before the occurrence of risk or harm to legal goods? Historically, assessment of such risks was conducted without such a strict awareness. This has given rise to the problem of early punishment. Most of the current theories rely on external restrictive principles as the basis of restraint against early punishment, such as criminal law as the last resort or the maintenance of freedom of civil life, although these principles are unrelated to legal goods. To maintain the function of the concept of legal goods in legislative regulation, it must be given an internal principle that resolves this problem. The capability approach is a useful tool for this purpose, as it can provide a clue for analyzing the extent of the risk and permissible degree of expansion for the interpretation of remote harm.

In the past, the main issue had been the extent of the remote harm. For example, in the traditional legislation of criminal laws, penalties for significant crimes such as murder and arson included acts of preparation and attempts at an earlier stage. This criterion remains effective. However, in the capability approach, the latent risk in the harm should also be considered. For example, terrorism prevention legislation should set forth the purpose of the regulation, considering the possible latent harms associated with the acts, and review them separately.

7.   Historically, the concept of legal goods and resources involved the creation of lists. Such lists are important as a basic starting point, but whether the degree of harm to each resource was made sufficiently clear for specific cases is questionable. On this point, components of specific harm that differ by case and person can be grasped separately through latent availability under the capability approach. This should enable the accurate measurement of the value of punishment, which is the foundation of the desert theory. Latent availability of resources may differ at each scene. By precisely reflecting this to the value of punishment, the penalty should become more appropriate.

8.   Against such approach, some who assert the limits of the legal goods theory argue that the concept of legal goods itself should be abandoned as a principle of legislature regulation, or a principle that forms the foundation of illegality.

In Germany, an approach that promotes the abandonment of the legal goods theory and presents the protection of norms commonly shared among the citizens as the mission of criminal law is gaining support. Scholars from Bonn, such as Günther Jakobs and Michael Pawlik, strongly assert this idea. This proposal is also becoming popular in South America, and has also received some support from Japanese academics.

Chapter 4 A Contribution to the Development of Criminal Theory based on the Desert Theory 55

This approach finds the basis of criminality theory in the shared understanding of the norm among the citizens. For those citizens who do not share the same understanding of the norm, it seeks to form such an understanding through punishment. Under this approach, the purpose of punitive sanction is to stabilize the norm. Punitive sanctions will be used as a means to indoctrinate the intentions of the citizens, and thereby create shared values for the social community.

This approach can also be found among the communitarian line of thought which focuses on "public value." However, it must be noted that criminal theories which emphasized "public value," such as the punitive sanction theory under Neo-Kantianism in Germany before WWII, were deployed in a manner that enforced specific moral and ethical values on its citizens. Surely the state and public are different; however, in terms of criminal law, it must be emphasized that public value is realized through the exercise of the right of punishment, which is exclusive to the state. Considering this history and structure, communitarian approaches are inappropriate, at least when applied to the criminal law.

9. Criminal theory should be created from a liberal position. The punitive sanction system is a system where the state imposes a significant burden on its citizens through strong enforcement. Under such a system, the freedom of thought for each individual citizen should be respected to the maximum degree. Punitive sanctions are hard treatment; however, they are there to clearly communicate the intent to the criminals, who are the recipient of the communication. For those who do not listen, the intention must be communicated in a stronger manner. In some cases, therefore, a hard treatment will be called for.

Based on such an approach, the present punitive sanctions system which relies on hard treatment should be eased further. That is to say, we should make efforts to create a more moderate punitive sanctions system which limits the maximum imprisonment to three years for general crimes, and five years for murder. This can be called the decemental strategy.

10. Against such a strategy, questions may be raised that it may be insufficient in terms of reproach or prevention, which are the essence of criminal law. Such questions can be addressed in the following manner. Firstly, on the issue of reproach. Reproach is an indication of denial of punishable acts by the state that "such act is impermissible," and is not an indication of vengeance or retribution. It seems that at the basis of interpretation of reproach as an indication of vengeance or retribution lies the understanding (whether conscious or subconscious) that the state should manage the system of reproach and act for its citizens, because allowing citizens to act upon their vengeance will create chaos. This may be considered a type of social contract theory. However, even if one was to follow the social contract theory, the right to retaliation is not given to the citizens as a civil right, and society cannot act for citizens in relation to something that is not given to them. Rather, reproach is an indication of denial of a criminal act, and does not necessarily mean that a punishment which corresponds to the amount of the criminal act should be given. There may be relative difference in strength, but there is no punishment that can be measured in absolute terms (i.e., absolute proportionality cannot be measured). As such, the allocation of punishment should follow justice (relative proportionality).

Next, on prevention. The fact that heavier penalties do not improve preventative effects has been proven by empirical science. Criminal theory should determine the scope of punitive sanctions from the perspective of defining the acts to be prevented, and provisions of criminal law should be interpreted by focusing on the effect on general prevention. However, punitive sanctions only have meanings as a method of communication of reproach. If so, it is important to secure the strength of communication so that the intent can be communicated effectively. If this is secured, a more moderate punitive sanction is desirable. From these perspectives, decemental strategy should be promoted.

11. A liberal punitive sanctions theory will lead to a criminal theory based on harming of interests. A communitarian punitive sanctions theory will aim to cultivate loyalty to order, and is based on the principle of violation of the norm. It has long been pointed out that the modern society is a risk society, so the tendency is to argue that maintenance of social life will be difficult unless risks are contained through punitive sanctions. Such argument may provide grounds to permit views on punitive sanctions that allow communitarian, ethicalist, or state values. We must stay alert against such tendencies.

Nazi criminal theory abandoned the legal goods concept, and focused on violation of obligations which were unrelated to legal goods. Abandonment of the concept of legal goods will clear the way for the state to criminalize the violation of norms as it sees fit. As history has proven, violations of norms theory do not have the means to prevent nationalism from taking over criminal law. It is important that we are naturally able to deploy common sense gained through history.

Chapter 5
Traces the History and Development of Japanese Criminal Law

I. Introduction[1]

It must be acknowledged that Japanese criminal law has not been well known to all Scandiavian or other European scholars. This may be due to the differences between Japanese and European languages. Japanese uses two-syllable alphabets and some characters from the Chinese language, which are in the nature of pictograms. Furthermore, Japanese syntax is quite different from that of the European languages. Despite this major practical obstacle, I believe that it must be interesting for Danes to know about Japanese criminal law as well, as there are some similarities. Considering only the content, Japanese criminal law is not as different from Danish law as some might imagine. Although Japan is an Asian country, in the 19th century it followed the traditions of European law. Japanese law can therefore be said to belong to a European legal tradition. This is particularly true of the Japanese Penal Code, which was adopted in 1907 under strong German influence and is still in force today, with amendments. It can therefore be said that the situation surrounding the adoption of the Penal Code has certain similarities with the adoption of the Danish Penal Code. However, there are also some very characteristic differences.

In this article I will describe the history and present situation of Japanese criminal law and also deal with some general aspects of Japanese criminal law. Since the most important area for many Japanese scholars has been the liability doctrine and since this is the most characteristic point of Japanese criminal

---
(1) This paper is an English translation of a paper written in Danish for a Danish audience. This is why there are some statements in the text such as "for Danes" etc.

law, I will concentrate especially on this. In Japan there are a large number of universities with law faculties and thus many legal scholars. Each scholar has his or her own professional opinion which is discussed among other scholars, leading to increasingly diverse interpretations of criminal law. Japanese criminal law is has developed under these special circumstances, which are very different from the Danish research environment. This scientific and interpretative disagreement is important to bear in mind when reading what follows. First, let me briefly outline the part of Japanese history that directly leads to the formation of a society based on the rule of law.

II. From the Meiji Restoration to the beginning of World War II

Until 1886, Japan was ruled by a shogun (ruler) residing in Edo (part of present-day Tokyo). The ruling family at this time was the Tokugawa family. Japan was already an empire at that time. The Emperor resided in the city of Kyoto, but had no power, which the Emperor had not had since the 12th century, when the military seized political power. The Emperor's role became symbolic, and he could not act without the approval of the shogunate.

Since 1639, the Tokugawa shogunate had pursued a protectionist policy, closing the 'gateway' to foreign countries with the aim of excluding Christian propaganda from Spain and Portugal. The Christian attitude that 'all were equal before God' was a poor fit with the Tokugawa government and the worldview of Japanese culture. There was a decisive emphasis on rank and almost an Indian-style caste system was practiced. The door to Japan was then closed to the outside world for about two hundred years.

In 1853, a naval invasion by the United States forced Japan to abandon its protectionist policy and open up to the world. The Americans wanted a larger trading market. The American threat was effective, and the large black frigates used in the invasion are still used today to symbolize threats in modern Japanese trade policy. The Tokugawa shogunate was pressured into many unfavorable trade agreements. In Japan, there was growing dissatisfaction with the Tokugawa's dealings. At the same time, there were also fiscal problems. A real opposition to the shogunate was emerging. Forces that cherished the belief that the Emperor was the son of the sun and that Japan was God's country felt threatened by America. A nationalist and imperialist movement began to take shape.

Warriors from Choshu (present-day Yamaguchi in south-western Japan) and warriors from Satsuma (present-day Kagoshima in the south) were the leaders of this resistance. France supported Choshu and Great Britain supported Satsuma. The Tokugawa shogunate was by this time greatly weakened, and these European powers were probably interested in influence over Japan's next government and a large new trade market.

In 1868 Japan reverted to the imperial system, which perhaps most closely resembled the single empire known in Europe. This was the so-called Meiji Restoration. It was the modernization of the legal system and the state that the Meiji regime considered most important. They had seen Asia being colonized by European nations and were aware of the threat. Japan had to become a modern state and improve the unequal agreements made by the Tokugawa shogunate.

The forces coming from Choshu had the greatest influence in the Meiji regime, and because of the French connection, the government invited Gustave Emile Boissonade (1825-1910), a professor at the University of Paris, to Japan and asked him to prepare a draft of the civil code, penal code, etc. In 1880 the first Japanese penal code was adopted and, as Boissonade was French, the law was influenced by French criminal law and the spirit of liberalism and the Enlightenment.

Hirobumi Ito (1841-1909) was inspired by Prussia and thought that the

Prussian model was a good example of an empire. He produced a draft constitution inspired by the Prussian system. He later became the first Prime Minister of Japan. In 1889, the government promulgated the Constitution of the Great Empire of Japan (Dai Nippon Teikoku Kenpo), which was highly imperialistic, and it was during this period that Japan's territory was expanded to include, among other countries, Korea. With the growing imperialist currents, the Penal Code of 1880 was found to be too liberal for Japanese society. As the Japanese constitution was modeled on the Prussian model, the Japanese penal code was therefore adapted under the influence of German criminal law. In 1907, the new Penal Code was adopted. It entered into force in 1908 and remains in force to this day.

At this time, Germany was at the forefront of the so-called modern school, which was inspired by the Italian school of criminal anthropology (Franz V. Liszt (1851-1919) and others). The influence of the modern school was strong in Japan. Japanese jurists, who played a central role in the drafting of the new criminal code, studied the modern school of criminal law in Germany during this period. The Japanese Criminal Code therefore reflects the modern school of thought in Germany during this period. One example is that there are only 264 paragraphs in the Japanese Penal Code. There are no narrowly worded provisions for each individual offense, as seen in the German Penal Code. The German Penal Code still regulates many kinds of homicide, such as 'Mord', 'Totschlag', and 'minderer schwerer Fall des Totschlags', while the Japanese Penal Code, like the current Danish Penal Code, had only one very broadly worded provision on homicide. An important feature of the new Japanese Penal Code was the absence of a principle of legality, and it is possible to observe a certain similarity between the Danish Penal Code and the Japanese Penal Code in this respect. The principle of legality is indeed prescribed in the Danish Penal Code, but it is significant that analogy is not prohibited in this country by Article 1 of the Penal Code. This flexibility in the Penal Code is characteristic of the modern school. Carl Torp, who wrote the influential Danish draft of the Penal Code of 1917, was also influenced by modernist currents. This fact implies similarities between Danish and Japanese criminal codes.

If one considers the role the modernists played in the preparation of the Penal Code, it is not difficult to imagine the authority and influence they had on its later interpretation. In particular, Eiichi Makino (1878-1970), who studied the thought of the modern school under Liszt's supervision in Germany, had a very great influence on Japanese criminal law theory. He believed in the theory of 'Zweckstrafe' (Purposeful Punishment) like Liszt. "Punish education", he said when discussing the theory of 'Erzieungsstrafe' (educational punishment). On the subject of guilt, he believed that the presumed dangerousness of the offender was important. He adopted the concepts of the 'offender principle' and 'subjectivism'. He discussed whether the principle of legality should be included in the law or remain unmentioned. Makino's theory of criminal guilt was very subjective and flexible.

Seiichiro Ono (1891-1986) and Yukitoki Takigawa (1891-1962) studied the so-called classical school in Germany. They adhered to the theory of 'retributive punishment' and, with regard to criminal guilt, they drew on the concepts of the 'act principle' and 'objectivism'. Ono and Takigawa were Makino's opponents. The conflict between different schools of criminal law, which had been seen in Germany, was thus transferred to Japan.

Although Ono and Takigawa both belonged to the classical school, there were major differences in their thinking. Takigawa took a liberalist view and believed that the principle of legality must necessarily be strictly followed. The Government felt that Takigawa's view of the doctrine was too liberalistic. For the national-imperialist government, anything other than Emperor-friendly thinking was to be considered communist, an attitude also known from U.S. McCarthyism after World War II. The government found a book written by

Takigawa to be communist and expelled him in 1933 from Kyoto University. In contrast, Ono argued that "law is national morality" and formulated the nationalist doctrine in the pre-war Fascist atmosphere.

In this situation, the Japanese government sought a complete revision of the Criminal Law of 1907. The government believed that a new law was needed which respected Japanese customs and at the same time adapted to modern criminal policy. A government draft of the general section of the Penal Code was presented in 1931, and the special section followed in 1940, but because of the World War the bills were never debated in Parliament.

III. The period immediately following Japan's defeat in World War II and the development of the 'formal responsibility doctrine'

After the surrender at the end of World War II, Japan's New Constitution (Nihon Koku Kenpo) was adopted and promulgated under the guidance of the United States. The Constitutional principles on which it is based are respect for human rights, democracy and peace. These were principles that were relatively new to Japanese criminal law in the Constitution. During the World War, political dissent and opponents of the war had been suppressed and punished. Many people who advocated liberal or communist views had been arrested, sometimes tortured and liquidated. The Japanese Constitution contained more specific provisions on criminal justice than are found in many other countries. They were put in place so that the events of the war would never be repeated. The American influence on the administration of justice led to the adoption in 1948 of a new Criminal Procedure Code which respected equality of treatment and the rights of the individual.

The Criminal Code was not thoroughly revised, but was amended by pointing to additions and omissions. For example, the section on crimes

Chapter 5 Traces the History and Development of Japanese Criminal Law

against the Emperor was deleted. The powers were placed on an equal footing under criminal law, and a section on the use of force by public officials was added. The principle of legality was not included in the Criminal Code, as it was already included in the Constitution, and thus the discussion on the use of analogy was also ended.

In the new Japanese society, the influence of the so-called modern school was greatly weakened. The Japanese modern school of thought was found to be too subjective and the descriptions of deeds too broad. It was now believed that this posed a danger of violating fundamental human rights.

The classical school became influential, but instead of the nationalistic Ono, who after the capitulation was banished from public work, Shigemitu Dando (1913-2012) became the leader of the Japanese classical school of criminal law. He found the description of the crime important for the typification of the crime and formulated many characteristics of the individual descriptions of the crime. For example, Dando found that intent and negligence were missing from the individual crime descriptions.

Dando believed that the more practical and systematic the structure of each provision, the less the risk of arbitrary sentencing and the better the protection of fundamental human rights. This theory is known in Japan as the Theory of "Tatbestand" and is widely accepted in practice today. Ono, who was Dando's supervisor during his studies, had a similar conception, but Dando developed it and elaborated on it and practiced the doctrine, which therefore became more significant than Ono's theory. Dando found that systematization and precision were important for the new Japanese society and developed several different theories.

Dando attempted to solve all problems related to criminal law theory through a deductive approach without deviating from a systematic construction. His model of solution was sometimes rarely suited to concrete cases, and this later led to criticism of the theory.

In the 1950s, the *'finale Handlungslehre'*, contributed by the German professor Hans Welzel (1904-1977), was introduced in Japan. According to this doctrine, an act includes not only the evilness of the external act, but also subjective factors such as the impulse or determination of the will. The systematic consequences of this doctrine has had a decisive influence on the idea that the illegality of a crime consists of both objective and subjective aspects.

Welzel's theory had a very strong influence on German criminalistic practice and jurisprudence. German penal theory imitated and absorbed some ideas derived from the doctrine of the 'Finalismus'. Some of Welzel's theories were widely adopted in Japan. Although only a few scholars adopted the 'final action doctrine', his theory of illegality became the prevailing doctrine in Japan.

Welzel's theory holds that illegality is not only the violation of the law and the infringement of the legal goods, but also the violation of national and social moral norms. Many Japanese scholars since Ono's time had thought that illegality was tantamount to the violation of national and social moral norms, and Welzel's ideas could therefore be easily transferred to Japanese criminal law scholarship.

IV. The influence of Anglo-American law and empirical criminal jurisprudence

In the 1960s, the influence of empirical Anglo-American law in Japan became stronger, and American influence also began to show itself in the field of jurisprudence. This development was first noticeable in the field of civil law and the sociology of law. It later developed into a discussion on the interpretation of the law in general. A more empirical and pragmatic interpretation began to be demanded. Ryuichi Hirano (born 1920), one of Japan's most important empirical oriented law professors, believed that it was necessary to consider the function of criminal law in society. Criminal law should not be analyzed in the abstract, but concretely for each problem. In particular, criticized Ono's nationalistic moral criminal law doctrine and Dando's formally systematic responsibility doctrine, and argued that Japanese society needed a more liberal doctrine consistent with the basic ideas of the new Constitution. Hirano was influenced by Takigawa and criticized the Japanese prevailing doctrine of illegality, which prescribed that illegality was a violation of national and social moral norms. Hirano considers that the direct, concrete interest of protection, the 'legal goods' (das *Rechtsgut*), is a fundamental principle of criminal law and that one can only speak of illegality if the 'legal goods' are violated. This discussion is related to the discussion of victimless crime. Ono and Dando considered that, despite the lack of a direct, concrete interest of protection, the violation of social and moral norms should be sufficient for the imposition of criminal liability. For example, in Japanese criminal law, in the case of pornography, there is often no violation of a direct, concrete interest in protection, but only of a social and moral norm. In the case of Ono and Dando, punishment could be imposed for dissemination of pornography, but not in the case of Hirano and Takigawa, as no direct, concrete interest in protection was violated. Hirano's arguments were supported by young scholars at the time and played a major role in the discussion on the revision of the Penal Code, discussed below.

  Hideo Fujiki (1932-1977) was one of the scholars who was influenced by American law. Fujiki was politically conservative and opposed to, for example, the decriminalization of victimless crimes. He developed many new theories and reflections on new crimes and issues that industrial society brought with it, such as white-collar crime, labor market crime, and environmental crime. Fujiki tried to develop a more substantive theory of responsibility than his supervisor, Dando, had done. Up to and including Dando's generation of scholars, the attitude was that the main function of the scholar was to contribute their own systematic theories and critiques of judicial practice, but after Fujiki, some scholars began to consider how their own theories could be applied and become useful in practice. This was an important turning point for Japanese criminal law scholarship. Not only theoretical German scholarship but also empirical Anglo-American scholarship began to be forged.

V. Failure of the Criminal Code Revision

As mentioned above, the new Japanese government did not revise the Criminal Code immediately after World War II. After the peace treaty with the Allies in 1952, Japanese society stabilized and the government began a complete overhaul of the penal code. In 1956, the Japanese Minister of Justice set up a commission to prepare the revision of the law. Ono, who was allowed to resume public service, became chairman of the commission. After some years of preparation for the revision, a new and larger commission was set up by the Ministry of Justice in 1963, again with Ono as chairman.

The discussions in the commission did not proceed smoothly. Ono and other conservative scholars felt that the function of the courts should be to uphold morality, and allowed stricter penalties and criminalization of additional offences. On the other hand, Hirano and young scholars held to a revision that was characterized by liberal views and involved decriminalization. The young scholars cited arguments by the British legal philosopher H.L.A.Hart and referred to comments on the 1957 English 'Report from Wolfenden Committee'. The young researchers found it necessary to make a clear distinction between criminal law and morality.

The Commission also included practitioners who differed widely in their views. The public prosecutors believed that there should be more provisions for strict liability as a consequence of the already introduced American-style procedural law. Eventually Hirano and some other scholars and lawyers set up their own working group to study the revision of the criminal code. In 1974, they published a counter-proposal to the Minister of Justice's draft in which they sharply criticized the official draft. In addition, there was strong criticism from psychiatrists against the draft regulations on insanity. The strong opposition and criticism made it impossible for the draft to become law.

VI. The present situation and future of Japanese criminal law

The controversy that arose in connection with the draft revision of the Penal Code continued in the 1970s and 1980s. The issues of the relationship between law and morality, victimless crimes and decriminalization were originally criminal policy problems. However, many Japanese scholars believed that there was a connection to the problem of the doctrine of criminal responsibility, especially with regard to whether illegality is due to the violation of national and social moral norms or to the violation of an individual protection interest. They therefore concentrated on discussing what illegality was. The discussion became more and more abstract and eventually turned into a metaphysical discussion about the whole doctrine of responsibility. For example, about what a criminal law norm is, what criminal dangerousness means, and whether the general subjective element of illegality is present or not. This previously heated discussion has now ended with many scholars coming to the view that illegality consists of a infringement of an individual protection interest. They find that using social and moral norms as a basis for criminal liability does not fit well with the liberal Japanese constitution.

As mentioned, Hirano's research had significance in two respects; one was a liberal conception of criminal law, and the other was an empirical, problem-oriented approach. In Japan, the liberal conception of radiological law became the prevailing doctrine, but not the empirical approach. Many

Japanese scholars still adhere to the German systematic approach. Today, almost all German scholars believe that illegality contains many subjective elements which were originally objective. Many Japanese scholars, however, still believe that subjective and objective elements must be divided in the same way that English-American criminal law distinguishes between actus reus and mens rea, and that subjective elements are generally related to the culpability issue. Although Japanese criminal law theory thus differed greatly from German theory today, the German systematic-complex theories continue to be introduced into Japanese liability doctrine. As a result, Japanese criminal law theory has become more and more complex, and some Japanese prosecutors and judges feel that it has become difficult at times to understand the theories of Japanese scholars. There is therefore some difference between practice and theory in Japanese criminal law. Many Japanese scholars have felt that it is important to demonstrate their own personal views on criminal law in their theory, especially since Dando, who made his own views clear in the theory. This is also one reason why practitioners found it difficult to accept scholars' theories. In the 1990s, a new movement began to give Japanese criminal law a more empirical disposition. Masahide Maeda (born 1949), for example, believes that it is necessary to make Japanese criminal law scholarship more pragmatic and functional. Maeda believes that the most important thing for Japanese criminal law is not complex and systematic theory, but 'feedback' between practice and theory. It was only in 1994 that the wording of the Japanese Criminal Code was changed to contemporary language for ease of understanding. Maeda's approach is necessary for Japanese criminal law in the future. If, as in the past, scholars find systematic German criminal law most important, the gap between Japanese theory and practice will become even wider. In fact, some Japanese scholars sometimes introduce German theory which has no connection with Japanese practice or social situation. In my opinion, this is a complex and unproductive discussion in Japanese criminal law. Japanese criminal law scholarship needs a more empirical and pragmatic approach, and this is one of the reasons for my research on Danish criminal law. With empirical and pragmatic thinking, I believe that Japanese criminal law scholarship can develop in a new direction.

Chapter 6
Death Penalty in Japan
——In light of the introduction of the mixed-panel system and recent developments in the criteria for applying the death penalty——

I. Introduction

The topic given to me is "Control of the Death Penalty and Effective Use of the Death Penalty in Japan". [1] In response to this, the content of this article will begin with an introduction to the current laws regarding the death penalty and the current status of executions in Japan as a prerequisite for controlling the death penalty. Next, as an aspect of death penalty control, the report will introduce recent developments in the role and function of the Minister of Justice, who ultimately issues the order for execution. The next section will introduce the criteria for the application of the death penalty as a means of controlling the death penalty in the application of the death penalty. Just this Monday, [2] the Supreme Court confirmed the death sentence in the Hikari-City Mother and Child Murder Case. It has been pointed out that the standard for the application of the death penalty in this case is different from the conventional standard. I will introduce this point. Then, I will introduce the criteria for the application of the death penalty under the so-called mixed-panel system, a landmark reform in Japan's criminal justice system in which citizens are allowed to participate in trials. Finally, I will introduce the debate in Japan regarding the effectiveness of the death penalty and its effective use, and present some ideas.

---

(1) This paper is a manuscript of a symposium on 'Judicial Control of the Death Penalty' held at Jilin University, China, in March 2012. It should therefore be noted that the situation in Japan described here is as of that time.

(2) Monday, 14th March 2012.

Since I am a specialist in criminal law (criminal substantive law), my discussion will focus on the death penalty as a theory of criminal law interpretation. In other words, my discussion will focus on the current status of the death penalty and the control of executions, as well as the criteria for applying the death penalty as a theory of punishment. It must be noted in advance that we cannot touch upon constitutional debates such as the constitutionality of the death penalty, or criminal policy debates such as the response to judges or the restoration of damages to victims.

II. Provisions in the Penal Code and Current Status of Execution of the Death Penalty

First, we would like to review the provisions on the death penalty in the Japanese Penal Code. Article 9 of the Penal Code stipulates the death penalty as the maximum punishment among the principal offenses. There are 12 types of crimes that carry the death penalty in Japan, but the actual cases in which the death penalty is imposed are limited to murder and robbery-murder.

Article 10 of the Penal Code regulates the execution of the death penalty. The method of execution is by hanging. The actual method of execution has long been shrouded in secrecy, but in 2010, former Minister of Justice Keiko Chiba opened the Tokyo Detention Center's execution chamber to the public so that the public could get some idea of how the death penalty is carried out. In 2010, former Minister of Justice Keiko Chiba opened to the public the execution chambers at the Tokyo Detention Center, giving the public some idea of what goes on there. The chambers opened to the public were: the "chapel" where the prisoners receive religious instruction; the "execution chamber" where the hangings are carried out; the "witness chamber" where the prosecutors watch the execution; the "front chamber" where the execution is announced; and the "button chamber" where the execution officer presses the button for execution. The front room is a religious facility with Buddhist paintings hanging on the walls. The front room can be separated from the execution chamber by a curtain. The ceiling of the execution chamber has a pulley embedded in it, through which ropes are threaded around the necks of executed prisoners, and a retractable "step board" approximately 1 meter square is installed on the floor directly below. The treads are operated in the "button room. There are three buttons on the wall of the button room, but only one button to open the treads. Three executioners press the button at the same time, so that it is impossible to tell whose button opened the step, thereby reducing the psychological burden on the prison staff. From the witness room, the prosecutor and the head of the penal institution can watch the execution through the glass.

Executions are carried out by order of the Minister of Justice in accordance with Article 477, Paragraph 1 of the Code of Criminal Procedure. Since the Minister of Justice has the final control over executions, we will introduce the attitude of the Minister of Justice toward executions. In Japan, executions were suspended for a short period of time after World War II. This was because the Minister of Justice did not sign the order. This was for three years and four months, from November 1989 to March 1993. Executions were then resumed when former Justice Minister Masaharu Goto signed the order. Ghotoda emphasized that the country is ruled by the rule of law, and he decided to carry out the executions. Since then, executions have been carried out every year. Since 2007, however, the number of death sentences has been on a gradual decline, and in 2011, no executions were carried out.

The current Minister of Justice, Toshio Ogawa, is said to be in favor of abolishing the death penalty. In an interview, he stated his thoughts on the death penalty. "If I had to decide whether I wanted to do it or not, I would say I didn't want to do it," he said. However, it is the responsibility of the minister of justice to carry out the death penalty. Failure to carry out his duties as required by law is unacceptable.

The idea for a study group on the death penalty set up by former Justice Minister Keiko Chiba at the ministry in 2010. In the study group, we often heard opinions about the existence or non-existence of the old system. It is not efficient to hear the same opinions over and over again. We would like to discuss the method of execution and the treatment of convicts on death row, rather than the existence or non-existence of the death penalty.

Next, in explaining the current status of the death penalty, it is necessary to discuss the criteria for selecting the death penalty, which will need to be addressed in relation to the mixed-panel system.

III. Criteria for death penalty selection under the mixed-panel system

3.1. Introduction of the mixed-panel system

In Japan, the mixed-panel system was introduced in 2009 to allow citizens to participate in criminal trials. Unlike the jury system in the U.K. and the U.S., the system is similar to the system on the European continent, in which the judge, in consultation with a professional judge, determines the guilt of the accused and the sentence. Citizens participate only in serious cases. This includes cases involving crimes punishable by death or life imprisonment or imprisonment without work (Article 2, Paragraph 1, Item 1 of the Mixed-panel Chamber Law) and cases involving crimes in which the defendant intentionally caused the death of the victim through criminal conduct (Paragraph 2, Item 2 of the Mixed Panel Law), so naturally, the participation of judges is required in cases where the death penalty is sought, and the death penalty is also applied. The death penalty is also to be applied. To date, a total of 12 death sentences have been handed down in mixed-panel trials. All of them were cases in which the death penalty was sought (in two cases in which the death penalty was sought but life imprisonment was imposed, it can be said that the sentences given were relatively close to those sought).

3.2. Nagayama Standard and the Hikari-City Mother and Child Murder Case

Traditionally, there has been what is known as the "Nagayama Criterion" regarding the selection criteria for the death penalty in Japan. The Nagayama Criterion, named after the defendant Norio Nagayama, is a death penalty selection criterion set forth by the Supreme Court in a case in which a defendant killed four people in succession with a gun he stole from a U.S. military base. The Supreme Court stated, "Under the current legal system, which has the death penalty, the defendant's guilt, motive, and manner of the crime, the persistence and brutality of the means of killing, the seriousness of the result, the number of victims killed, the victim's bereaved family, social impact, the age of the offender, previous criminal record, and post-crime circumstances must be considered in combination with various other circumstances, and the defendant's guilt must be so serious that the death penalty is the only option for the offender. The death penalty is also permissible if the crime is so serious that the death penalty is unavoidable from the standpoint of the proportionality of punishment and from the standpoint of general prevention". [3]

Generally speaking, the following factors are often summarized: 1) the nature of the crime, 2) the motive for the crime, 3) the manner of the crime, especially the persistence and brutality of the killing method, 4) the seriousness of the result, 5) the victimization of the bereaved family, 6) social impact, 7) the age of the criminal, 8) previous criminal record, and 9) the post-crime circumstances. Theoretically, however, attention should be paid to the second half of the sentence, which deals with (1) the proportionality of crimes and

---

(3) 1981 (A) 1505 Keishu Vol. 37, No. 6.

sentences and (2) general prevention.

In the Nagayama case, the relationship between (1) and (2) was not necessarily explicitly stated. However, the expression "When the maximum penalty is found to be unavoidable, it must be said that the choice of the death penalty is permissible," suggests that the court was very cautious about choosing the death penalty, or that it would seek to avoid the death penalty if possible.

Recently, however, the Supreme Court, in the appeal hearing of the so-called Hikari-City Mother and Child Murder Case, while quoting the Nagayama standard, changed the wording of the Nagayama decision to "In cases where the maximum punishment is found to be unavoidable, it must be said that the choice of death penalty must be allowed," and after stating the facts of the case, held that "The defendant's guilt is so grave that, unless there are extenuating circumstances, he must be given the choice of death penalty. After stating the facts of the case, the court concluded that "the defendant's guilt is so serious that, in the absence of extenuating circumstances, it must be said that the death penalty is the only option.

This holding can be understood as providing a framework for judgment in which (1) the choice of the death penalty is considered as the primary factor from the viewpoint of the proportionality of crimes, and then (2) extenuating circumstances, i.e., whether the death penalty can be avoided from the viewpoint of general or special precaution (Toshihiro Kawaide).

In the Hikari-City Mother and Child Murder Case, an 18-year-old boy, with the intention of raping a woman (mother), entered her apartment complex, killed her when she strongly resisted his attempts to rape her, then committed adultery with her, and when her child (baby) cried, he beat her to death on the floor. It was an unplanned and brutal case that attracted a lot of public attention. The first trial court sentenced him to life imprisonment and the high court also sentenced him to life imprisonment, but the Supreme Court reversed and remanded the high court's decision based on the aforementioned criteria, and after the reversal, the high court sentenced him to death. Although the case is timely, it is understood as a case that demonstrates the difficulty of applying the death penalty, as far as the media reports, especially on TV, are concerned.

3.3. Mixed-panel System and Criteria for Applying the Death Penalty

Assuming that the criteria for the selection of the death penalty are as described above, what kind of discussion is taking place regarding the criteria for the selection of the death penalty under the mixed-panel system? In particular, it has been pointed out that the criteria in the Nagayama standard are unclear (as mentioned above), and attempts are being made to clarify them.

For example, the following criteria have been proposed by one prominent criminal judge In general, (1) the criminal circumstances (facts that determine the existence or non-existence of the right to punishment, mostly but not exclusively the responsibility) determine the general framework of the sentence. (2) general circumstances (criminal policy considerations such as the defendant's age and motive, which fall under general and special precautionary considerations, but are not limited to them) to determine the final sentence, and then, with regard to the death penalty, (1) whether the death penalty can be chosen only on the basis of criminal circumstances, and (2) General circumstances should only be taken into consideration in order to avoid the death penalty (Harada Kunio). This view has already begun to be adopted in some mixed-panel trials and is expected to serve as a certain standard in the future.

It has been pointed out that the upper limit is determined according to responsibility and general circumstances are taken into consideration in the direction of avoiding the death penalty, which is consistent with the "negative responsibility principle" that "if there is no responsibility, there is no penalty" (Yuji Shiroshita), and from the standpoint of criminal law theory, this should be evaluated positively.

IV. Effects of the death penalty and its use

The effectiveness of the death penalty has always been an issue in the debate over the existence or abolition of the death penalty. Although it has been pointed out by some (Norio Takahashi) that there has been no theoretical progress in this area for a long time and that the issue of the death penalty is not a theoretical issue but a policy issue, we would like to reexamine this issue here. In other words, the death penalty from the standpoint of rationale.

Criminal law or punishment can be likened to a deleterious drug with strong side effects. Therefore, punishment must be rigorously justified theoretically. The classical justifications for punishment are the theories of retributive punishment, education, and ameliorative punishment, but recently, these two theories are generally discussed as special prevention and general prevention, integrating and exalting the two aspects. First, from the viewpoint of the special precautionary theory, the death penalty is a system that gives no future to the accused, so there is no room for justification from the special precautionary theory, either from the aspect of improvement or from the aspect of punishment. In contrast, according to the general prevention theory, there is room for justification for both passive and active general prevention. For the former, it can be said that the death penalty will keep the public away from crimes, and for the latter, it can be said that the death penalty will confirm the norm and imprint a sense that people should not commit crimes in their consciousness. It has long been known, however, that there is no empirical evidence of the effects of punishment. Rather, it may be easier to justify the lack of empirical opportunity from a positive general precautionary theory. Taking a more extreme position, or perhaps justifying the death penalty on the basis of maintaining the public's confidence in the judiciary (especially if the public consciousness is strongly inclined toward the existence of the death penalty, a distrust of the judiciary could be generated with regard to the absence of the death penalty).

The above justifications are possible, however, from a theoretical standpoint, it is difficult to utilize the death penalty. This is because the death penalty is the most deleterious drug in the criminal or penal system, and its effectiveness has not been proven to be comparable to the side effects of deleterious drugs. The fact that there are even defendants who state that they committed crimes because they want to be executed can even be said to have the opposite effect of the deterrent effect (Kanako Takayama). In addition, it must be said that it is difficult to effectively utilize the death penalty, a system whose effectiveness is not always indispensable.

At the same time, however, it is also difficult to lead the discussion only in a theoretical direction, since the penal system and criminal law, not only the death penalty, are very strongly underpinned by public consciousness, culture, ethics, history, and religious views (recall, for example, the difficulties of harmonizing criminal law in the European Union).

In 2011, for the first time in 19 years, there were no executions in Japan. Considering that the only postwar years with no executions were 1964, 1968, and 1990-1992, it is not impossible that this could be an opportunity to stop the death penalty (as of December 31, 2011, there were 130 convicts on death row, the highest number since the war). As the Minister of Justice has the authority to order executions, the death penalty should not be carried out like a conveyor belt (in fact, one Minister of Justice recently stated that the death penalty should be carried out like a conveyor belt, but his insight should be questioned), but should be carried out after repeated discussions. With the Hikari-City verdict now finalized, further discussion is needed, but it is also true that the materials for discussion are not yet in place. In particular, it has been pointed out that there is a lack of information on the current state of executions.

V. Conclusion

Finally, I would like to conclude my report with my own analysis.

It is said that many countries in Europe, the United States, and Africa have abolished the death penalty, while many countries in Asia have the death penalty. This is an example of how the death penalty is not completely linked to the theoretical development of human rights, but rather, criminal law is closely related to ethics, religion, history, and culture. On this basis, why does the death penalty exist in Japan? I personally believe that the idea of "revenge" is a major factor. This is the culture of the samurai, who believed that to remain killed was to lose face and honor, and this idea is very strongly ingrained in the Japanese people. As long as this point does not change, the Japanese people's expectations of the death penalty will not disappear.

How can the abolition of the death penalty be achieved in Japan? If so, it is likely to be through external pressure. When major social structural changes occur in Japan, they are often the result of external pressure. For example, if the current situation in South Korea regarding the death penalty were better known, it would have a great impact. Also, if the U.S. abolishes the death penalty, it will almost certainly lead to the abolition of the death penalty in Japan.

Chapter 7
Low-level Penalties in Japan: Fines and Petty Fines

I. Introduction

1.1. Objective

This article discusses low-level penalties in Japan through fines and petty fines. Unlike other countries that allow community service and electronic tagging (i.e., ankle monitors) as another form of low-level penalty, Japanese criminal law establishes that low-level penalties in Japan solely take the form of financial punishment. In other words, financial punishment is the only other option after the maximum penalties (death penalty and imprisonment).

Japanese criminal law establishes four categories within financial punishment: (1) fines (Art. 15), (2) petty fines (Art. 17), (3) confiscation (Art. 19), and (4) collection (Art. 19). The first two categories are principal punishments, which are punishments imposable standing alone. The last two categories are supplemental punishments, which are only imposable on top of a principal punishment. Confiscation and collection as supplemental punishments serve to deprive financial assets and exist in the name of "punishment." It is difficult to see these as more conventional types of punishment because their legal character is vague. Some say that supplemental punishments are not penalties but more of a security measure (measures to remove the cause of crime). In light of this, this article will explore fines and petty fines as principal punishments in the context of traditional low-level penalty.

Additionally, a suspended sentence (with probation) can also be considered a low-level penalty. However, Japanese case law does not consider this as a type of punishment. This view could be criticized, but this article will follow case law and consider suspended sentences as a method of imposing punishment and will not further pursue this issue.

1.2. The difference between fines and petty fines

This section will give an overview of fines and petty fines. Fines and petty fines are similar in that they are considered financial punishments. They can be distinguished by the price tag. Financial punishment in excess of 10,000 yen is a fine. If it is in excess of 1,000 yen but less than 10,000 yen, it is a petty fine.

The first difference is, a suspended sentence can be given for fines but not for a petty fines (Art. 25-1). Second, if an offender commits another crime during probation and is subject to another fine, probation is voidable *only for fines*. Third, the statute of limitations for fines is three years compared to one year for petty fines. Fourth, when an offender is imposed a punishment heavier than a fine, it can result in limitations to licenses and certifications (i.e., suspension of a medical license).

II. General Knowledge of Sentencing in Japan

2.1. Sentencing in Practice

Japanese criminal law does not have general provisions on sentencing.[1] For this reason, the sentencing standard in Japan is left to practitioners, specifically judges, to set. This standard is known as "punishment in accordance with *tatschuld*." *Tatschuld*[2] is the degree of harmfulness and blameworthiness, or

---

(1) Article 248 of the code of criminal procedure states that "[w]here prosecution is deemed unnecessary owing to the character, age, and environment of the offender, the gravity of the offense, and the circumstances or situation after the offense, prosecution need not be instituted." Some have explained the listed situations to be references for sentencing; but we should only recognize these as references and nothing more.

(2) This is a German word with no available English translation. For this reason, the German word will be used as it is.

in other words, the seriousness of the offenders' conduct. In the European continental law context, it is the degree of illegality or responsibility. Punishment in accordance with *tatschuld* is the basis for sentencing.

Let me further explain what *tatschuld* is. In Japanese criminal law, when we are determining whether something is a crime, we only consider the conduct itself. In other words, circumstantial facts surrounding the conduct is irrelevant to *tatschuld*. However, after crime status is established and we move on to the sentencing stage, where we determine the degree of punishment, we start considering the circumstantial facts surrounding the conduct in addition to the conduct itself. For example, in addition to the crime itself, we will consider the events leading up to and motivations behind the crime or the wrongfulness of the crime. In Japan, we call this *"hanjo"* which roughly translates to "criminal circumstances." The degree of the criminal circumstances is the starting point in sentencing.

After *"hanjo"* is determined, we look to the circumstantial facts related to the offender. For example, we will consider factors such as the degree of the offender's remorse, the need of restitution, whether the victim is inclined to forgive, and whether the offender has a support system. This is known as "general circumstance."

In this way, practitioners in Japan decide sentences.

2.2. Theoretical Analysis

The controlling theory (academic theory) in Japan adds an explanation to Japanese sentencing. *Tatschuld*, or the seriousness of the crime, has some room for interpretation to a certain extent. Within that room, there are considerations of individual special prevention and, depending on the situation, general prevention with societal impact of the crime in mind – and eventually, the final sentence is decided. This explanation is similar to the "playing room" theory, which is the dominating theory in Germany. Japanese judges also, at least from their published articles, hold the same opinion.

However, the playing room theory comes with its faults. To begin with, the notion that responsibility has some breadth for interpretation is problematic in the context of legal consistency. Furthermore, the justification for this broad interpretation is unknown. If anything, responsibility should be decided not on a broad scale, but at one point. This is known as the "point theory". The theoretically better explanation is this: at that "point", sentencing should be adjusted based on practical considerations related to the offender themselves. In other words, we are adjusting sentencing out of "equity factors" [3] that includes humanity and tolerance, rather than the unrelated preventative considerations. This theory can be said to be a derivative of a sentencing principle based on the desert model, otherwise known as the principle of proportionality. [4]

This theory is not only theoretically superior but is more compatible with the reality of practice in Japan. With *tatschuld* as its foundation, analyzing mitigating factors from the perspective of humanity and tolerance is a plausible approach as an explanation by Japanese practitioners (Matsuzawa, 2018).

Sentencing for fines and petty fines as low-level penalties should, per se, follow this standard. However, that seems difficult in a real-world setting. I will return to this topic in later sections.

III. History of the Punishment System in Japan

The Japanese legal system was originally modelled after the Chinese system, but it experienced a significant change after the Meiji Restoration, where the system was reformed to inherit western concepts. Financial punishments

---

(3)　See, Swedish Criminal Code (BrB1962:700) Chapter 29, Article 5.
(4)　A more detailed explanation of this theory will not be addressed here in light of spatial constraints, but it is worth exploring its main proponents including von Hirsch, 2017.

existed before the Meiji restoration, but it is not a predecessor to the current fines and petty fines.

The first "Criminal Code" (not as a category of law, but as a name) in Japan that inherited western concepts was enacted in 1880, modelled after French law. This law divided crime into misdemeanor and felony. As for fines and petty fines, it had fines as a principal punishment of misdemeanor (Article 8), petty fines as a principal punishment of police offense (Article 9), and fines as a supplemental punishment (Article 10).

Later, in 1907, a new "Criminal Code," this time modelled after German law, was enacted. This law is criminal law as we know it today in Japan. Fines and petty fines are established as principal punishments. The amount fined, in consideration of inflation, has increased since it was first enacted. Currently, fines and petty fines are established as financial punishments. Fines are in excess of 10,000 yen, and petty fines are in excess of 1,000 yen but less than 10,000 yen. Moreover, a sentence for a fine can be suspended. Suspended sentences for fines were first recognized after World War II.

IV. Current Fines in Japan

4.1. Fixed-amount System

Fines in the current criminal law take the fixed-amount system. When the current criminal law was first enacted in 1907, the fixed-amount system was the only system in existence even at the international level. [5] Even after the daily fine system came into existence, it was never implemented.

When you implement the fixed-amount system, there is a problem as to how to handle offenders who do not have the financial ability to pay fines. In Japan, delayed payments or payments by installments have been allowed in

---

(5) The daily fine system did not exist yet.

practice (depending on the circumstances) but are not recognized by the system. For this reason, Article 18 of the criminal law provides for the "detention in a workhouse in place of payment of fines" system [6]. This system is for those who do not have the financial ability to pay their fines or petty fines and remedied this problem by detaining them in workhouses. As implicative by its name, workhouses impose labor. Through this system, the fine system is complemented. Moreover, the time spent in these workhouses is limited. Fines require at least one day but less than 2 years, and petty fines call for at least one day but less than 30 days (Article 18).

4.2. Main Typologies

The following shows the main typologies that underlie the establishment of fines:

Criminal Charge	Number of Guilty Persons/ Persons Fined	Statutory Penalty
Total Penal Code Offenses	847	
Crimes of Obstruction of Performance of Public Duty	34	(Obstructing Performance of Public Duty) Imprisonment with labor for no more than three years / imprisonment or a fine of no more than 500,000 yen
Crimes of Harboring Criminals and Suppressing Evidence	1	(Harboring of Criminals, Suppression of Evidence) Imprisonment with labor for no more than three years or a fine of no more than 300,000 yen
Arson	0	(Arson of Inhabited Buildings) Death penalty or life imprisonment / imprisonment with labor for no less than five years
Crimes of Arson and Fire Caused Through Negligence	0	(Fire Caused through Negligence) Fine of no more than 500,000 yen
Crimes of Obstruction of Traffic	0	(Obstruction of Traffic) Imprisonment with labor for no more than two years or a fine of no more than 200,000 yen

[6] However in 2006, article 18 paragraph 6 created a provision that assumes payment by installments.

Crime	Count	Penalty
Crimes of Breaking Into a Residence	34	(Breaking Into a Residence) Imprisonment with labor for no more than three years or a fine of no more than 100,000 yen
Counterfeiting of Official Documents	0	(Uttering of Counterfeit Official Documents) Imprisonment with labor for no less than one year but no more than ten years
Counterfeiting of Private Documents	0	(Uttering of Counterfeit Private Documents) Imprisonment with labor for no less than three months but no more than five years
Crimes Related to Electromagnetic Records of Payment Cards	0	(Unauthorized Creation of Electromagnetic Records of Payment Cards) Imprisonment with labor for no more than ten years or a fine of no more than 1,000,000 yen
Crimes of Obscenity, Rape and Bigamy	10	(Public Indecency) Imprisonment with labor for no more than six months / a fine of no more than 300,000 yen or misdemeanor imprisonment / a petty fine
Crimes Related to Gambling and Lotteries	0	(Gambling) Fine of no more than 500,000 yen or a petty fine
Crimes of Bribery	0	(Acceptance of Bribes) Imprisonment with labor for no more than five years
Crimes of Injury	292	(Injury) Imprisonment with labor for no more than fifteen years or a fine of no more than 500,000 yen
Crimes of Injury Through Negligence	5	(Causing Injury Through Negligence) Fine of no more than 300,000 yen or a petty fine
Crimes of Intimidation	29	(Intimidation) Imprisonment with labor for no more than two years or a fine of no more than 300,000 yen
Crimes Against the Credit of Businesses [Defamation of Businesses]	3	(Damage to Credit) Imprisonment with labor for no more than three years or a fine of no more than 500,000 yen
Crimes of Theft	334	(Theft) Imprisonment with labor for no more than ten years or a fine of no more than 500,000 yen
Breach of Trust	0	(Breach of Trust) Imprisonment with labor for no more than five years or a fine of no more than 500,000 yen
Crimes of Embezzlement	21	(Embezzlement of Lost Property) Imprisonment with labor for no more than one year or a fine of no more than 100,000 yen / a petty fine

Criminal Charge	Number of Guilty Persons/ Persons Fined	Statutory Penalty
Crimes Related to Stolen Property	0	(Acceptance of Stolen Property) Imprisonment with labor for no more than three years
Crimes of Destruction and Concealment	52	(Damage to Property) Imprisonment with labor for no more than three years or a fine of no more than 300,000 yen / a petty fine
Criminal Regulations to Control Explosives	0	(Use of Explosives) Death penalty or life imprisonment / imprisonment with labor for no less than seven years or imprisonment
Act Relating to Duels	0	(Engaging a Duel) Imprisonment with labor for no less than two years but no more than five years
Act on Punishment of Physical Violence and Others	26	(Collective Assault·Intimidation·Damage to Property) Imprisonment with labor for no more than three years or a fine of no more than 300,000 yen / a petty fine
Other Penal Code Offenses	6	

Criminal Charge	Number of Guilty Persons/ Persons Fined	Statutory Penalty
Total Special Law Offenses	757	
Public Offices Election Act	0	(Acquisition of and Induction of Interest/Bribery) Imprisonment with labor for no more than three years / imprisonment or a fine of no more than 500,000 yen
Anti-Prostitution Act	4	(Provision of Location) Imprisonment with labor for no more than three years or a fine of no more than 100,000 yen
Law on Control and Improvement of Amusement Businesses [Adult Entertainment Business Law]	16	(Unauthorized Operation of Business ect.) Imprisonment with labor for no more than two years / a fine of no more than 2,000,000 yen
Firearms And Swords Control Law	36	(Organized Groups Firing Handguns) Life imprisonment / definite term imprisonment with labor for no less than five years or life imprisonment / definite term imprisonment with labor for no less than five years and a fine of no more than 30,000,000 yen
Child Welfare Act	0	(Causing a Child to Commit an Obscene Act) Imprisonment with labor for no more than ten years / a fine of no more than 3,000,000 yen, or a cumulative imposition of both

Cannabis Control Act	0	(Cannabis Possession, Receipt, Transfer) Imprisonment with labor for no more than five years
Stimulants Control Act	0	(Stimulants Possession, Receipt, Transfer) Imprisonment with labor for no more than ten years
Narcotics and Psychotropics Control Act	0	(Diacetylmorphine or a Similar Substance Packaging, Transfer, Receipt, Delivery, Possession) Imprisonment with labor for no more than ten years
Opium Control Act	0	(Cultivation of Opium Poppy) Imprisonment with labor for no less than one year but no more than ten years
Law Concerning Special Provisions for the Narcotics and Psychotropics Control Act	0	(Illegal Imports Conducted for Business) Life imprisonment or imprisonment with labor for no less than five years and a fine of no more than 10,000,000 yen
Income Tax Act	0	(Tax Evasion ect.) Imprisonment with labor for no more than ten years / a fine of no more than 10,000,000 yen or a cumulative imposition of both
Corporation Tax Act	57	(Tax Evasion ect.) Imprisonment with labor for no more than ten years / a fine of no more than 10,000,000 yen or a cumulative imposition of both
Liquor Tax Act	0	(Unlicensed Manufacturing) Imprisonment with labor for no more than ten years or a fine of no more than 1,000,000 yen
Consumption Tax Act	16	(Tax Evasion ect.) Imprisonment with labor for no more than ten years / a fine of no more than 10,000,000 yen or a cumulative imposition of both
Customs Act	4	(Importation of Illegal Cargo etc.) Imprisonment with labor for no more than ten years / a fine of no more than 30,000,000 yen or a cumulative imposition of both
Act Regulating the Receipt of Contributions, Receipt of Deposits and Interest Rates	3	(Punishments for High Interest Rates) Imprisonment with labor for no more than ten years / a fine of no more than 30,000,000 yen or a cumulative imposition of both
Horse Racing Act	0	(Use of Drugs on Racehorses) Imprisonment with labor for no more than three years or a fine of no more than 3,000,000 yen
Bicycle Racing Act	0	(Dishonest Acts Involving Bribery) Imprisonment with labor for no more than three years

Road Traffic Act	202	(Driving Under the Influence of Alchohol) Imprisonment with labor for no more than five years or a fine of no more than 1,000,000 yen
Act on Assurance of Car Parking Spaces and Other Matters	0	(False Application of Car Parking Spaces) Fine of no more than 200,000 yen
Punishments for Driving Casualties Act	75	(Negligent Driving Causing Death or Injury) Imprisonment with labor for no more than seven years / imprisonment or a fine of no more than 1,000,000 yen
Immigration Control and Refugee Recognition Act	99	(Illegal Entry, Illegal Stay) Imprisonment with labor for no more than three years / imprisonment / a fine of no more than 3,000,000 yen or a cumulative imposition of all
Prefectural (Including Municipal) Ordinances	81	(Tokyo Nuisance Prevention Ordinance) Imprisonment with labor for no more than one year or a fine of no more than 1,000,000 yen
Other Special Law Offenses	164	
Total	1604	

4.3. Current State of Implementation

The following shows the current state of implementation of fines:

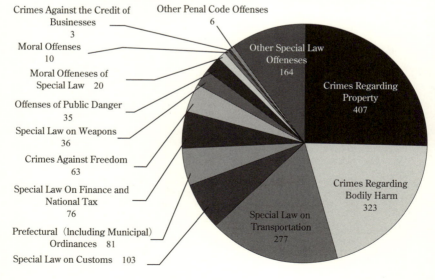

Guilty Persons/Persons Fined on the First Instance

Guilty Persons/Persons Fined on the First Instance for Special Law Offenses

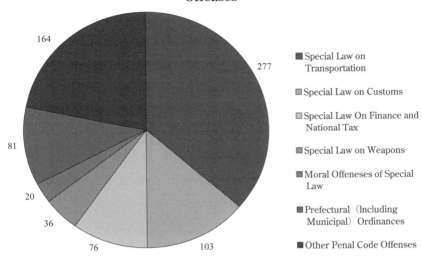

Guilty Persons/Persons Fined on the First Instance for Penal Code Offenses

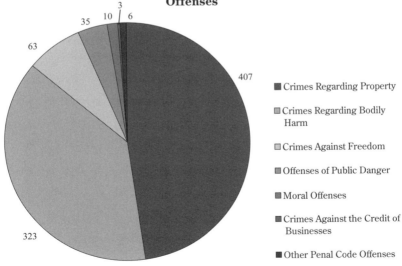

4.4. Analysis of Operation
4.4.1. Overview

Because fines are a type of punishment, it is reasonable to assume that it should follow general standards for sentencing. In other words, sentencing should be decided by considering each individual's circumstances with tatschuld as its basis. The problem is, in imposing fines, it is usually unclear as to what exactly is *tatschuld*.

The definition of *tatschuld* is clear because it is formally the degree of seriousness. However, for example, if the fine is less than 1,000,000 yen, the degree of seriousness of the wrongful act or the wrongful typology is typically unclear.

On the other hand, when we are dealing with imprisonment, the case itself is usually organized and standards that set the degree of sentencing in response to the degree of the wrongful conduct is well-established. This is called as *Ryoukei-souba*, the "sentencing market", but this is only legal jargon and not formal legalese. This means that sentences can be decided with relative consistency by comparing the current case to a similar prior case.

In high-profile cases in Japan, there are three professional judges and six lay judges, who are private citizens who were randomly picked. [7] Because lay judges only participate in that one trial, they do not have prior knowledge of sentencing. [8] To solve this problem, the courthouse created various databases containing information on sentencing for the lay judges to refer to. With these databases, theoretically, lay judges should have an idea of what type of sentencing is appropriate for a particular case to a certain extent. However, as said before, because lay judges only experience trials for high-profile cases, these databases tend to cover cases of crimes that resulted in imprisonment. Because of this,

---

[7] Similar to the Anglo-American jury system.
[8] European continental law, on the other hand, has a system where lay judges have a term wherein, they can serve in several trials.

Criminal Charge	Number of Guilty Persons/Persons Fined
Crimes Regarding Property	407
Crimes Regarding Bodily Harm	323
Special Law on Transportation	277
Special Law on Customs	103
Prefectural (Including Municipal) Ordinances	81
Special Law on Finance and National Tax	76
Crimes Against Freedom	63
Special Law on Weapons	36
Offenses of Public Danger	35
Moral Offenses of Special Law	20
Moral Offenses	10
Crimes Against the Credit of Businesses	3
Other Penal Code Offenses	6
Other Special Law Offenses	164
Total	1604

Criminal Charge	Number of Guilty Persons/Persons Fined
Crimes Regarding Property	407
Crimes Regarding Bodily Harm	323
Crimes Against Freedom	63
Offenses of Public Danger	35
Moral Offenses	10
Crimes Against the Credit of Businesses	3
Other Penal Code Offenses	6
Total Penal Code Offenses	847

Criminal Charge	Number of Guilty Persons/Persons Fined
Special Law on Transportation	277
Special Law on Customs	103
Special Law on Finance and National Tax	76
Special Law on Weapons	36
Moral Offenses of Special Law	20
Prefectural (Including Municipal) Ordinances	81
Other Special Law Offenses	164
Total Special Law Offenses	757

the "market" for sentences related to cases involving fines is not as clear cut. In more technical terms, the ordinal proportionality is not as clear.

Furthermore, the considerations made for imprisonment is usually different from that of fines. General convention is to avoid imprisonment. If this were so, fines are the more desirable form of punishment. There are situations where a certain type of conduct warrants imprisonment, but fines are chosen anyway. In these cases, the amount of the fine is difficult to determine.

Moreover, defendants of cases that warrant fines tend to be financial or economic criminals, or traffic violators. Some think that judges must impose fines that are seen from offenders as disproportionate, or that the fine is not worth the criminal conduct. For example, some may think a 1,000,000 yen fine for a 1,000,000yen illegal transaction is not a punishment, but others think that some kind of strict sentencing is necessary to, for example, discourage taxi drivers from thinking that traffic violation fines are part of the job. These types of punishment are interpreted as preventative in the context of sentencing and are seen to break the structure of "punishments proportionate to *tatschuld*."

4.4.2. Judge's Thinking

To further discuss this point, we have analyzed judges' articles (Osaka Keijijitumu Kenkyukai, 2011) and directly interviewed them. First, it is primarily advanced, in what we think is the most important document published by a judge, that making an offender understand that deprivation of unlawful gain is not economical is primarily advanced. With this in mind, Munehisa Sugita, a renowned Japanese judge, is said to have charged twice the amount of any profits gained. However as far as I have heard from Sugita himself, his methods were not mainstream. If anything, most judges' sentencing is probably based on *tatschuld*, the principal form of sentencing.

In practice, fines are usually imposed as demanded by the prosecution. However, this does not necessarily hold for fines over 1,000,000 yen. The prosecution is said to demand punishments in accordance with *tatschuld* because their demands are based on a detailed and elaborate sentencing market, a product of the accumulation of prior cases. Moreover, as an exception, the sentencing market for fines for illegal drug use has a relatively clear standard.

As for fines, judges consider sentencing difficult. Some even say that "decision making behind sentencing can be on a whim." If this invokes considerations other than *tatschuld*-based punishments and proportionality punishments, it is not desirable as a consequence of a desert model based sentencing theory. Even in practice, these decisions are seemingly inevitably made, and for this reason, this requests supplemental explanation from an academic standpoint.

V. The Daily Fine System: A discussion of legislation or legal policy

5.1. Discussion During Criminal Law Reform

In the 1960s and 1970s, implementation of the daily fine system was discussed as part of criminal law reform in Japan. A draft of a daily fine system was proposed in 1964 and 1966 to the legislative council. However, including the daily fine system, this criminal law reform never reached fruition.

Today, as legal policy, the daily fine system is still occasionally discussed. It is, however, not very realistic. This is because Japanese criminal legislation is not flexible and, although the Ministry of Justice leads fundamental legislative reform, it is presently not inclined to do so.

In this section, I would like to present a discussion on the daily fine system in Japan by referencing academic discussions made during criminal law reform and later significant discussions.

First, I will organize criticisms against the daily fine system made during criminal law reform discussion, when such discussions held an actual meaning:

(1) This system heavily considers the financial circumstance of the offender in comparison to other sentencing matters, but there is no reason to do so.
(2) Generally, typologies that impose daily fines and fixed amount fines are different, but this system is too complicated.
(3) If we implement the daily fine system, the amount is dependent on the offenders' situation, which means that fines imposed on wealthy offenders may be a much higher amount than those who are not. This is in conflicts with objective justice.
(4) It is difficult to accurately grasp an offender's true financial situation and there is a possibility that the punishment will be unfair.

Those who support the daily fine system (Onosaka, 1965-66) responded to these criticisms as follows:

(1) In the daily fine system, fines will be sentenced in days. This means that for an offender who committed the same crime (or same criminal liability), we can consistently follow the principle to impose the same punishment. Furthermore, for the amount fined, we can realize fairness by calculating the amount based on the offender's financial situation. In this way, the daily fine system achieves justice internally and externally.
(2) In the case of Japan, traffic violations are typically punished by fines and so it renders the daily fine punishment inapplicable. For this reason, we can only implement the system for crimes expressly indicated in the criminal code and other specific crimes. This does make this system complicated, but if we specifically outline the outer boundaries of the system, it should present no problem in practice.
(3) There is certainly a possibility of unfairness for wealthy offenders. To

prevent those situations, we should allow limits on the amount fined per day at the expense of a certain degree of systematic consistency.
(4) We can solve this problem if we commission hearings to the tax office, like in Sweden.

5.2. Discussions After Attempted Criminal Law Reform

After the attempted criminal law reform, formal criticisms against the daily fine system started to emerge from the fundamental theory of punishment. This is the theory presented by Kazuo Yoshioka (Yoshioka, 1996).

According to Yoshioka, the purpose of fines is to deprive one's purchasing power. Based on the belief that denies general prevention and special prevention as effects of punishment, he argues that the amount of fines can stay at a lower standard even when general commodity prices increase. And because the daily fine system cannot withstand these price increases, Yoshioka is a staunch opponent of this system. Furthermore, he lists the following justifications for his arguments against the system:

(1) By implementing the daily fine system, punishment by fine can be taken as something similar to punishment by curtailment of liberty and will tighten the ropes on private citizens' daily lives.
(2) Punishment by fine is a system that imposes financial pain by taking a portion of living expenses away (this is based on Yoshioka's argument that fines punish by depriving purchasing power) but there is no guarantee that the daily fine system will have the same result.
(3) Those who diligently work and save money are at a disadvantage compared to those who moderately work but spend extravagantly.
(4) Investigation of financial situation is necessary, but this proves itself is questionable because of individual privacy.

5.3. Analysis

Yoshioka fundamentally believes that the desert model is the correct theory of sentencing. Jurists who support the desert model are rare in Japan. In this sense, Yoshioka and I share common ground. However, I do not think Yoshioka's theory is very convincing. I believe it is more logical that the daily fine system is a consequence of the desert model.

When Sweden, which currently has a desert model sentencing provision, first implemented the daily fine system, punishment theory was centered around individual treatment. However, it was ultimately found that the daily fine system is the most fitting system with the desert model/principle of proportionality. According to the desert model/principle of proportionality, punishment serves as a communication tool to convey punishment as hard treatment. If this were so, we must avoid adjusting the degree of hard treatment per offender. If we implement the daily fine system, we can avoid these situations. On the other hand, if we use the fixed amount system, the degree of hard treatment can vastly change depending on the offender's financial ability. It is inevitable that the fixed amount system is completely incompatible with the principle of proportionality.

VI. Detailed Analysis of Fines

6.1. Fines and Crime Prevention

In Japan, many theorists discuss fines with the assumption that they have crime preventative effects. These discussions are especially held in the following situations; (1) in the context of white-collar crime, criminal conduct by elite company executives may be prevented by setting a very high fine as a symbolic fine; (2) in the context of traffic violations, where fines are considered a necessary expense as a driver, drivers' criminal conduct may be prevented by setting a high fine for those who believe traffic violations are a part of driving; (3) in the context of criminal organizations such as gangs, criminal conduct may be prevented by high fines to lead the organization to think asset building is not possible. For example, in the fall of 2019, it was reported that the fine for smuggling eels will be multiplied by 100 and that policymakers are hopeful of its effects.

These notions are supported by the idea that crime can be prevented with higher fines. However, there is no empirical evidence that heavier punishment in general (not only fines) actually prevents crime.

Of course, the act of punishing criminal conduct itself has preventative effects. Criminal law is a system that works with the human mind and motivates people to remove themselves from criminal activity. If we deny this, it will mean that criminal law has no meaning and is useless. When criminal law proclaims that a certain conduct warrants punishment, the police, local governments, and society at large will use that as justification to prevent that conduct without punishment.

However, when something is already a crime and the amount fined is increased, the same response does not necessarily follow. Neither are there any supporting data. For this reason, these discussions are, inevitably, meaningless.

Does this mean that increasing the fine is also meaningless? Not necessarily. There are circumstances where the fine must be increased, such as when the penal value was incorrectly measured. Eel smuggling, as previously stated, is a basic example. The fine attached to eel smuggling was not a reflection of the penal value - and for this reason, the punishment for eel smuggling seemed light.

In any other circumstance, increasing fines seem to be meaningless. Very few drivers perceive traffic tickets as a necessary expense and increased fines do not affect those drivers anyway. These drivers tend to think that they will never be caught in the first place. In white-collar crime, the symbolic high fine is probably an abnormal situation where the absolute proportionality of punishment is unknown. These fines are literally symbolic punishments and they are rarely imposed in practice.

6.2. Differentiating Fines and Other Similar Sanctioning

In Japan, there are other sanctions that are similar to fines. One example is punishment for disturbing administrative order, which is a sanction established under administrative law. Administrative law can impose administrative punishments and can be divided into administrative criminal punishment and punishment for disturbing administrative order. The former is applicable to administrative criminal law and is categorized as a type of fine. The latter is known as an administrative or non-penal fine and is not a punishment. Punishment for disturbing administrative order/non-penal fines are imposed when certain conduct does not warrant a fine but should be deterred.

Because fines and administrative fines seem to have a similar purpose, drawing their differences and limits is an issue. In modern times, criminalization theories take issue when determining what types of conduct warrants fines and what warrants an administrative fine.

This issue is especially difficult when we perceive criminal punishment and punishment for disturbing administrative order (and further, civil sanctions) as serving a fundamentally same purpose; and that the former should be imposed for conduct we want to deter the most and the latter for conduct that calls for less deterrence (and for conduct thereafter, civil sanctions). This is because all punishments are based on the degree of the conduct, which in turn makes drawing upper limits a difficult task. If we think of criminal law as a preventative device, this is an important issue that must be resolved, notwithstanding its difficulty.

Ultimately, the only way to resolve this issue is to return to principles. Punishment is, as a principle, imposed against conduct wanting of moral censure - other sanctions are irrelevant to moral censure. According to this principle, criminal law is not a device to prevent crime. Criminal law is a system that punishes in accordance with *tatschuld*. Punishment in general (not just fines) is a communication tool to convey moral censure to the actor. On the other hand, punishment for disturbing administrative order as set forth in administrative law is not a sanction based on moral censure. If anything, its central character is in correcting unfairness. Here, we find a clear difference between criminal and administrative law. Even if the conduct is something the government wants to deter, unless that conduct warrants censure, punishment by fine is inappropriate.

Of course, if the discussion reaches the bottom limit of petty fines (1,000 yen), it will probably turn into a discussion of whether certain conduct warrants a petty fine or not. However, it does not mean that, if the conduct does not warrant petty fine, we will continue our analysis into punishment for disturbing administrative order. Criminal punishments and punishment for disturbing administrative order each strive to control conduct that is substantively different.

In this way, punishment by fine and punishment for disturbing administrative order are two very different things.

References:
Japanese
- Nagata, Kenji, *Zaisanteki Keijiseisai no Kenkyu*, Kansai University Press, 2013 (including English Summary).
- Onosaka. Hiroshi, *Bakkinseido no Saikento 1-4*, in Hougaku 29.3, pp.64-101, 1965, 29.4, pp.77-100, 1965, 30.2, pp.10-77, 1966, 30.3, 1966, pp.19-50.
- Yoshioka, Kazuo, *Keijigaku*, 2nd ed., Seirin-shoin, 1996.
- Osaka Keiji Jitsumu Kenkyukai ed., *Ryoukei Jitsumu Taikei vol.4.*, Hanrei-Times-Sha, 2011.

English
- Von Hirsch, Andreas, *Deserved Crimial Sentences*, Hart publishing, 2017.
- Matsuzawa, Shin, *Using Equity Reasons to evaluate Mitigating Circumstances-An Explanation of Sentencing Principles*, in Waseda Bulletin of Comparative Law Vol.31, pp. 1-12.

Chapter 8
Using Equity Reasons to evaluate Mitigating Circumstances
──An Explanation of Sentencing Principles──

I. Preface

Many "soft" factors are considered in the process of sentencing, and they can be separated into two large groups; the first is the factors surrounding the severity of the criminal conduct itself, and the second is the circumstances surrounding the perpetrator. The second group is usually regarded, at least in Japan, as something based on general prevention or special prevention.

The same could be said for the *Spilraumteorie* of German theories,[1] which Japanese law frequently references.[2] Briefly explained, *Spilraumteorie* is a theory which suggests that the standard by which penalties are determined is indicated within a specific scope, and within that scope, mitigating circumstances (especially those that satisfy general and special prevention) must be considered.

However, *Spilraumteorie* is inevitably a theory that is lacking in the clarification of sentencing standards. The first reason is because of the premise of *Spilraumteorie*; it is based upon the volatility of the sentencing standard. In a way, it is a contradiction to call this a "standard." Secondly, the details about the consideration of prevention methods is very vague. From the perspective of criminology theories, nothing has been empirically tested to prove this as a reputable theory. Since this is an unproven theory, making it a standard equates any discussion using this theory as something based on impression. We seek to know the extent to which a sentence can influence prevention, but achieving

---
(1) Bruns (1985) s.105 ff.
(2) See, Shiroshita (2010) p.243.

that is impossible without concrete data.

What is really in need are the two of the following theories; first, a theory that allows sentencing (proportionate to the gravity of the crime) to be judged within a certain scope, and second, a theory that does not consider prevention in sentencing.

Theories that include both of these already exist in Anglo-American Law; a sentencing theory based on the principle of proportionality. I believe sentencing theories based on the principle of proportionality to be the most effective, even when compared with all other existing theories (this theory has been refined and reconstructed by Andreas von Hirsch [3] etc.).

So the question is, if we were to utilize the principle of proportionality, does that mean that keeping penalties proportionate to the crime becomes the sole sentencing standard? If this were to be true, I believe the sentencing will become too rigid. For instance, is it acceptable to equate a situation where compensation is possible with one where it is impossible? Is it acceptable to consider a situation where the defendant shows remorse, the same as one where none is shown? Is it acceptable to treat a first offender with the same consideration as a repeated offender? The consequences are endless.

In this case, it becomes necessary to consider the circumstances of these people with a more practical approach in sentencing.

However, another problem arises. Where is the basis that makes the consideration of these circumstances possible, when the principle of proportionality fundamentally rejects the consideration of prevention? If this remains unsolved, it will possibly render the principle of proportionality to a theory "that is looks great on paper but not practical" no matter how superior the principle itself makes itself out to be.

---

(3) For example, v Hirsch (2017).

II. Which factors are important in sentencing?

It could be safely assumed that similar circumstances are considered in sentencing processes in any country. It is easy to simply call this "common sense." However it is necessary to theoretically analyze the true implications within these circumstances.

Let us look at what types of circumstances could potentially exist:

· Existing criminal records
· The defendant's age and health
· The defendant's degree of remorse or admission
· When the defendant is largely disadvantaged by his or her own doings
· When the defendant is already subject to other societal punishments
· When some time has already passed from the date of the criminal act

The inclination to consider these circumstances is most likely shared between all countries. The real problem is, why these are able to become the foundation of sentencing principles.

As said before, in many cases in Japan and Germany, the above problems has been assessed from the viewpoints of general prevention and special prevention; but is it really appropriate to explain this problem from a prevention-based view?

In evaluating this problem, let us say that it is possible to explain the above circumstances from the perspective of the principle of proportionality, or that it is more appropriate to explain these form perspectives other than prevention. In other words, it is possible to make practical and appropriate sentencing without considering prevention, and it is possible to make this a rationale for sentencing. If it were that these were indeed possible, it could be predicted that the result would be that there is no room for *Spilraumteorie*.

III. Humanity —— a fundamental viewpoint

The Swedish legal system has already solved the problems we face.[4] Swedish criminal law provides provisions for sentencing standards that are based on the principle of proportionality (BrB chap.29.art.1,2.), and as a principle to practically adjust the achieved results, there are also provisions that lessen the severity of sentencing for individual cases. These provisions are said to be rooted from "equity reasons."

As a fundamental rule, Swedish criminal law proportionally penalizes criminals based on the penal value (*"strafvärde"*) of their crime. After sentencing, these penalties are readjusted by the above "equity reasons."

According to Nils Jareborg and Josef Zila, equity reasons are formulated from justice.[5] Some examples of justice are humanity, respect, sympathy, acceptance an its values.[6]

What become interesting is the relationship between humanity and the principle of proportionality. These questions arise because, if we were to formally carry through the principle of proportionality, it seems as if there is no space for the consideration of humanity.

In 2015, Jack Ågren published a detailed research report on the above relationship.[7] According to Ågren, the foundation upon which the principle of proportionality stands is the realization of justice, and hence the consideration of "equity reasons," which is consistent with justice, does not clash with the fundamental structure of the principle of proportionality, but it allows for

---

(4) Cf. v Hirsch & Jareborg (2009).
(5) Jareborg & Zila (2007) p.129.
(6) About these ideas, see, Jareborg & Zila (2007) p.91 ff.
(7) Ågren (2013).

further development. If the principle of proportionality is derived from the fundamental principle of the realization of justice, it should not contradict "equity reasons" as this i also derived from the same fundamental principle.

Adding on to what Nils Jareborg and Josef Zila has already proposed, Ågren sought to make a more detailed explanation of humanity.[8] In other words, the concept of "humanity" is unique to Swedish law, and is also a key concept in explaining "equity reasons. However, the word "humanity" makes an impression consistent with the generally accepted meaning of it, despite its ties with the criminal jurisprudence world, and for these reasons some people are not enthusiastic about theoretically including this concept in penal theories. In contrary to these opinions, "humanity" became a fundamental principle in Swedish criminal law after its reform in 1864. To this day, it is a comprehensive principle in penal theories and is regarded as an important authority. Ågren asserts that "humanity" is an understanding of others and others' situations and implies acceptance and dignity. It exists in many forms in order to achieve the goals of acceptance and dignity.

With these viewpoints in mind, I would like to closely examine the above circumstances in the next chapter.

IV. Existing criminal records

A sentence is usually more severe when the defendant has a criminal record. This is a strong factor that is backed by a strong sense of conviction, since it is a result that naturally comes with the sentiments of the general public. Take this for an example; let us say we are disciplining child. Generally we are more forgiving when the child makes a certain mistake for the first time, and let them go; the second time, we may make them write a letter of

---

(8) Ågren (2013) s.86 f.

apology; from the third time and onwards, we may stop their monthly allowance.

These actions are generally accepted as a normal way to discipline a child, but it is difficult to justify them from the principle of proportionality. The principle of proportionality calls for penalties that are proportional to the severity of the crime committed, and it is common to think that as long as the crime is the same, the same penalty will be placed regardless of how many times it has been committed. In Sweden, where sentencing provisions are based on the principle of proportionality, it is said that the defendants' criminal records are not really considered in the process of sentencing (there are, however, provisions that allow to "add-on" the severity of penalties; ref. BrB chap.29, art.4.). Special prevention provides a simpler explanation; in other words, repeated offenders have dangerous personalities, or are people who need to be heavily penalized in order to stop them from repeating the offense(s) and thus the demand for special prevention is high which leads to heavier penalties.

It is possible to explain this situation through the principle of proportionality as well. The crime, for which the defendant is to be punished, not only includes the wrongness of the crime, but also the gravity of responsibility and blameworthiness. If one were to have more blame, it is appropriate to regard the crime as graver than it was before.

There is another explanation through this principle. If the consequences after the third offense is more severe than after the second offense, the second after the first, it can be said that the consequences after the first offense is lighter than after the second offense and the same applies for the second and third. In other words, the if penalty proportionate to the crime should be based on the third offense, but by lessening the intensity of the intensity from the third to second, second to first, we could claim that we are treating the defendant with humanity. We could say that criminal records do not necessarily increase the intensity of penalties, but it may serve as a circumstance that alleviates, in part, the intensity of the penalty.

The special prevention explanation is unnecessary if it were acceptable to think in this way. Again, the special prevention explanation is appealing, but there is no objective data to allow to measure the intensity of the penalty that will prevent the defendant from committing further crimes or repeating them. Everything is determined through subjectivity, or feeling. Additionally, even if we were to consistently double the intensity of the penalty every time a crime is repeated, that still does not make it a component of special prevention. The requirements of special prevention differs from every case and cannot be dependent upon a consistent rule like above. Special prevention can only be justified through the principle of proportionality.

V. The defendant's degree of remorse or admission

(1) Preventative measures to localize damage and damage compensation

How much remorse a defendant shows is an important factor in sentencing. More specifically, such remorse is shown through measures to prevent further damage and how much damage compensation is offered. In Japan, in order for these circumstances to be considered, there are three types of justifications; (a) it is explained through responsibility, (b) it is explained through prevention, or (c) it is explained through a third party independent form responsibility or prevention. Since option (b) is not compatible with the premise of the principle of proportionality, let us start with the explanation for option (a).

Ågren explains his theory from option (a). [9] He claims that actions to prevent further damage from a certain crime is deserving of a lighter penalty, and therefore the level of blame towards the defendant is also lightened. The premise for this claim is that the principle of proportionality is interpreted

---

(9) Ågren (2013) s.138 ff.

more broadly to include factors that are outside the scope of the consequences of the crime in question. With this explanation in hand, whether the post-crime activities had the effect of reviving or repairing damages becomes a very important factor and whether the offender had regret or remorse and other moral emotions becomes irrelevant.

Ågren's theory seems like it is trying to revise the interpretation of a criminal act itself. If it were so, the prevention of the harmful effects of crime becomes an obsolete explanation, since this does not affect the penal value of a premise that requires a completed criminal act. However, Ågren's theory probably does not deal with these explanations. What he was trying to say is, even if the prevention of the harmful effect of crime is executed, this does not change the penal value of an already committed crime, but by the defendant executing these actions, it lessens the need to give a culpability sentence proportionate to the penal value of the crime. In other words, if the offender's criminal acts were interpreted broadly (including the time immediately before and after the crime itself), the penalty that seems appropriate to the penal values loses its proportionality.

Ågren's theory deftly steers away from having to explain special prevention, which is rejected by the principle of proportionality. However, it is quite questionable; (1) Does the fact that remorse, regret and other moral emotions are not considered a viable result that could be accepted? (2) Is not true that no matter what theoretical structure is used, making the defendant's behavior (including those immediately before and after the crime) and the penalty proportionate to each other is not something that is included in the definition of proportionality in the principle of proportionality?

Truthfully, question (2) requires Option (c) (explained through a third party independent form responsibility or prevention). Namely, these kind of circumstances are consistent with the goals of criminal policy. In the case of criminal theory in continental law, it may be explained that *Strafbarkeit* and

Strafwürdigkeit will both disappear.

(2) Surrender

A sentence becomes lighter if an offender surrenders or admits his or her crime(s). Ågren gives the same explanation [10] as above, for the justification of this case.

In Japan, there is a legal provision that accepts surrender as a circumstance to be considered to lighten a penalty. Its justification can be proven through policy and the lessening of culpability, but, as with Ågren, it is most appropriate to say that the blameworthiness is lightened. From this, *Strafbarkeit* and *Strafwürdigkeit* also deceased in intensity.

Subsequently, if provisions like Japan were placed, where a penalty will be lightened if one surrenders, it could be predicted that more people will admit to their crimes in hopes of a lightened penalty. In this sense, it is possible to justify these circumstances being included in provisions as general considerations through the rationality of criminal policy. With these provisions, the efficiency of the prevention of further harmful effects by crime and criminal legislation will undoubtedly be addressed, and for this reason, the assertion that the advantages of these policies will be reflected in sentencing and subsequently seek to achieve the realization of these advantages is plausible as an example of justification to include these circumstances as a determining factor of sentencing.

VI. When the defendant is largely disadvantaged by his or her own doings

A characteristic example of the defendant largely disadvantaged by his

---

(10) Ågren (2013) s.158.

or her own doings is when one is severely injured (physically). It is possible, in this case, for the inflicted injuries to be personal responsibility. However, in the long run, comparing those who actually got injured versus those who did not, it is clear the the former tends to be regarded as a harsher consequence. In reality, these types of circumstances are interpreted as a sentencing factor in most cases.

Ågren, from the viewpoint of the former, bring up "humanity" as its justification.[11] Humanity should be understood as a moral philosophy and fundamentally calls for respect for the individual that is stresses the value of the independent individual. It does not imply that anyone should not be rejected from the concept of "humanity." Generally, there are no criticism towards the claims that protect the victim's rights, but the offender is as human as the victim is and should be respected as a human being as well.

In Japan, severe physical injuries tend to influence a sentencing to be of a lighter degree. Again, there are three types of justifications; (a) it is explained through responsibility, (b) it is explained through prevention, or (c) it is explained through a third party independent form responsibility or prevention. Swedish criminal law theorists including Ågren may be categorized to take the perspective of option (c).

Yuji Shiroshita, who takes option (b), criticizes that "implementing viewpoints other than 'responsibility' and 'prevention' as the foundation of sentencing factors must be carefully considered, as it translates to the acceptance of the new penal theory that is nearly equivalent in prominence with existing penal theories regarding the justification of penalties."[12] However, it is possible to consider humanity (as part of justice) without clashing with the principle of proportionality, since the very root of the principle of proportionality is the realization of justice. It is possible to theoretically and logically

---

(11) Ågren (2013) s.107 ff.
(12) Shiroshita (2009) p.74 f.

explain the mitigation of the sentence in the case of the defendant being subject to disadvantages.

VII. The defendant's age, health, and occupation

If the defendant is of old age and/or in poor health, these are usually considered mitigating circumstances in sentencing. In Japan, old age is an advantageous factor because special prevention includes the protection of the elderly and the same applies to poor health because it may exacerbate the suffering in prison or require consideration of treatment and these are factors of special prevention. In both cases, concluding that they are advantageous because they are part of special prevention is questionable as an explanation, since the goals of special prevention is reformation and rehabilitation.

Ågren analyzes old age and poor health as categories for defendants, but should be mitigating circumstances from the perspective of humanity.[13] Compared with those who are younger and healthier, those who are of old age and poor health will experience more suffering even with the same penalty, and therefore should mitigate the penalty for humane reasons.

VIII. When the defendant is already subject to other societal punishments

In many cases, being already subject to other societal punishments is considered in sentencing, such as when one is laid off of a job.

Ågren claims that this holds a double-layered personality to it and should be implemented for the sake of humanity.[14]

In Japan, many interpret this as independent of responsibility and pre-

---
(13) Ågren (2013) s.129.
(14) Ågren (2013) s.212 ff.

vention. For example, many stand for the neutral adjustment principle with neutral values and argue that by receiving a certain type of punishment, the need for retributive penalties is clearly diminished.

These explanations, which can be inferred from previous ones, is consistent with the principle of proportionality. Explaining this circumstances from prevention is impossible.

The neutral adjustment principle can be said to have a background with a similar structure with the principle of proportionality which seeks to readjust disproportionate sentencing, and for the latter, explanations based on the principle of proportionality functions properly as with the case of Ågren's explanations.

IX. When some time has already passed from the date of the criminal act

When there has been a ridiculously long time since the occurrence of the actual crime, this may become a mitigating circumstance.

Ågren divides this circumstance into two types of situations; [15] firstly, when there has been a long time between the actual occurrence of the crime and the start of lawsuit, and secondly, when there has been a long time between the start of lawsuit and the conclusion of the lawsuit. The former case calls for mitigation because the necessity for penal diminishes as the penal value diminishes, and the latter does because it should be considered an "equity reason" for the stability of the law.

In Japan, there has not been much discussion regarding the elapse of time, but it has been a topic of research. Its relationship with the statute of limitation, its decreased influence on society, and its influence on the defendant

---

(15) Ågren (2013) s.274.

have been discussed, but these cases cannot be explained through prevention. Similar to Swedish law, this is appropriate and can be explained without associating it with prevention and placing the principle of proportionality at its foundation.

X. Conclusion

The principle of proportionality as a premise for equity reasons seems like a drastic claim similar to the "an eye for an eye" retribution and the absolute retributive theory, since it does not consider prevention and emphasizes penalties that is proportionate to the criminal act. However, the principle of proportionality is based on penalties consistent with formal justice (or penalties equivalent with penal value, as said in Sweden) and rejects subjective prevention theories that do not have any room for empirical testing, and by utilizing "equity reasons" based on "humanity" for revision, it enables the realization of penalties that is consistent with justice and is theoretically and practically a theory that is much more distinguished than Spilraumteorie.

Further, the principle of proportionality is an easier concept to be understood by the general public, and may be instrumental in explaining sentencing standards to lay judges by professional judges. It also does not utilize prevention, which is a concept that lacks in empirical evidence, and thus avoids the unnecessary an inconclusive debate about the degree of sentencing that will definitively prevent future crimes.

In Sweden, its criminal law stabilized after its provisions were revised by lay judges' sentencing standards which were based on the principle of proportionality and equity reasons. There is great value in considering this method for future reference in countries where there are problems surrounding how sentencing standards should be set with the participation of lay judges.

There is a clear difference between Sweden and Japan, in that Swedish law has a provision where it verbalizes the principle of proportionality whereas Japan does not. In Sweden, sentencing inconsistent with the principle of proportionality is seen as illegal, but in Japan, even if the principle of proportionality was implemented, it would only be regarded as another example of interpretation. However, I believe there is great value in familiarizing the principle of proportionality by suggesting to utilize a new standard for interpretation at the same time as showing and explaining to the judges the reality by organizing and pursuing the theoretical foundation of the principles of interpretation, even where there are no existing written provisions.

References:
- *Ashworth, Andrew & Roberts, Julian* (Ed.), Principled Sentencing, 3.ed., 2009.
- B*runs, Hans-Jürgen,* Das Recht der Strafzumessung, 2. Aufl., 1985.
- *von Hirsch, Andreas,* Deserved Criminal Sentences, 2017.
- *von Hirsch, Andrew & Jareborg, Nils,* The Swedish Sentencing Law, : in *von Hirsch, Andrew.*
- *Jareborg, Nils & Zila, Josef,* Straffrättens Påfjoldslära, 3.uppl., 2007.
- *Shiroshita, Yuji,* Ryokeiriron No Gendaitekikadai [Present Issues on Sentencing Theory], enlatged ed., 2009.
- *Shiroshita, Yuji,* Current Trends and Issues in Japanese Sentencing, Federal Sentencing Reporter vol.22 no.4 pp.243-248., 2010.
- *Ågren, Jack,* Billighetsskälen i BrB 29:5, 2013.

Chapter 9
Judicial Persons as Victims: An Introduction from a Japanese Perspective

I. Introduction

First, I would like to elaborate on topics that I find interesting because I believe that this knowledge might make it easier for the readers to follow the paper. I specialize in dogmatic analyses of material criminal law with a greater focus on dogmatic legal matters than on matters such as criminology or victimology. However, I will attempt to bridge the gap between dogmatic criminal law and empirical criminology. While this is a very difficult goal to achieve, I will attempt it in this paper.

When we discuss the status of a judicial person, particularly when referring to a company, in the context of criminal law, we generally regard the judicial person as a criminal rather than as a victim. For example, compliance programs are designed to prevent judicial persons from committing crimes; however, we do not have any such mechanism in place to avoid the victimization of judicial persons.

I propose certain legal frameworks for judicial persons who are victims and point out certain examples from the Japanese perspective.

The term judicial person, in this paper, refers to a company. There are certain complications related to whether or not a judicial person should be registered with the appellation "judicial person" in order to be protected by the legal system. However, in this present study, these complex problems have been ignored.

II. Legal dogmatic analyses

I would like to begin with the topic of "intimidation of a judicial person." Intimidation is known as kyohaku-zai and is regulated under Article 222 of the Japanese Criminal Code.[1] The following case is provided as an example:
This example involves a Japanese man and a company. We shall refer to the man as Mr. M and the company as T Corporation.

In the recent past, Mr. M, a long-time employee of a famous electronics maker, T Corporation, was laid-off by the company. Mr. M was disgruntled and angry and soon thought of different ways to harass the management. Exasperated, he approached the president of T Corporation and informed him of his intention to supply a large quantity of T-radios that were broken and not functioning to showrooms across Japan. The president, who was aware of the fact that his company had just launched a substantial commercial campaign based on tradition, quality, and trustworthiness, was intimidated; he was worried that his company's good name would be ruined. On account of his anxiety, he took an extended sick leave.

Who is the victim in this scenario—T Corporation or the president? Who suffers from harm in this fictitious example? Since the president was intimidated and suffered from anxiety, does that make him the victim?

If Mr. M proceeds to distribute the dysfunctional products to as many stores as possible, T Corporation might be at serious risk of losing its sales and market share; moreover, its high-profile commercial campaign could become

---

(1) Article 222 (Intimidation).
    (1) A person who intimidates another through a threat to another's life, body, freedom, reputation or property shall be punished by imprisonment with work for not more than 2 years or a fine of not more than 300,000 yen.
    (2) The same shall apply to a person who intimidates another through a threat to the life, body, freedom, reputation, or property of the relatives of another.

redundant. Does this make T Corporation, in its capacity as a judicial person, the victim?

According to the criminal justice system in Japan, in legal terms, criminals are only able to intimidate a physical person, and not a judicial person. This is because a judicial person does not have private life and, therefore, cannot be "threatened."

In the above example, the president's personal interests were not threatened in any way; as a matter of fact, it was the company's interests alone that were under threat. Therefore, as it can be argued that no harm has been done, should Mr. M be permitted to go free?

As per the Japanese law, Mr. M will be punished. He will be punished for the forcible obstruction of business. This is termed as iryokugyomubogai-zai (Article 234 of the Japanese Criminal Code).[2] It is very easy to prosecute under this provision; however, the law pertaining to the forcible obstruction of business (iryokugyomubogai-zai) is not characterized in definite terms. In the Japanese, Scandinavian, and German law, this type of crime is referred to as an "abstract endangering crime."

However, unfortunately, the definition of the "forcible obstruction of business" is not entirely clear; it is vague, making it difficult to understand which actions merit punishment. Is the shoplifter obstructing business or the person who murders a CEO?

If we are to introduce another aspect to the former case, where an irate Mr. M threatens, to place useless T Corporation radios in shops across Japan unless he is paid ¥20,000,000 is he punishable for obstructing business? The answer is no. Under the Japanese criminal justice system, according to section 249 of the Japanese Criminal Code,[3] kyokatsu-zai, Mr. M is charged with

---

(2) Article 234 (Forcible Obstruction of Business).
A person who obstructs the business of another by force shall be dealt with in the same manner as proscribed under the preceding Article.

extortion (blackmailing a judicial person in the form of T Corporation).

Considering this example, why is it that the abovementioned crime against T Corporation is punishable as blackmail, while the intimidation in the former case is not punishable? To a certain extent, both these cases are identical. In both examples, the president is intimidated. The only difference is in whether it is the funds or the trust of the company that is in jeopardy.

I believe that the reason for this problem is the failure of the Japanese criminal law theory to distinguish between the management of the company (CEO, boards, etc.) and the actual judicial person (the company). If the management of the company and the judicial person do not have the same interests, they should not be treated as one.

I claim that the cases wherein judicial persons are victims should be categorized into the following three types.

- Type A: A judicial person is attacked and harmed by another judicial person.
- Type B: A judicial person is attacked and harmed by a physical person who is independent of the said judicial person.
- Type C: A judicial person is attacked and harmed by a physical person who is employed by the judicial person.

The following are examples of the abovementioned types.

- Type A: Manufacture and sale of imitations
- Type B: The intimidation or blackmail of a judicial person

---

(3) Article 249 (Extortion).
  (1) A person who extorts another to deliver property shall be punished by imprisonment with work for not more than 10 years.
  (2) The same shall apply to a person who obtains or causes another to obtain a profit by the means proscribed under the preceding paragraph.

- Type C: Embezzlement or breach of duty [faith]

I believe that this categorization provides us with a type of legal framework; subsequently, we should research and formulate theories based on these three categories.

III. Empirical research

3.1. Introduction

In Japan, we have yet to observe any thorough empirical research on this topic. However, Waseda University has conducted some minor research. I will be addressing this issue later. I am aware that Price Waterhouse Coopers has conducted extensive research on the issue of economic crime. However, in this paper, I am referring to research where the type of harm caused to the victim is taken into consideration.

In the research conducted by Waseda University on "the CSR (Corporate Social Responsibility) rules and the compliance programs" in Japanese companies, [4] the focus was only on the victims of type A, namely, the cases where a judicial person is harmed by another judicial person. Although only limited data is available on the topic, I would still like to elaborate on Waseda's research.

3.2. Questions and results

Our project team, the 21st-century Center of Excellence, Waseda Institute for Corporation Law and Society (COE), administered a questionnaire on CSR and the measures against it to 3,103 leading corporations in Japan. We received responses from 942 corporations.

---

(4) The survey of the Japanese corporations regarding their attitudes toward CSR, corporate compliance programs, and corporate governance was conducted by the project team of the School of Law, Waseda University, in 2003. The results are not officially published in English.

The questionnaire contained 30 questions on issues such as CSR, corporate ethics/compliance of laws and regulations, damages incurred or experienced as a victim in a business process, evaluation of legal dispositions, and future legal systems. The questionnaire provided space for respondents to comment on the theme of the survey.

Below are the questions and responses on the damages incurred or experienced as a victim in the business process.

The questions were as follows:

- Q17: Have you suffered damages resulting from other companies' violations of laws and regulations? If "Yes," what type of company was responsible for such violations—domestic or foreign?
- Q18: If you have had such an experience, can you explain the type of damages that you suffered? (Please differentiate the cause of the damages between domestic and foreign companies.)
- Q19: If you answered in the affirmative to Question 17, how would you evaluate the relief measures provided as compensation for the damages in the civil procedure? (space provided)
- Q20: If you answered in the affirmative to Question 17, how would you evaluate the criminal justice system when they were involved in a criminal case as a victim? (space provided)

Below are the responses to Q17 and Q18 that were indicated by Yes/No or as multiple-choice answers.

- With regard to Q17, 74.41% stated "No" and 25.59% stated "Yes" as their answer to the first part of the question. For the second part, 14.24% identified the company as a domestic one, while 82.23% identified the company as a foreign one; 3.10% indicated both and 0.43% were unsure.

- With regard to Q18, the respondents indicated the type of damage they had suffered. The number of cases is indicated in parenthesis (domestic (Japanese) corporation, foreign (non-Japanese) corporation).
1. Formation of cartels (3,3)
2. Prearranged bidding (6,0)
3. Under bargain sales (12,2)
4. Resale price restrictions (0,0)
5. Delay in the payments of subcontractors (10,1)
6. Misleading representation (34,11)
7. Patent infringement (91,42)
8. Similar trademark (54,56)
9. Defective products (61,21)
10. Bribery (1,0)
11. Violation of reporting requirements to the regulatory authority (8,1)
12. Other (41,17)

Since Q19 and Q20 do not correspond to statistical and quantitative analysis, their answers have been provided below.

3.3. Analysis and discussion
3.3.1. Quantitative research

From the data provided (see Table 1), it appears that companies adhering to CSR rules tend to be victimized more often than companies that do not adhere to them. This appears strange, since it can be assumed that companies that adhere to these CSR rules take special interest in attempting to prevent causing and avoid becoming victims of corporate crime. However, no cross research was conducted on the reasons for the CSR rules being formulated. In many cases, I assume that the experience of having dealt with corporate crime would naturally lead to the formulation of CSR rules.

Let us now consider another example based the survey data (see Table 2). When companies, which have been victimized in the past, conduct business with other companies, they often inquire if their counterpart adheres to CSR rules. This might be an attempt to try and avoid being victimized again by selecting partners based on whether or not they adhere to CSR rules. Thus, they presume that having a CSR program is a symbol of genuineness.

Other data (see Table 3) from the survey indicates that the more detailed a company's compliance program, the less is the risk of victimization.

By cross tabulating, I have attempted to create a table on the basis of Q17 and the following questions:

1. Do you follow internal company rules that emphasize the importance of the so-called corporate social responsibility (CSR) to your employees? (Q1)
2. Do you have an in-house system to educate your employees in order to make them comply with the related laws and regulations? (Q8)
3. Do you have a specific system to find and prevent cases wherein an individual employee of yours or your corporation, by having violated related laws and regulations, is involved in illegal conduct? (Q9)
4. Do you have a well-defined procedure that allows employees who would like to report a possible violation of the compliance program to be heard? (Q14)
5. Do you attempt to voluntarily disclose your compliance program to shareholders? (Q11)
6. Do you attempt to voluntarily disclose your compliance program to consumers? (Q12)
7. Do you have a specific third-party audit system to check for possible

scandals that might occur within your corporation? (Q13)

There were no differences in the results of the first three questions; however, certain differences were observed in the results of the last four questions. The last four questions mainly deal with whether respondents have detailed compliance programs that are meant to disseminate the corporation's information among outsiders. Corporations that have suffered damages on account of laws and regulations being violated by other companies tend to have detailed compliance programs that are meant for public presentation.

Generally, compliance programs are effective in preventing crimes that fall within the category of Type C, namely, where a person within the company is the offender.

3.3.2. Qualitative research

As part of the survey, the companies were encouraged to comment on the topic and share their experiences of victimization. The response rate was unexpectedly high, that is, many corporations responded to Q19 and Q20.

Several companies have commented on the possible consequences of a case being brought forth. Typically, the company is awarded damages. Some companies find the damages to be sufficient; however, most point out that in cases wherein the company stands to lose the trust of its customers and is possibly forced to halt its activities, the damages awarded are never sufficient.

3.3.3. Analysis based on the three types of harm

From the perspective of victimology, we may be able to state something with regard to how companies can be prevented from being victimized. In general, when a physical person is being referred to with respect to him/her being an easy victim of crime, they are often perceived as (1) kind individuals who do not tend to doubt others, (2) individuals who lack physical strength, and (3) individuals who find it difficult to communicate and maintain good relationships with others. If these characteristics are applied to judicial persons (corporations), then the corresponding types of judicial persons are (1) corporations that pay attention when conducting trade with others, (2) healthy corporations that have sufficient capital and are sensitive to illegal matters, and (3) a popular corporation which has no troubles with others is not tending to be victims easily.

Next, I will provide a detailed explanation by analyzing the three different types of harm.

First, let us examine Type A, wherein a judicial person is attacked and harmed by another judicial person. In attempting to avoid becoming a victim of a Type A crime, the abovementioned steps can be undertaken. That is, knowing one's trade partner, disseminating information regarding compliance programs to others, and avoiding illegal matters. Thus, it becomes difficult for a trade partner to abuse the corporation.

A typical example of a Type A crime is the manufacture and sale of product imitations. Another example is the stealing of trade secrets. In Japan, in 2006, regulations to punish those who stole trade secrets were provided for under the Unfair Competition Prevention Act. Although these regulations are relatively new, harsher punishments were introduced in 2007. However, it is extremely interesting to note that these regulations have never been employed. In fact, most conflicts are resolved through civil cases, and the punishments only serve a symbolic function.

Moreover, the stealing of trade secrets may also correspond to Types B or C. However, the Unfair Competition Act mainly punishes perpetrators of the Type C category, namely, where a corporate employee colludes to pass on his corporation's trade secrets to others. As a matter of fact, a Type C category of crime is most common; however, at the same time, it is possible to adequately discipline this type of crime within the corporation. Therefore, I doubt the effectiveness of punishment being meted out for the Type C category of crime. In addition, to say the least, this is not the proper method for meting out punishment.

Second, we examine the Type B category, wherein a judicial person is attacked and harmed by a physical person who is independent of the said judicial person.

A typical Type B crime involves intimidation or blackmail of the judicial person. It is usually carried out by the mafia (or the so-called yakuza) in Japan. The so-called "sokaiya," meaning racketeer in Japanese, can be referred to as an example. Most of them are members of the mafia, and they often intimidate judicial persons by disturbing stockholders meeting. If a corporation offers them certain benefits, such as money or stocks, then the corporation itself will be prosecuted (rieki-kyoyo-zai). Thus, it is very important for corporation to stay away from the mafia.

In order to avoid becoming victims of this kind of crime, CSR and/or compliance programs may serve an effective measure. In Waseda's survey, the companies were asked to offer their opinions with regard to the kinds of issues that should be considered as appropriate subjects of CSR (Q2). Of the corporations that have a CSR program in place, 78.3% suggested the severing of relationships with antisocial groups. This implies that a considerable number of Japanese corporations attempt to break their existing relationship with the mafia, and this should prove helpful in trying to avoid becoming victims.

Here, I would like to point out that Types A and B are relatively similar. When a corporate employee harms the corporation to which he belongs, his crime is categorized as a Type A crime. However, if he does so after having left the corporation, that is, after he has resigned, his crime will be categorized as a

Type B crime.

Lastly, we examine the Type C category, wherein a judicial person is attacked and harmed by a physical person who is employed by the judicial person. Examples include embezzlement and/or the breach of duty [faith]. Type C crimes occur within the corporation; therefore, at times, these problems can be resolved within the corporation itself. In the Japanese criminal law theory, a considerably important principle is that criminal law must be employed as the ultima ratio, or in other words, as the last option for resolving conflicts. Further, it should not intervene in normal everyday life. Thus, resolving a conflict within the corporation itself is regarded as a better alternative. However, this is not the case when the damages caused are extensive. Large scale embezzlement is an extremely serious crime. It is believed to be the most common problematic type of economic crime. If corporate workers are sincere, a Type C crime will never occur. This implies that if the compliance programs are effective and rules and regulations are followed, corporations can avoid becoming victims of crime.

IV. Conclusion

The only manner in which justice can be administered to these companies is to prevent them from becoming victims in the first place. This can be achieved through criminal law. We need to establish victimology for judicial persons; criminology, or the science of criminal law, and victimology can also work together in this regard. This request is the essence of this paper; moreover, this paper is only an introduction. Further criminological and legal dogmatic researches are necessary.

I hope to construct the framework for this innovative and interesting research area and contribute to its development.

Tables

(Table 1)

	Experiences of victimization	No experiences of victimization
Yes	29.5% (185)	70.5% (443)
No	17.6% (54)	82.4% (252)
Total	239	695

(Table 2)

	Experiences of victimization	No experiences of victimization
Yes	17.8% (42)	6.4% (44)
No	82.2% (194)	93.6% (645)
Total	236	689

(Table 3)

	Victimization		Relative frequency	No victimization		Relative frequency
Have CSR	189	79%	1.00	449	65%	1.00
Educate employees	191	80%	1.01	429	62%	0.96
Specific systems that prevent harm	186	78%	0.98	446	64%	0.97
Well-defined procedures	137	57%	**0.72**	287	41%	**0.64**
Information for shareholders	99	41%	**0.52**	195	28%	**0.43**
Information for e-customers	62	26%	**0.33**	97	14%	**0.22**
Specific third-party audit systems	45	19%	**0.24**	73	11%	**0.16**
Total	239			695		

Chapter 10
Specialized Frauds in Japan

I. What are "Specialized Frauds"?

1.1. In Japan, there have been numerous cases of fraud against the elderly. For example, the following case is typical.

A planned to cheat an elderly woman C out of 1,000,000 yen with the help of B. A called C and said, "Hello, I'm your son, A. I failed in my company's business and lost 1,000,000 yen. I need to make up the loss, but I don't have enough money right now. My friend B will come to your house to collect the money, and you will give him 1,000,000 yen in cash? C wanted to help his son and immediately prepared 1,000,000 yen in cash. A short time later, B, who claimed to be her son's friend, came to C's house, and C gave B 1,000,000 in cash.

Elderly people often have impaired listening skills, and because they are speaking on the phone, they are often unable to accurately determine if it is their own child's voice. Also, if their child tells them they are in trouble, they will often trust them. Although Japan has a pension system, many elderly people believe that the pension alone is not enough to live a comfortable life. As a result, the elderly often have a considerable amount of money on deposit in banks, making them easy targets for fraud.

1.2. This type of fraud is commonly known as *specialized fraud*. There are different types of specialized fraud. For example, in the example above, the scammer may contact the victim by email instead of telephone, or they may ask the victim to transfer money to a bank account instead of receiving it in person, or they may ask the victim to send cash by courier to a specified location. In addition to being tricked into believing that their own child is calling, there are also cases where the person is made to believe that a bill has not been paid, or that it is a financial instruments transaction.

Therefore, a more general definition of this form of fraud has been developed. *Specialized fraud* is a generic term for crimes of defrauding an unspecified number of persons of cash or other assets by making the victim trust them by telephone or by other means without meeting them face-to-face, and then defrauding them by transferring the money to a designated savings account or by other means.

1.3. Specialized frauds are often organized. For example, they are often perpetrated by gangs or similar criminal groups. They plan their crimes meticulously and assign roles carefully, with the elderly being their main target.

Criminal groups are adept at successfully avoiding detection. In the example given above, the person most likely to be apprehended by the police is the person in the role of physically collecting the money. For this role, students and people without a regular job are hired under the guise that they will be given a lucrative part-time job. As the person hired is a temporary employee, he or she is not linked to any criminal group and has no knowledge of his or her employer. As a result, the police are often unable to penetrate the criminal group, even if they catch the person in the role of collecting money.

1.4. Specialized fraud has become a major problem in recent years. Statistics from the National Police Agency in Japan concerning specialized frauds are as follows. [1]

---

(1) This data can be found on the Japanese National Police Agency's website (https://www.npa.go.jp/english/).

Year	Number of Cases	Total amount of damage (Yen)	Number of Arrests
2022	17,570	37,081,354,580	6,640
2021	14,498	28,199,462,547	6,600
2020	13,550	28,523,359,039	7,424
2019	16,851	31,582,937,585	6,817
2018	17,844	38,286,761,222	5,550

1.5. With regard to specialized frauds, there is a question of interpretation when it comes to the provisions involving fraud in the Japanese Penal Code. Several important precedents [2] have been issued in recent years:

(1) 2017(A)322 Keishu Vol. 72, No. 1
(2) 2017(A)1079 Keishu Vol. 71, No. 10
(3) 2017(A)44 Keishu Vol. 72, No. 6

First, precedent (1) has established the point at which the conduct punishable as attempted specialized fraud can be considered committed. Next, precedent (2) addressed the issue of whether complicity can be established with respect to a person involved after the fraud was initiated. Lastly, precedent (3) deals with the issue of intent in specialized frauds. [3]

This article reviews these cases and examines the theoretical issues they raise. These precedents deal primarily with general criminal law issues. [4]

---

(2) These precedents can be read in English by searching the Japanese Supreme Court website (https://www.courts.go.jp/english/index.html.).
(3) Precedents to the same effect as Precedent (3) are at 2016 (A) 1808 Keishu Vol. 72, No. 6 and 2018 (A) 1224 Keishu Vol. 73, No. 4.
(4) The resolution of these issues should be seen as inherent in the interpretation of the fraud provisions. This is because the provisions on fraud are characterized differently from those of other crimes. In order for an act to fall under the fraud provisions, it is necessary to follow a certain causal chain: the act of deception, the victim's mistake, the act of delivery and the occurrence of material damage. The conclusions reached here should not be extrapolated to the

II.　Consideration of Attempted Crime of Specialized Fraud

2.1.　Precedent (1) involved the following facts.

One day, the victim was the target of a specialized fraud and was cheated out of 1,000,000 yen in cash. The next day, a person with an unknown name claiming to be a police officer called A. The man asked the victim to "confirm the loss". The man told the victim that he should withdraw all of his deposits in order to confirm the amount taken, and that he wanted the victim's cooperation with the investigation. A short time later, the unidentified person called the victim again and told him that he would be there at 2:00 PM. In other words, the criminal group was trying to con the victim out of her money again. However, the victim also realized that the call was a fraud. So, the victim contacted the police. The victim pretended to be deceived and waited for perpetrator A to come to the victim's house to collect the cash, where the police officer arrested him. In this case, perpetrator A is not guilty of a completed fraud because he was caught by the police before receiving the fraudulent money. The question is whether the crime of attempted fraud has been committed.

2.2.　In order for the crime of attempt to be committed, the perpetrator must have commenced the commission of the crime of fraud. Now, let us look at the provisions of the Japanese Penal Code for the attempted crime and the provisions for the crime of fraud.

(Reduction or Exculpation of Punishments for Attempts)
Article 43

---

whole general theory of criminal law.

The punishment of a person who commences a crime without completing it may be reduced; provided, however, that voluntary abandonment of commission of the crime, shall lead to the punishment being reduced or the offender being exculpated.

(Fraud)
Article 246 (1)
A person who defrauds another of property shall be punished by imprisonment with work for not more than 10 years.

The act of committing fraud is the act of demanding the delivery of property in order to defraud. In this case, however, the perpetrator did not demand delivery of property. Therefore, is it possible for an attempt to defraud, such as in the above case, to also constitute a criminal offense?

In this regard, the Japanese Supreme Court stated: "An act of making the victim, who had already been defrauded of 1,000,000 yen, believe the lies as truth can be said to have significantly increased the danger of the victim's delivering cash immediately in response to a requirement made by the defendant, who was going to visit the victim's residence in a short time".

2.3. Scholars have offered various analyses of this precedent. There are also criticisms of this precedent. Some scholars say that since the act of fraud is seeking delivery of property, there can be no attempted crime as long as the act has not been commenced. Such a conclusion is not unnatural when one reads the numerous fraud precedents which have been issued in the past.

However, from a practical standpoint, this case has sufficient value to be punished as an attempt to commit fraud. In particular, considering that specialized frauds are an organized crime targeting the elderly and that there is a high need for deterrence, the conclusion that this case is punishable as an attempted crime is generally seen as acceptable.

How, then, can such a conclusion be explained? Theoretically, it could be explained as follows. Why is the attempted crime punished in the first place? It is because the attempted act creates a real and concrete danger of infringement of legal interests. Since criminal law is primarily intended to protect legal interests, it should be triggered only when legal interests are infringed. However, it need not do so unless that legal interest is an important one. The state is permitted to use criminal law when there is an imminent danger that an important legal interest will be infringed.

If this is the case, then the attempt can be punishable as soon as there is an imminent danger of the legal interest being infringed. In other words, even if the criminal act itself has not yet begun, it may be punishable as an attempted crime at the preparatory stage.

In the first place, the initiation of a criminal act does not always coincide with the occurrence of an imminent danger to the legal interest being infringed. Normally, the initiation of a criminal act is accompanied by an imminent danger to the legal interest being infringed. However, this is not always the case.

In this precedent, A, in collaboration with an unidentified person, attempted to demand delivery of the property after telling the victim a series of lies. According to this plan, by telling a series of lies, the danger that the property would be defrauded was greatly increased. In this light, the defendant's actions should rightly be punished as an attempt to defraud.

Additionally, it should be considered that the precise point at which a crime becomes punishable as an attempted crime is a matter of policy. It is fair to say that the timing of the imminent danger of infringing legal interests is determined by a series of precedents. And the precedents referred to here certainly recognize that the timing at which a person becomes culpable as an attempted offender is at a much earlier stage than previous Japanese precedents. In that respect, this precedent signals a new approach taken by the Supreme

Court regarding the crime of attempted specialized frauds.

III. Consideration of Complicity of Specialized Fraud

3.1. Precedent (2) involved the following facts.

B phoned the victim and lied to her, telling her that she could take part in a special lottery draw in which she was certain to win if she paid a fee, and asked her to send money by courier to a specified location. The victim realized that B's call was a scam because it was suspicious. B, on the other hand, instructed C, who was unaware of the situation, to go to the destination and collect the package, which C accepted because he would receive a large reward from B. C became suspicious of the large reward, and realized that he might be involved in a Specialized Fraud that he had often heard about in the media, but C received the package which he was sent to collect at the target address.

In this case, can C be punished as an accomplice to the crime of fraud? The crime of fraud is committed when goods are delivered with the intent to defraud. On the other hand, C is not involved in such an act of fraud. Initially, at the time of the fraudulent act, C does not even know that the fraud is being committed.

3.2. Let us look at the provisions of the Japanese Penal Code on co-principals.

(Co-Principals)
Article 60
Two or more persons who commit a crime in joint action are all principals.

Japanese courts have interpreted this provision to mean that if one of the conspirators commits the crime after communicating his intentions to the others, they are all criminally liable for the entire criminal result.

C was not involved in the fraud from the beginning, but only in the course of it. In such a case, would he still be a co-principal?

3.3. The Supreme Court ruled that C was a co-perpetrator of attempted fraud for the entire fraud in question, including the fraudulent acts before C joined the fraud.

The Japanese Supreme Court stated: "…in connection with the fraud, the defendant was engaged in the Receiving Act, which was contemplated to be integrated with the Deceitful Act in order to accomplish the fraud, in conspiracy with accomplices, without being aware that the pretending-to-be-deceived operation had commenced, after the Deceitful Act was conducted by an accomplice. From these points, it is adequate to construe that the defendant bears the responsibility of a co-principal in attempted fraud in connection with the fraud, including the Deceitful Act conducted before the defendant's engagement…".

However, this does not explain why the accused is considered a co-principal. In this precedent, the reasoning for the finding of co-principals is unclear. Why did the Supreme Court deem the defendant to be co-principal?

In fact, prior to this decision, the Supreme Court has dealt with cases involving the culpability of persons who, while not initially involved in a crime, participated in the commission of the crime at a later stage. The following is the explanation given by the Supreme Court when it ruled on this issue with respect to physical injury (2012 (A) 23 Keishu Vol. 66, No. 11).

The Japanese Supreme Court stated: "In that case, it is reasonable to construe that the accused is not culpable as a co-principal of the crime of injury for the injuries that P and Q had already caused before he conspired and joined with them because his involvement in conspiracy and his acts arising therefrom have no causal relationship with said injuries, and he is culpable as a co-principal of the crime of injury only for having contributed to causing injuries to R and S by assaulting them so violently as to result in injuring them, after conspiring and joining with P and Q".

Here, the Supreme Court has explained that a person is liable as a co-principal for the consequences arising from acts committed by others because he or she has participated in the conspiracy, acted on it, and causally contributed to the consequences. Such a theory is known in Japan as t*he causal complicity theory*. The causal complicity theory has been a firmly accepted theory in academic discourse for the past 30 years. In practice, there are a number of precedent setting cases that are thought to be based on this concept.

On the basis of this causal complicity theory, how would the above precedent on fraud be explained? This is extremely difficult to explain from the causal complicity theory. This is because defendant C was not involved in the act of committing the fraud, and the conspiracy of the defendants and their acts based on it do not have a causal relationship with respect to the fraud as a whole. If that were the case, C would be liable only for his act of receiving the package, and would not be a co-principal with respect to the fraud as a whole. This new precedent would not be consistent with the Court's previous thinking.

How, then, should this precedent be reconciled with previously decided cases? Some have suggested that this precedent has negated the theory of causal complicity. However, in view of the entirety of criminal law practice to date, this is unlikely to be the case. Although there is no room here to go into detail, the Supreme Court's precedent to date has accumulated decisions over the years based on the causal complicity theory. Moreover, in 2012, the Court explicitly articulated the causal complicity theory as described above and issued a precedent that did not affirm co-principal offenses with respect to perpetrators who became involved later, so it is exceedingly unlikely that, five years later, the Court would adopt a theory of complicity based on a completely different theory.

The question is how to explain this precedent from the perspective of causal co-influence theory. Many academic theories modify the causal co-involvement theory in various ways. However, since causal relationships do not flow from the future to the past, causal contribution cannot be attributed to an act in which one was not involved in to begin with. If this is the case, then co-principals should only be liable for consequences after their own acts of involvement. In the end, it must be said that this precedent cannot be logically explained.

If so, the only possible explanation is that this precedent created a new category of crimes, limited to cases of Specialized Frauds. I know this is certainly a very strange explanation from the perspective of the principle of legality in continental law, since new laws must be enacted by the legislature, i.e., the Parliament. The Supreme Court should never have issued such a precedent. Quite simply, it is the wrong precedent. However, there would be no practical point in criticizing it for being wrong. [5] From a practical standpoint, it is better to think of this precedent as an exception to the rule of fraud, and to use it on a limited basis.

IV. Consideration of Intent of Specialized Fraud

4.1. Precedent (3) involved the following facts.

On the instructions of an acquaintance, the accused received a parcel sent to a room in a block of flats from an employee of a delivery company by pretending to be someone else. The package contained cash which had been sent by the victim of a specialized fraud. At trial, the defendant claimed that he

---

(5) If the Supreme Court, i.e., the judicial power, makes an illegal decision, it is the legislative or executive power that can admonish it. This is the concept of separation of powers. Here, however, there is a practical problem of legislative technique, which prevents the Diet from legislating appropriately on specialized frauds. Considering this, it is possible to view the courts as supplementing the legislation that the Diet was unable to pass, in the form of case law. In common law countries, such a response may not be viewed as particularly strange.

thought the package contained illegal drugs and weapons. In addition, the defendant had repeated the act of receiving similar packages several times, each time receiving a reward.

This case deals with the intent to commit specialized fraud. This is because the defendant in this case does not have a definitive and binding awareness that he is participating in the crime of fraud. Of course, he is aware that the item in the package or envelope he receives is some kind of illegal item. However, he believes that it might be a prohibited drug or a handgun. In such a case, would he still be found guilty of intent to defraud?

4.2. The Japanese Penal Code defines intent as follows.

(Intent)
Article 38 (1) An act performed without the intent to commit a crime is not punishable; provided, however, that the same does not apply unless otherwise specially provided for by law.

From a jurisprudential point of view, this provision alone does not clarify exactly what intent is. Japanese criminal justice practice and scholarship have developed the concept of intent theoretically. It is important to define what intent means here. In Japanese criminal justice practice and academic theory, intent is defined as the recognition and admission of the fact of a crime.

In this precedent, the Japanese Supreme Court stated: "The accused then stated that the accused believed that the packages contain guns and drugs, but did not confirm that the packages contain guns and drugs, and there are no circumstances that eliminate the possibility that the accused was aware that the accused's own acts might constitute a fraud". The Supreme Court then concluded that the accused had the intent to commit fraud.

Japanese academic theory describes Intent as follows. Intent is the recognition and admission of the fact of a crime. This criminal fact is framed by the constitutive requirements that typify the crime (*Tatbestand*). Thus, it is not enough to have an awareness that something is illegal in relation to some crime. In the case of this precedent, it is necessary to recognize that the object may have been acquired as a consequence of the crime of fraud. Of course, the recognition that it may be a handgun or that it may be an illegal drug may also exist in parallel with the recognition that it may be fraud.

Put another way, in this case, there are no circumstances which eliminate the possibility that the accused was aware that the accused's own acts might constitute a fraud. Therefore, the conclusion is that the accused had the intent of fraud. The majority of the academic literature evaluates this precedent as justifiable.

However, on further reflection, the above idea can be somewhat questionable. If we simply accept that the intent to commit several offenses exists in parallel, there is a risk that the determination of intent will be extremely crude. Of course, if the conclusion is accepted that the fraud cannot be established in this case, the problem which arises is that the police will not be able to obtain any evidence to proceed with the investigation of the specialized fraud. It is therefore understandable that both practitioners and academics agree on the conclusion that fraud should be established in this case. However, it seems certain that there is an important theoretical problem here. It seems that Japanese scholars do not take this issue very seriously, but I would be interested to hear what the readers of this paper (non-Japanese readers) think about it.

V. Final Remarks

Properly punishing and deterring special frauds such as those described in this paper is of great importance for the protection of the elderly. It is assumed that such frauds occur not only in Japan but also in many other countries. While what is described here may be a local problem stemming from

Japan's fraud provisions, it is possible that similar problems occur in other countries as well.

In addition, the criminal law interpretative issues examined in this paper present important challenges with regard to the fundamental issues of attempt, complicity, and intent. It is hoped that this paper will be of use to readers interested in these issues.

Chapter 11
An analysis of Japan's Foreign Public Official Anti-Bribery Act

I. Introduction

The most important international convention for anti-corruption is the United Nations Convention Against Corruption. This convention was adopted at the United Nations General Assembly held in Mérida, Mexico in October 2003. Japan has since been making efforts to ratify this treaty. In June 2017, with the reform of the Act on Punishment of Organized Crimes and Control of Crime Proceeds, the components of the convention became incorporated in the law and ratification became a reality.

If explained this way, this event creates an image that Japan's anti-corruption efforts experienced a turning point in 2017. Unfortunately, it was not as significant a turning point as it was anticipated to be. The Act on Punishment of Organized Crimes and Control of Crime Proceeds, the domestic law reformed in response to the United Nations Convention against Corruption, has some components that are very similar to the domestic law pertaining to the United Nations Convention against Transnational Organized Crime. Diet deliberations regarding the similar points, together with discussions on conspiracy, proved to be a difficult one and caused the conclusion of this convention to be delayed.

Creating the provision on "Harboring a criminal and other matters involving organized crimes" (Act on Punishment of Organized Crimes and Control of Crime Proceeds, Article 7 (2)) was the extent of the ratification of the United Nations Convention against Corruption. A more prominent effort on part of Japan regarding transnational corruption prevention had already occurred in 1997 – the conclusion of the Convention on Combating Bribery of Foreign Public

Officials in International Business Transactions, also known as the OECD Anti-Bribery Convention. Through this convention, a domestic law, the Foreign Public Officials Anti-Bribery Act, was enacted. This act may have been much more significant than the most recent law reform.

Keeping in mind the above factors, I would like to give an introduction about Japan's efforts of preventing world-wide corruption by using the Foreign Public Officials Anti-Bribery Act as the foundation and adding on analyses from the perspective of criminal law theory.

II. The Enactment of the Foreign Public Officials Anti-Bribery Act

In October 1997, the OECD Anti-Bribery Convention was adopted. This is what the objective of the convention was: Being said that dishonest "benefits" bestowed to foreign public officials involved in international transactions creates unfair international competition, if each participating country criminalizes this act, combatting dishonest international transactions becomes possible through international cooperation and thus protecting fair and just competition. In order to conclude this convention, Japan established the Foreign Public Officials Anti-Bribery Act.

The Foreign Public Officials Anti-Bribery Act is essentially a provision on bribery, which may have made it possible for this law to be established as a subcategory of bribery. However, in 1998, Japan reformed the Unfair Competition Prevention Act by establishing, as part of it, the Foreign Public Officials Anti-Bribery Act. The protected interests of the Foreign Public Officials Anti-Bribery Act, according to the framers of this law, is different from bribery in the penal law sense. In other words, again referencing the framers of this law, the protected interests of bribery in penal law are the fairness of Japanese public officials and the public's trust toward said Japanese public officials. On the other hand, the punishment of those who bribe foreign public officials, made mandatory by the OECD Anti-Bribery Convention, is based upon protecting fair competition in international transactions. Thus, since the protected interests are very different in the two instances, it is said that the Foreign Public Officials Anti-Bribery Act should not be categorized with penal law (For more information on the legal framework for corruption prevention in general, see Oyamada 2015; p.26-29).

III. The Foreign Public Officials Anti-Bribery Act and its Application

We will now take a look at the details of the Foreign Public Officials Anti-Bribery Act. In Article 18 (1) in the Unfair Competition Prevention Act, bribery of foreign public officials is described as follows:

"No person shall give, or offer or promise to give, any money or other benefit to a Foreign Public Official etc., in order to have the Foreign Public Official, etc. act or refrain from acting in relation to the performance of official duties, or in order to have the Foreign Public Official, etc., use his/her position to influence another Foreign Public Official, etc. to act or refrain from acting in relation to the performance of official duties, in order to obtain a wrongful gain in business with regard to international commercial transactions. "

In response to this article, the offender will be punished with either imprisonment or a fine according to Article 21(2) (vii), which provides that a person who gave, etc. an improper benefit to a foreign public official, etc. in violation of Article 18(1) shall be subject to imprisonment with work for a period not exceeding five years or for a fine not exceeding 5,000,000 yen.

For juridical persons, the Dual Criminal Liability Provision will be applied. Article 22 of the Unfair Competition Prevention Act provides that where a representative, agent, employee or any other staff, etc. of a juridical person has committed a violation in connection with an operation of the said juridical person, a fine not exceeding 300,000,000 yen will be imposed on that juridical person, which is in addition to punishment for the offender himself/herself.

There are several cases where this law has been applied in practice (For details, see Manabe, K., Umetsu, H. R., & Ono, S., 2018; p193-194).

IV. Theoretical Analysis —— Dogmatics/Doctrine

Now I would like to add in dogmatics/doctrine of criminal law. I would also like to place an emphasis on the theory of criminalization (Readers interested in this crime from a comparative legal perspective may find it useful to refer, Kai 2020).

When analyzing the Foreign Public Officials Anti-Bribery Act from the perspective of criminalization, there are two important points we must address – (1) The creation of this Act was not in direct response of the public voice, but to ratify the convention and (2) The Foreign Public Official Anti-Bribery Act was enacted to protect competition fairness and order – in other words, the protected interest of society is the protected interest of the law, and this is different from "bribery" in the sense of penal law, which lays its protected interest with the protected interest of the state.

The problem with (1) is that this act of bribery was criminalized through international law (convention). The entity that concludes conventions is the government (Executive branch), which may make this seem like a problem of separation of powers, since the government must execute the convention and that execution involves criminalization of a certain action. Traditionally, the government (Executive branch) is responsible for enforcing the law, but in this instance, it seems to be that the government has control over the Diet (Legislative branch), which is responsible for enacting laws. At the end of the day, however, it is up to the Diet to enact laws – even if the government concludes a convention, without the Diet's involvement, the convention cannot be used as a rationale to directly punish civilians. Further, the convention does determine the rough outlines of a certain law, but the Diet is not required to comply with every single detail of the concluded convention. As long as penalties or laws that punish actions covered in the convention are enacted, any other minor differences or disparities between the convention and the domestic law does not create any problems. In this way, the first problem should be resolved.

The second issue is whether the understanding of "legal goods" established by the Foreign Public Official Anti-Bribery Act in Japan is appropriate. As mentioned before, lawmakers have already said that the legal goods of this act is to protect fair competition in international transactions. Needless to say, if a corporation involved in an international transaction bribes a foreign public official, it becomes impossible to maintain competition fairness. A similar concept can be seen in the United Nations Convention against Corruption. Article 15 of the same convention is as follows:

> "Article 15. Bribery of national public officials Each State Party shall adopt such legislative and other measures as may be necessary to establish as criminal offences, when committed intentionally:
> (a) The promise, offering or giving, to a public official, directly or indirectly, of an undue advantage, for the official himself or herself or another person or entity, in order that the official act or refrain from acting in the exercise of his or her official duties;
> (b) The solicitation or acceptance by a public official, directly or indirectly, of an undue advantage, of the official himself or herself or another person or entity, in order that the official act or refrain from acting in the exercise of his or her official duties."

The next article, Article 16, calls for the criminalization of bribing foreign public officials:

"Article 16. Bribery of foreign public officials and officials of public international organizations
1. Each State Party shall adopt such legislative and other measure as may be necessary to establish as a criminal offence, when committed intentionally, the promise, offering or giving to a foreign public official or an official of a public international organization, directly or indirectly, of an undue advantage, for the official himself or herself or another person or entity, in order that the official act or refrain from acting in the exercise of his or her official duties, in order to obtain or retain business or other undue advantage in relation to the conduct of international business.
2. Each State Party shall consider adopting such legislative and other measures as may be necessary to establish as a criminal offence, when committed intentionally, the solicitation or acceptance by a foreign public official or an official of a public international organization, directly or indirectly, of an undue advantage, for the official himself or herself or another person or entity, in order that the official act or refrain from acting in the exercise of his or her official duties."

If criminalization is executed in accordance with these articles, it can said that the existing Japanese domestic law (criminal law) that punishes bribery has very different rationales. According to the most commonly accepted theory and judicial precedents, the protected interest of the Japanese bribery law is the society's trust toward the fairness of public duty (the "trust-protection" theory). In other words, bribery is an action that destroys the trustworthiness of public duty – the breach of fair public duty or the potential of a breach does not trigger punishment. The "OECD Convention" and the "United Nations Convention against Corruption" is something that calls for punishment of a corrupt action that allows or disallows a certain public duty to be executed, and thus in this case, the potential of a breach of fair public duty can be interpreted as the rationale of punishing corrupt behavior.

There certainly is an ounce of truth in this logic. It adheres to the harm principle, which holds that criminal law should only be exercised when some kind of right is under attack. The harm principle is central to the criminalization theory in Anglo-American law but it also has its similarities to the European Continental law (especially German; Japanese criminal law theory adheres to this as well) which holds that penal laws and standards can be used to suppress or ban the protected interests of law from being attacked or exposed to danger.

However, this logic proves itself to be insufficient to evaluate punishment of corrupt behavior. According to this logic, corrupt behavior cannot be punished when bribery was committed after dishonest or unfair public duty was executed, since this dishonest or unfair behavior was not caused by bribery. Furthermore, in the case where a public official executes an inappropriate duty by selling favors to criminal organizations, punishment for bribery is not possible simply due to the fact that no actual "bribery" was involved.

In order to fill these potholes, it is advisable to evaluate both the protection fair competition in international business transactions together with the protection of trust at the international level toward the fair and just execution of public duties in each country. In other words, there is a need for each country to come up with a legal policy that transcends the limitations of the convention and is stricter with the punishment of corrupt behavior.

It is certainly desirable for Japan to follow suit and cultivate further discussion about this topic, but it seems to be that Japan's Foreign Public Official Anti-Bribery Act is embedded within the Unfair Competition Prevention Act, which is the very thing that is blocking any further discussion. If the Foreign Public Official Anti-Bribery Act is considered a dogmatic/doctrine of the Unfair Competition Prevention Act, dogmatics/doctrines from a "legal goods" perspective, such as the one previously mentioned, is easier to be passed unnoticed. In order to allow these discussions to develop, it is best that Japan creates an independent law, for example, "(International) Act on Punishment of Corrupt Behavior," and to place its legal standard within the criminal code.

V. Evaluation from a Criminal Policy Perspective
　——　The Function of Criminal Law

　　Needless to say at this point, the criminalization of the Foreign Public Official Anti-Bribery Act is based upon the notion of "using criminal law as a means to prevent corrupt behavior." What the problem now is, to what extent do we need to evaluate prevention as a basis of criminalization? Usually, the basis of criminalization is different to that of the same criminalization itself. In other words, a certain behavior has harmed another individual and that it is also worthy of blame (Simester and von Hirsch state "The censuring response of the criminal law is appropriate only culpable wrongdoing". See Simester, A.P. & von Hirsch, A., 2011; p.30). It is more about how to deal with the aftermath of the harm, rather than prevention.

　　However, with this perspective, it may be appropriate for traditional crimes such as homicide and robbery, but it may not be appropriate for newer types of crime. Crimes such as bribery of foreign public officials is a type or financial crime in the sense that it is the prevention of unfair competition, and it is also international crime in the sense that it is the expansion of international transactions. Furthermore, since public officials are involved, it may also be seen as political crime. Newer crime such as bribery of foreign public officials cannot be controlled by merely blaming the offender, but to inform them that that behavior is a crime against civilians and by association, it is inevitable to think about preventing and suppressing crime. By creating penal regulations, it becomes the perspective of preventing and suppressing crime becomes more evident.

　　However, even if penal regulations are created, that alone will not prevent crime. That alone will have next to no preventative effects. This has been shown by prior research of criminology, which effectively hold that general preventative effects of penalty does not exist. What is important is that penal regulations exist. With its mere existence, it makes prevention and suppression by other means (based on punishment by criminal law) possible. Penal regulations function as the foundation of prevention and suppression by other means. Only by following this process can preventative effects by way of penal regulations come to light.

The Ministry of Economy, Trade and Industry has drawn up the "Guideline to Prevent Bribery of Foreign Public Officials," which provides a more specific example. This guideline mentions its objective as to support the autonomous and preventive approach to prevent bribery toward foreign public officials, etc. who are associated with corporations involved in international transactions, and proposes specific measures, especially that of internal structuring within corporations. Some of those measures include the enforcement of corporation compliance, the fostering of corporate ethics, and transparency among different sectors or practices. This can be interpreted as belonging in corporate or economic law more than criminal or penal law. For this reason, I will refrain fro pursuing this any further, but I would like to emphasize again that placing penal regulations alone do not prevent or suppress crime — it is most important to be aware of other means, and additionally place penal regulations.

VI. Conclusion

Finally, allow me to introduce one perspective of the European interpretation of anti-bribery. My primary interest is Danish criminal law, and Denmark is regarded as one of the least corrupt countries in the world. If I were asked if this is because of its exceptional criminal legal standard, however, I will have to say no. It is also the same case if I were asked if this is because of exceptional internal structuring of corporations. I believe Denmark is one of the least corrupt countries simply because of Scandinavian culture. In Scandinavia, the pressure for transparency of politicians and public officials is especially strong. In a society where voter turn-out is more than 80%, any politician or public official who becomes the target of any suspicion will be unsparingly voted out of office. Additionally, Scandinavia maintains their reputable social security through very high taxes, which places these politicians and public officials under scrutiny of the tax office. Any suspicious transaction will be watched by the tax office, so, in essence, the people live with the sense that it is very impractical and counterintuitive to both give and receive bribes.

In order to protect the rights of citizens, it is necessary to establish a system that does not allow self-serving behavior by public officials. All citizens must be given the rights they deserve, without distinction. The "right to life," the theme of this book, should not mean "the right to survive," but "the right to live while receiving the full range of legitimate rights as a human being. To this end, anti-corruption is a very important issue.

Punishment by way of criminal law is the first thing that comes to mind when we want to stop a certain behavior, and this thought process by itself is a very important one. However, the problem is, criminal legal standards tend to be enacted before that can be done. Utilizing penalties to prevent corrupt behavior is only the first step toward complete prevention. Penalties alone do not hold preventative or suppressive effects. Jurists of criminal law, or an institution that enacted criminal legal standards should keep these concepts in mind and work toward refining more effective criminal legal standards.

References:
- Kai, Y. (2020). Japan. Anderson Mori & Tomotsube. (aveilable on the website; https://www.amt-law.com/asset/res/news_2020_pdf/publication_0022031_ja_001.pdf)
- Manabe, K., Umetsu, H. R., & Ono, S., (2018). Chapter 15 Japan. *The Anti-Bribery and Anti-Corruption Review,* 7th ed., p.187.
- Oyamada, E., (2015). Anti-Corruption Measures the Japanese Way: Prevention

Matters. *Asian Education and Development Studies*, Vol.4(1), p.27.
- Ministry of Economy Trade and Industry of Japan (2021). Guideline to Prevent Bribery of Foreign Public Officials (aveilable on the website; Only Japanese, https://www.meti.go.jp/policy/external_economy/zouwai/pdf/GaikokukoumuinzouwaiBoushiShishin20210512.pdf
- Simester, A.P. & von Hirsch, A., (2011). Crimes, Harms, and Wrongs. Hart Publishing.

Chapter 12
A consideration of the protection of trade secrets in Japan

I. Introduction

Every company has confidential information which it does not wish to be disclosed or taken out. This type of information is referred to as a 'trade secret'. Disclosure or taking of trade secrets is an ethically problematic act. At the same time, if the damage caused is significant, it is punishable as a crime called 'trade secret infringement'. So, when does this become a crime under Japanese law? Let us consider this question by looking at the development of criminal law relating to the protection of trade secrets and the current state of trade secret infringement offences.

In considering this issue, one [case study] will be given, and the following discussion will be based on this case study in detail. Note that this [case study] is fictitious.

[case study]

X, a regular employee of temporary staffing agency A, was dissatisfied with the amount of overtime work he was required to do on a daily basis and wanted to move to another temporary staffing agency if he could. Around March 2021, he had an opportunity to meet Mr C, the sales manager of staffing agency B. X and C hit it off immediately. Around July of the same year, when C's subordinate D decided to retire, C began to think that he would like to employ X as his subordinate, explained the situation to X and proposed that he change jobs at Company B. X, who was becoming increasingly dissatisfied with the situation at Company A at the time, immediately agreed. In order to maintain the benefits of his position at Company B, X thought of taking out some information that would be advantageous to Company B. He remembered that Company A had information on temporary workers (a file containing names, addresses, contact details, etc.) and accessed the company's server with a password that he took from his boss's desk without permission. He duplicated the data in the file marked "[Confidential] Temporary Worker List [Strictly prohibited to take out or copy]" to his USB memory by transferring it. In August of the same year, X resigned from Company A and transferred to Company B. Immediately afterwards, he transferred the data to Company B's computer and copied the file to his own USB memory. Is X's conduct a criminal offence?

II. International situation regarding confidential information

In recent years, the leakage of confidential information occurring in companies and research institutions has become an increasingly important social problem. For both the party keeping the secret and the party providing the secret, the leakage of secrets is a major problem that cannot be easily overlooked, as it can cause significant damage.

Japanese companies and research institutions have traditionally held highly technical information. It is generally understood that this confidential information is the subject of intelligence-gathering activities by other countries. This means that any company or research institute, large or small, legitimate or illegitimate, can be targeted if it has advanced technical information.

Additionally, with recent developments in IT technology, information has become increasingly digitised, making it far easier to take it out than ever before. For example, even significantly large quantities of data can be taken out almost instantaneously by transfer via email or storage on a cloud drive. You can also transfer data to a smartphone or tablet with a lightning cable, and with direct transfers over Wi-Fi, you probably won't even need a connecting cable.

In the worst-case scenario, the leakage of advanced technical information could be diverted to research and development of weapons of mass destruction, and even if this is not the case, it could result in the loss of technological superiority for Japanese companies and research institutions. This could also lead to a significant loss of confidence in the companies and research institutions from which the information is leaked, and ultimately to a decline in the international competitiveness of Japan as a whole. The economic loss caused by leaving this unchecked is incalculable.

III. The situation in Japan regarding confidential information

Even in Japan, companies and research institutions with sophisticated technical information are constantly targeted. The number of arrests for trade secret infringement in Japan has been consistently increasing in recent years. In the USA, trade secret infringement has become a major social problem, particularly in relation to China, where there are far more arrests than in Japan. In Japan, the situation has not yet reached this level, but it is expected to do so in the future, requiring measures to be taken to deal with it. Under such circumstances, companies and research institutions are becoming more and more strongly aware of how to protect confidential information. At the same time, however, the risk of confidential information being compromised is now much higher than before, in line with the evolution of IT technologies mentioned earlier.

Specifically, in 2013, there were 11 arrests, but this number increased to 22 in 2019. Only 30% of these cases resulted in prosecution. Of these, only about 30% actually lead to prosecution, and of these, less than 10% of the cases concerned the taking of information abroad. The situation is still not critical, but that is why it is necessary to act now.

IV. What is meant by protection of confidential information?

The problem lies in how to prevent this and how to protect confidential information. When we think of confidential information, we usually think of technical information. For example, new technologies developed by a company or a new market design may come to mind. Of course, these are included in confidential information and are important information. However, it is often confidential information relating to individuals, such as employee or customer lists that are problematic in real life situations. In the [case study], we have ventured to focus on such cases, which are common incidents and happen on a regular basis.

In recent years, the corporate culture that was once considered uniquely Japanese, such as lifetime employment (a system in which companies do not lay off employees and continue to employ them until retirement unless the company goes bankrupt) and the seniority system (a personnel evaluation system in which older employees with more years of service receive better treatment), has gradually diminished. Reflecting the social situation, there has been a marked increase in the mobility of human resources. Many businesspeople share a common desire to change jobs to companies with higher salaries and better working conditions, and there are increasingly cases of people using confidential information about their former employer to gain an advantage when changing jobs. The customer lists in question in [case study] are a particularly important example of this.

Note that the information in question here is "non-public" information. The question in this [case study] is what punishment pertains to the leakage of undisclosed information, and whether the offence in question here is the offence of "trade secret infringement".

V. What is the offence of trade secret infringement?

The offence of trade secret infringement is a relatively newly created offence: it was provided for in a 2003 amendment of the Unfair Competition Prevention Act. Since then, it has been amended several times. The amendments were carried out exclusively to increase statutory penalties.

Around 1985, a number of well-known cases appeared. One example is the case known as the "New Drugs Industrial Espionage Case". In this case, A and B, who were both executives of a pharmaceutical company at the time of the offence, conspired with C, a health engineer at the National Institute of Health and Preventive Medicine, to take a new drug manufacturing approval application file that C had stored in his boss's private cupboard and hand it to B, who made a copy at the pharmaceutical company and returned it to C the same day. The case was heard by the Tokyo District Court. The Tokyo District Court found C guilty of theft, focusing not only on the value of the file that he took out, but also on the value of the information embodied in the paper medium (This judgment was issued by the Tokyo District Court on 28 June 1984 and can be found in Hanrei Jihou No 1126, p. 3). Certainly, in such cases, the crime of theft can be applied because the paper medium was taken outside the company. However, it is now possible to take information outside the company without removing paper media from the company premises. Information can be copied onto a USB memory stick, sent by email, pasted into LINE, Facebook Messenger, etc. Theft (and other property offences under the Criminal Code), which is a crime against "property", would then make taking information out of the country unpunishable. This is why the offence of infringement of trade secrets was created to deter such situations.

VI. The concept of trade secrets

The offence of trade secret infringement is provided for in the Unfair Competition Prevention Act. In other words, it does not protect information in general, but rather "trade secrets". The important question is what constitutes a "trade secret".

The Unfair Competition Prevention Act defines a trade secret as 'a production method, sales method or other technical or business information useful for business activities that is managed as a secret and is not openly known' (Article 2(2) (2) (vi) of the Unfair Competition Prevention Act). Since the content of a secret is "technical or business information useful for production methods, sales methods and other business activities", the list of dispatched workers in question in [case study] is also included in this category.

This definition is then organised into three categories: (i) confidentiality, (ii) usefulness and (iii) non-publicity. I will explain them in turn. (i) Confidentiality means that the information is controlled as a secret. The holder of the information must not only have the subjective intention to keep it secret, but must also be in a state where it is objectively recognised as being managed as a secret by employees and outsiders. In other words, the holder's intention to maintain confidentiality must be indicated by specific confidentiality management measures implemented by the holder, and the employees and outsiders must be able to recognise the holder's intention to maintain confidentiality.

Secondly, (ii) usefulness means that the information is technical or business information that is useful for the activities of the business in question. Usefulness here means that the information is useful for business activities, such as being useful for the production, sale or research and development of goods and services.

Finally, (iii) non-publicity means that the information is not publicly known, namely that the information is not generally available except under the control of the holder, e.g. the information is not described in a publication. It can be said to mean that the information is not normally available within the scope of reasonable efforts.

VII. Three objective requirements

These three are known as the three requirements of a trade secret. So which of these three requirements is, in practice, the most problematic? In practice, the most problematic is actually (i) confidentiality. This can be seen from responses given to a consultation service set up by the Life Safety Bureau of the Metropolitan Police Department for business-related persons concerning damage caused by trade secret infringements. Statistics over the past few years show that 71 cases, or 43.3% of the total, involved confidentiality issues. The number of cases involving usefulness issues was 2, accounting for 1.2% of the total. There were 5 cases of non-publicity issues, accounting for 3.0% of the total. This shows that of the three trade secret requirements, confidentiality is by far the most important issue.

In [case study], confidentiality is also an issue. In [case study], the file taken out by X was stored on Company A's server, titled "[Confidential] Temporary Worker List [Strictly prohibited to take out or copy]" and also had a password set. This indicates that Company A was aware that the file was confidential information and had placed appropriate access restrictions on it. In such cases, confidentiality would be recognised without any problem.

Conversely, for example, if Company A's temporary worker information was placed in a state where any employee could easily access it, and there were no notes saying that the information was "confidential" or "must not be taken out or reproduced", would X's culpability be different? In this case, even if Company A considered this information to be confidential, it lacked confidentiality management because it did not have a management system in place. Therefore, in this case, X would not be guilty of trade secret infringement. And in real cases, this situation is surprisingly common due to companies not properly managing their secrets.

VIII. Subjective requirement - "the intent to gain an unfair advantage or to cause damage to the holder of the trade secret"

In order for the offence of trade secret infringement to be established, the offender must have subjectively had a special intent (special subjective requirement). In other words, the offender must have "the intent to gain an unfair advantage or to cause damage to the holder of the trade secret".

The requirement of a figurative aggravating purpose excludes the use of trade secrets for whistleblowing, research purposes, reporting purposes, etc. However, this purpose is understood to be relatively thin in content, so it is better to understand when it does not constitute a purpose than to consider when it does. Specifically, the following are mentioned. (i) whistle-blowing for the purpose of realising the public interest; (ii) disclosing within the trade union trade secrets of the holder acquired for the purpose of realising the legitimate rights of workers; and (iii) taking documents or USBs containing trade secrets home without permission from an authorised superior for overtime purposes.

In [case study], X took information on temporary workers in order to gain an advantage in his new job, and then used it to extract temporary workers in his new job. In this case, it would be clear that X has a premeditated and harmful purpose.

However, let us imagine instead that X had no intention to change jobs but discovered that his bosses has required him work long hours in a black company-like manner without any consideration for the employment conditions of temporary workers, and he keeps a record of this on a file listing these workers, which he accesses to gather evidence for the purpose of whistleblowing. In such cases, X's conduct does not constitute a criminal offence, as there is no intent to cause harm.

IX. What constitutes trade secret infringement?

Infringements of trade secrets can be broadly divided into (i) unauthorised acquisition or receipt, (ii) disclosure and (iii) use (Article 21(1) and (3) of the Unfair Competition Prevention Act).

In [case study], X illegally obtained temporary worker information and used it to recruit temporary workers. In this case, an act of trade secret infringement can be assessed as having taken place.

If the offence of trade secret infringement is established, the penalty is considerably heavier than for ordinary crimes. The statutory penalty is imprisonment for up to 10 years or a fine of up to 20 million yen, or both (Article 21(1) of the Unfair Competition Prevention Act (Article 21(1) of the Unfair Competition Prevention Act). In addition, if the offence relates to taking the goods out of the country, the penalty is imprisonment for up to 10 years or a fine of up to 30 million yen, or both (Article 21(3) of the Unfair Competition Prevention Act). Attempted offences are punishable (paragraph 4) and, depending on the case, criminal offences may also be committed under the Criminal Code (paragraph 9). Property obtained by or as a reward for the same offence is forfeited (paragraph 10).

X. How can trade secret infringement be detected?

In order to protect companies and research institutions from trade secret infringement, a trade secret leak must first be promptly detected. There are usually signs that information has been leaked. For example, in the case of [case study], it is likely that Company A's temporary workers will begin to leave one after another, because temporary workers are being drawn away from the company. Of course, resignations will often occur, but if they occur at a significantly different rate than in the past, caution is needed.

If technical information is leaked, for example, the quality of a competitor's product may suddenly improve. A supplier may suddenly cut off business without giving a reason. Common to both would be, for example, rumours of information leaks on the internet, or suspicious information circulating on SNS or anonymous forums such as Twitter. With the development of the online society, it is now necessary to check your company's reputation and gossip.

XI. How can companies defend themselves against trade secret infringement?

As mentioned above, the most problematic of the three trade secret requirements is confidentiality. Many companies and research institutions are still not very conscious of protecting their trade secrets and often have inadequate secret management. As a result, when trade secret infringement actually occurs, it may no longer be protected under the trade secret infringement offence because it was not managed as a secret, even though an infringement clearly occurred.

Until now, Japanese companies have tended to handle trade secret infringements internally as much as possible, considering such infringements to be an embarrassment to the company. In particular, many company officials may feel embarrassed if the cause of the breach was revealed to be inadequate secret management. However, this is not the case. Trade secret infringement used to be a crime of intimate knowledge (a crime that cannot be prosecuted without a complaint from the victim), but that provision has also disappeared. Trade secret infringement can cause significant economic loss to society as a whole. It is necessary to take appropriate countermeasures, rather than thinking of it as a problem that affects only one's own company.

For example, it is necessary to strictly limit access to confidential information, to manage passwords well (because it is difficult to limit access if the information is used constantly in regular business), to ensure that retirees delete information in e-mails and files appropriately, to prevent recruits from bringing in information from their former employer, to sign non-disclosure and confidentiality agreements at the outset, and so on.

XII. Conclusion

With the mobility of human resources, information is also becoming more fluid. Information exists in computers and cannot be held in one's hand as an object, so its importance is often not fully understood. The temptation to misuse trade secrets may be even stronger if, as in the case of X in [case study], the information will be useful after changing jobs, or will be rewarded by the boss of the new company and will help to improve one's position. We need to understand that it is a crime to do so, and it is very important that those in a position to manage companies educate their employees and make sure that trade secrets are positioned and clarified as secrets so that everyone can understand them.

References
- Ministry of Economy Trade and Industry of Japan. "*Management Guidelines for Trade Secrets*" https://www.meti.go.jp/english/policy/economy/chizai/chiteki/pdf/0813mgtc.pdf
- Suzuki, M. "Japan: Overview and Summary", in Liu, K. and Hilty, R., Trade

Secret Protection: Asia at a Crossroads, Frederick, Wolters Kluwer Legal & Regulatory, 2021.
- Yamane, T., "Japan: The Criminal Punishment for Trade Secrets Infringement and the Element of Purpose of Wrongful Gain in Japan", in Liu, K. and Hilty, R., Trade Secret Protection: Asia at a Crossroads, Frederick, Wolters Kluwer Legal & Regulatory, 2021.

Chapter 13
The Case of Criminal Regulation as a Strategy to Control the Covid-19 Pandemic in Japan

I. Introduction

This paper examines the theory of criminal regulation in the new era, taking Criminal Regulation as a Strategy to Control the Covid-19 Pandemic in Japan as an example.

The mentioned "theory of criminal regulation" can be distinguished from criminal legislative theory. In recent years, there has been a flurry of research in Japan on what is called "criminal legislative studies" or "criminal legislative theory". Under these theories, the desirable form of criminal legislation and regulations are discussed in a manner which includes the proposition, "this is the way it should be," and proposals are made on how to structure articles and the specific scope of punishment. In some cases, even proposals for new articles are presented.

This paper is not aimed at putting forward a "theory of criminal legislation" involving such *normative* propositions. Rather, it is intended to discuss the propositions related to the *fact* of how far criminal law can intervene in society when considered theoretically as criminal law theory.

I refer to this type of discourse as the "criminalization theory," as distinguished from the "criminal legislation theory." Criminalization theory defines which acts can be considered crimes in terms of criminal law theory.

Let us consider an example. An infectious disease scientist/medical scientist can state what symptoms Covid-19 causes, how the infection occurs, and what methods are available to block the route of infection. This is an analysis as a natural scientist and a statement regarding facts. However, what specific measures should be taken to prevent infection based on such facts is a statement of duty and a political judgment. That decision is made by politicians and bureaucrats. These two types of statements must be strictly distinguished. As criminal law scholars, what we can state is the fact of how effectively the criminal law deters crime. How to use this fact to make criminal legislation is not our task, but that of the legislators.

With the above in mind, I would like to discuss here the "criminalization theory" from the perspective of theoretical criminal law studies (and, moreover, pragmatic theory of criminal law).

II. Criminal Regulation as a Strategy to Control the Covid-19 Pandemic —— The Situation in Japan

According to Professor Tokikazu Konishi, the issues involved in criminal regulation as a strategy to control the Covid-19 Pandemic can be divided into three types. [1] The first is the prevention of infection in the criminal justice system. Although this is a criminal law issue, it is not intended to control the behavior of the public through punishment, so it is excluded from consideration here.

The second is the use of criminal law as a means of preventing fraudulent acts. For example, the Law on Emergency Measures for Stabilization of National Living Standards prohibits the resale of "masks" and "rubbing alcohol" by government ordinance, and imposes criminal penalties (imprisonment for up to one year, a fine of up to 1 million yen, or both). Article 1, Paragraph 1 of the Law on Emergency Measures for Stabilization of National Living Standards further prohibits hoarding and selling of goods highly related to the livelihood of the people or goods of national economic importance (hereinafter referred to as

---

(1) Tokikazu Konishi, 'Shingata Korona-ka ni okeru Keijihoujou no Shomondai' (2022) 52 Hanzaigaku Zasshi, vol.88 No.2.

'livelihood-related goods, etc.'). The purpose of this law is to contribute to the stability of people's lives and the smooth operation of the national economy by providing for emergency measures against hoarding and selling of goods that are highly relevant to people's lives or important to the national economy. The current pandemic has caused masks and rubbing alcohol to be designated as such 'livelihood-related goods, etc.'. This law imposes criminal regulations on the resale of such goods. Criminal regulations are imposed on the resale of these goods on the grounds that they are closely related to people's daily lives. If this is so, the reason for criminal regulation is clear and does not require special consideration in this paper. Therefore, we shall leave this issue out of the discussion.

The third is when criminal law is used as a measure to prevent the spread of infectious diseases. This is a "direct restriction on freedom of action as it restricts people's outings, movements, business activities, etc."[2] Specific examples include: (1) a person who has Covid-19 and does not comply with a request to be admitted to a hospital or flees from a hospital, or (2) a person who does not comply with a request to change store hours or restrict the use of a facility. Expanding on this, the discussion turns to whether criminal penalties can be imposed on those who do not comply with the so-called lockdown movement restrictions when they are implemented. These issues should be at the core of criminal regulation as a strategy to control the Covid-19 Pandemic.

In Japan, the introduction of criminal penalties was considered in the legislative deliberation process for (1) and (2) in the third case above. Ultimately, however, the introduction of criminal penalties was abandoned, and only a non-penal fine as administrative penalty was introduced. Administrative penalties, unlike criminal penalties in Japan,[3] are considered sanctions that do not have

---

(2) *Konishi* fn (1) 53.
(3) Article 80 of the Act on Prevention of Infectious Diseases and Medical Care for Patients with Infectious Diseases (abbreviated as "KANSENSHO-HO, Infectious Disease Control Act")

censure or/and moral reproof in their background. Moreover, a large-scale lockdown was never implemented in the first place, and so the introduction of criminal penalties for its violation was never even considered.

Considering the above, how can the attitude of the Japanese legislature in taking such anti-Covid-19 pandemic strategies be viewed from the perspective of criminal law theory?

III. Under what circumstances are criminal penalties permissible? —— An Examination from the Perspective of Punishment Theory

3.1. Genealogy of Punishment Theory

In order to answer the above question, it is necessary to consider the fundamental theoretical question, "In what cases is punishment permissible?". There is a way to approach this question from the viewpoint of "what is punishment? ". This approach should provide a straightforward answer to the question, "Under what circumstances are criminal penalties permissible?" Therefore, we

---

provides that if a person hospitalized by a measure for hospitalization, etc. escapes within the period of hospitalization, or if the person subject to a measure for hospitalization is not hospitalized by the beginning of the period to be hospitalized without any justifiable reason, he/she shall be liable to a non-penal fine not exceeding 500,000 yen.

In addition, the Law Concerning Special Measures against Influenza Pandemic, etc. (abbreviated as "TOKUSO-HO, Special Measures Law") provides that when priority measures are taken to prevent the spread of influenza, etc., non-compliance with requests to change business hours, etc. without just cause may result in an order being issued, and if the order is violated, a fine of up to ¥200,000 may be imposed (Special Measures Law). In addition, if a request is made during the declaration of a state of emergency to restrict the use of facilities, etc., and the request is not complied with without justifiable reason, an order shall be issued, non-compliance with which shall result in a fine of no more than 200,000 yen. In the event of a violation of such an order, a non-penal fine of up to 300,000 yen may be imposed (Article 45, Paragraph 2, Article 45, Paragraph 3, Article 45, Paragraph 3, Article 45, Paragraph 3, and Article 79 of the Special Measures Law).

first need to refer to the model of the penal system.

When tracing the genealogy of punishment theory to the present day, the first thing which comes to mind is the conflict between the classical school, which is based on the theory of retributive punishment, and the modern school, which is based on the theory of correctional and incapacitating punishment.

However, this conflict was quickly resolved in the second half of the 20th century. The theory of correctional and incapacitating punishment declined. The modern school of criminal law is a positivist criminal law theory, the nature of which is that the theory is defended only because it is proven by evidence. The argument of the modern school criminal law theory (i.e., that punishment is not a meaningless retribution, but a corrective and incapacitating measure that prevents future crimes) loses its persuasive force if it is not proven.

In the 1970s, it became clear that, despite years of effort, the corrective and incapacitating effects of punishment were not nearly as apparent as expected (this became apparent in the Nordic countries which had most actively promoted such punishment systems, namely Denmark, Norway, Sweden, and Finland). Strong doubts were then cast on the effectiveness of the modern school of correctional punishment. The famous phrase "Nothing works" uttered in the U.S. at the time expressed great disappointment with correctional and incapacitating punishment. As a result, the theory of punishment once again moved in the direction of retributive punishment. This time, however, retributive punishment was not merely taken up conceptually, as in the classical school, but a more sophisticated theory of retributive punishment was presented. The two approaches which emerged in this regard are the *Justice Model* and the *Deterrence Model*.

The *Justice Model* and the *Deterrence Model* are two theories of punishment which emerged in the United States at the end of the 20th century. Both of these theories can be said to originate from the theory of retributive punishment, but their ideas are contrasting.

The *Justice Model* holds that: since the correctional punishment theory has failed, it is wrong to respond to the cause of a crime with punishment. Having said this, it is important to ensure procedural fairness, to give judges less discretion in their decisions, and to eliminate arbitrary sentencing. The less discretion exercised by judges, the more likely it is that sentences will be imposed in just desert. Thus, the *Justice Model* argues that the very nature of punishment is that it should be proportionate to the act of the crime.

The *Deterrence Model,* on the other hand, is based on the following idea: as we can see from the failure of the correctional sentencing theory, it is impossible to identify where the causes of crime lie. However, the policy goal of threatening and deterring crime through punishment is still meaningful in and of itself. It is important, then, to provide for general prevention by defining the acts one wishes to deter as crimes, threatening them with punishment, and ensuring that perpetrators of criminal acts are punished. Thus, according to the *Deterrence Model*, the very nature of punishment is that of deterrent punishment.

Both of these models are conceivable in terms of the consequences of the frustration of the correctional sentencing theory. Which of these two theories was superior was a major controversy in American penal theory at the end of the 20th century.

In my opinion, the *Justice Model* is superior, as the *Deterrence Model* has a number of serious flaws.

First, the *Deterrence Model* relies on the effects of heavy punishment, which may or may not still be effective. According to criminological findings, punishment has no correctional effect, nor does heavy punishment have a deterrent effect.

Second, the threat of severe punishment used in the *Deterrence Model* may, on the contrary, cause the loss of its crime-prevention effect. This point has already been argued in Japan by Professor Kazuhiko Tokoro, [4] and more recently by Professor Paul Robinson [5] of the U.S., who has made the point more empirically. According to Professor Robinson's research, extreme threats of punishment, as advocated for in the *Deterrence Model*, instead cause a public backlash and a loss of law-abiding awareness.

3.2. Empirical Desert Theory

Let us now take a closer look at Professor Robinson's theory. With regard to punishment, there has been a conflict between approaches based on balanced punishment and those based on deterrent punishment. Professor Robinson argues that these two principles can be fully reconciled. The crux of his argument is as follows:

(1) It has been proven that future crimes can be avoided most effectively and efficiently by achieving justice through punishment according to people's empirically confirmed ideas about justice (i.e., punishment based on "empirical deserts"). In so doing, the penal system can establish moral trust from the people and use the power of social influence, community support, and internalized norms.

(2) It has been proven that a criminal system that is perceived to be contrary to people's ideas about justice generates resistance and subversion. Conversely, a criminal system that is perceived as realizing justice by incorporating people's ideas about justice will, through its moral trust, gain more respect, cooperation, and endorsement, thus allowing for the internalization of social norms about reprehensible modes of behavior.

An empirical investigation (fact-finding survey) to prove these facts is being conducted by Professor Robinson himself, with his own team of researchers, the details of which are not discussed here for the sake of brevity. However, according to Professor Robinson's empirical research, the efficiency

---

(4) Kazuhiko Tokoro, Keijiseisaku no kisoriron [Basic Theory of Criminal Policy] (1994 Taisei shuppansha), 85-87.
(5) Paul H. Robinson, Intuitions of Justice and the Utility of Desert (2013 OUP).

of crime control essentially depends on the community's trust in the criminal law. When the criminal system is widely recognized as dependable in dispensing justice and preventing injustice, it gains moral support and promotes compliance with it and the internalization of its norms.

Thus, according to Professor Robinson, a criminal system that institutionalizes people's ideas about justice, or "empirical deserts," is the most efficient way to control crime.

Powerful intimidation, as in the *Deterrence Model* traditionally thought of, is not effective in controlling crime sufficiently. Although deterrence through intimidation can theoretically be an efficient crime control mechanism, it does not work in practical application. In other words, if we want to deter crime in the most efficient manner, the most proportionate punishment (i.e., according to the *Justice Model*) is the most effective.

Chinese President Deng Xiaoping once said, " It doesn't matter whether a cat is black or white, as long as it catches mice." The theory of pragmatist criminal law, I argue, is based on precisely this kind of thinking. At least in terms of crime prevention, it became clear that the cat that most successfully captured rats was the white cat, i.e., the cat that best met the criteria of legality.

IV. Again, under what circumstances are criminal penalties permissible?

4.1. The concept of "wrongdoing"

The above indicates that the answer to the question of whether it is permissible to impose criminal regulations to control the Covid-19 pandemic depends on whether the public believes that it would do justice. The next question is: How does it become evident whether or not the public believes that justice would be done? To answer this question, a different approach is needed from the side of crime.

Here, we may understand various concepts from the viewpoint of pragmatist criminal law theory, for which I am advocating, by first ascertaining the facts which are the source of those concepts. Therefore, we must start by determining the facts corresponding to the concept of crime.

I refer in this regard to two prominent scholars. Firstly, according to the English philosopher P. F. Strawson, people reactively express an attitude of censure in response to being treated badly. The mistreatment referred to by Strawson is the prototype of crime, and the "resentment/reactive attitude" [6] which occurs reactively, is the prototype of punishment.

Secondly, according to French sociologist Emile Durkheim, violation of sacred values always provokes a reaction of outrage. [7] The archetype of crime is anything that violates deeply ingrained sentiments and feelings in society and makes a healthy consciousness feel insecure. Crime also elicits a strong psychological reaction in those not directly involved (a sense of rage, anger, indignation, and violent vengeance), which is the archetype of punishment. [8]

Thus, when considered on the basis of facts, the essence of punishment and crime is as follows: the essence of punishment is the transmission of blame, and since it is a reaction supported by "resentment," it is conveyed through the vehicle of harm. The essence of crime is "mistreatment," i.e., an act that "stokes the feelings of the people," an act that the people perceive as morally wrong. In criminalization theory, this concept of "wrongdoing" is important, and is used in Anglo-American criminal law theory.

---

(6) P F Strawson', Freedom and Resentment' in Freedom and Resentment and Other Essays (first published 1974, Routledge 2008) 10.
(7) Émile Durkheim, The Division of Labor in Society (2nd ed, WD Halls tr, Steven Lukes ed, Palgrave Mcmillan 2012) 67.
(8) As a clear exposition of Durkheim's theory, see, e.g. David Garland, Punishment and Modern Society: A Study in Social Theory (The University of Chicago Press 1990) 30.

4.2. Difficulty of a theoretical explanation through the concept of "legal goods"

Traditionally, it was the concept of "legal goods" to which we Japanese criminal law scholars had to refer. The legal goods concept originally served an important function in limiting the invocation of the criminal law to cases in which a legal good, a factual or causally alterable interest, was violated, so as not to punish acts of moral turpitude.

The result has been the rejection of legal moralism, for which the legal goods concept has had some success (today, for example, a criminal law that punishes homosexual acts would be found almost nowhere else in the world if one were to search).

In recent years, however, it has become increasingly difficult to determine what is punishable as a crime based on the concept of legal interest, due to crimes associated with the development of advanced technology and the expansion of terrorism crimes. This is because it is impossible to explain why these crimes are punished without diluting the content of the concept of legal interest.

Thus, if the legal interest concept is diluted, on the contrary, it is possible to explain the reasons for punishing almost all acts, with the exception of mere moral violations. For example, it is possible to explain that the development of advanced technology of any kind can be punished because of the social dangers which it may pose in the future. Similarly, the purchase of a tool sold in an ordinary store could be punishable on the grounds that it might be used in a terrorist crime.

In such a situation, it seems important to consider the concept of "wrongdoing" mentioned above, as it can limit the appropriate range of penalties to be imposed. Thus, the answer to the question of whether it is permissible to impose criminal regulations with respect to the control of Covid-19 pandemic is given by whether the public would consider the regulated acts to be morally wrongful, i.e., whether their feelings would be stoked or reactive resentment would arise when they knew that such acts had been committed.

V. Evaluation of Criminal Regulation as a Strategy to Control the Covid-19 Pandemic in Japan

5.1. Discussion

Based on the conclusions drawn from the above discussion, we may now examine whether the criminal regulations related to control Covid-19 infection are "wrongful" acts for which the public wants to be punished, and whether the public considers that such punishments would do justice.

As we have already seen, the acts for which the imposition of criminal penalties was considered in Japan were the following: (1) a person who has Covid-19 and does not comply with a request to be admitted to a hospital or flees from a hospital, or (2) a person who does not comply with a request to change store hours or restrict the use of a facility.

First, let us consider (1). These behaviors are likely to include several typologies. Some people may be infected with Covid-19, but continue to live in places where many people reside and do not mind infecting others, while others may live in places where they see almost no one and take great care not to infect others. This would mean that not all of these cases are "wrongful". However, there are certainly some "wrongful" acts that are included. When regulating the posting of these acts, it would be necessary to fully examine their "wrongfulness" and narrow down the types of acts to be punished.

Next, let us consider (2). Here, whether or not the government provides compensation when changing store operating hours or restricting the use of facilities seems to have a significant impact. In Japan, the government's compensation was inadequate and the public was often sympathetic to stores and facilities. Under such circumstances, few citizens would perceive these actions as "wrongful".

Thus, the conclusion would be that behavioral restrictions to prevent the spread of Covid-19 infection, if any, need to be well typified.

5.2. Conclusion

From the perspective of criminalization theory, we may conclude that the introduction of criminal penalties to control Covid-19 infection is feasible, albeit limited. Japan, however, has not taken the step of introducing criminal penalties for behavioral restrictions to prevent the spread of Covid-19 infection. This is a policy decision that resulted from deliberations in the Japanese Diet. This is a criminal legislative debate and, indeed, a policy decision. As stated at the outset, we as criminal law scholars should not speak to issues of politics.

In this paper, we have shown what conduct is punishable with respect to the restriction of behavior to prevent the spread of Covid-19 infection. This is a theoretical examination and a discussion of factual perceptions. As noted at the outset, what criminal law scholars can do is to indicate this range. It seems important, then, to leave it to policy judges to decide whether or not to actually punish this, i.e., the theory of criminal legislation.

Chapter 14
Protection of Victims of Crime
——The case of Japan——

I. Introduction

1.1. The Significance of Victims

Here's a prominent sentence; "The victims were forgotten people". Almost every article on the victims in Japan begins with these words. I will begin this paper in the same way. What does it mean to be "forgotten"? It means that the victim had lost his or her place in the criminal justice system. To begin with, criminal law is a branch of public law. What is public law is one difficult question, but in its most general definition, it is the law that governs the relationship between the state and the individual. Criminal law is the law that governs the relationship between the state and the individual in the sense that the state recognizes and punishes the wrongdoing of criminals. Therefore, when the principle of public law is thoroughly enforced, there is no room for victims to come in. In other words, because the Criminal Code regulates wrongdoing, the victim (the injured party), is outside the protection of the Criminal Code. But the victims are real. Placed outside the protection of criminal law, they were not entitled to any protection other than that afforded by damages in civil matters.

1.2. Victim found

However, this is no longer the case in Japan today. A number of victims' support groups have been established and are working for their protection. Criminal legislation can no longer be enacted without taking the victim into account. Instead, victim support groups have begun to seek protection for victims, calling for harsher penalties and more severe punishment for the accused. For most of the victims, the perpetrators are unforgivable. In a sense, they are the enemy. The victims often resent the perpetrators deeply and call for severe punishment. For example, the current situation in Japan is such that it is difficult to say that the death penalty should be abolished if the criminal justice system seeks not to displace the victims. As they say, "Those who have never had a family member killed can't understand how they feel. The death penalty is necessary. Can those who support the abolition of the death penalty proudly say in front of victims that the death penalty should be abolished? Definitely not". It could be argued that a very different situation has arisen than when the victims feel that they are "forgotten" by the criminal justice system.

1.3. Issue of this paper

What has happened from the time when the victims were "forgotten" to the present? What has happened in the last few decades? This article examines various issues of victim protection in Japan by tracing their historical development. Specifically, the protection of victims in criminal proceedings is the central topic of discussion.

II. The development process of victim protection

2.1. General Remarks

According to Japanese criminologist, Akira Segawa (Makoto Mitsui et al. 2020; p.318), the development process of Japan's victim support system can be divided into four periods. The first is the period when the victim compensation system was established (Phase 1), which is the period when the Crime Victims' Benefit Payment Act of 1980 was enacted. This was the first time that victims who had not previously received much attention received compensation under the legal system in Japan. The second was a period of stagnation (Phase 2), during which there was no significant movement of victim support in the decade following the enactment of the Crime Victims' Benefits Payment Act of 1980. The third was the period of "discovery of victims" in Japan (Phase 3), when a number of victim support groups were established and the status of victims was measured from 1990 onwards. In 1999, the Code of Criminal Procedure was partially amended to create specific provisions for the protection of victims when they take the stand in court. The fourth was the period in which the legal development took place (Phase 4). The two laws for the protection of victims of crime and the Basic Law for Victims of Crime were enacted. With the former, a more substantial system of protection for crime victims was created within the Code of Criminal Procedure. The latter law provided victims with strong support from the state.

After the above four phases, it can be said that since 2006, there has been a system of participation of victims of crime in criminal proceedings and financial support for further victims (Phase 5: current).

The following is an overview of these periods, following them chronologically.

2.2. Phase 1— Enactment of the Crime Victims' Benefits Payment Act

The system for the protection of crime victims in Japan began in 1980 with the Payment of Crime Victims' Benefits Act. Until then, victims were only compensated by the perpetrators on an individual basis in accordance with the Tort Law in the private sector. From the standpoint of the separation of public and private law, this system of compensation for damages is a correct way of thinking. However, in reality, the perpetrators are often not in a good financial position to provide adequate compensation to the victims. Therefore, there is a need for a system in which the state provides financial compensation to victims.

Since the 1960s, Japan has been conducting research into the actual conditions of crime victims, and in several high-profile cases, victims were unable to receive adequate compensation (e.g., the Mitsubishi Heavy Industries case in 1974). These incidents led to a debate in the Diet about the need for a system to provide victims with compensation. In 1980, the Law on Crime Victims' Benefits was enacted. Under this system, crime victims have been able to receive monetary compensation, albeit to a certain extent.

2.3. Phase 2 — Stagnation period

After the enactment of the Crime Victims' Benefits Payment Act in1980, victim protection in Japan entered a period of stagnation for almost a decade. There may have been some relief in the creation of a system for victim protection, albeit to a certain extent. Despite some sporadic research on crime victims, no new debate concerning the provision of greater protection for victims' human rights was sparked off.

However, it was acknowledged that monetary compensation alone was not sufficient to meet the real needs of victims. In 1990, a symposium was held to commemorate the 10th anniversary of the Crime Victims' Benefit Payment Act, and it is said that the symposium raised awareness of the need for psychological support for victims. This led to developments in the third phase of the 1990s.

2.4. Phase 3 — The Beginning of Victim Support

In the 1990s, as a result of the above, the movement to support crime victims began in earnest. In Japan, this stage is regarded as the stage at which the victims were found.

In 1990, the Society for Victims' Studies was established under the leadership of Koichi Miyazawa. Miyazawa and others conducted a large-scale research on crime victims, and the results were published in 1996. This research served as the basis for subsequent research on crime victims.

At the private sector level, crime victim support groups have begun to organize in earnest: the Crime Victims Network, established in 1998, is a nationwide support network of crime victim organizations in Japan. Eight support organizations that already existed in Hokkaido, Ishikawa, Tokyo, Ibaraki, Aichi, Wakayama, Osaka and Hiroshima collaborated in improving victim support.

In the legislation, some amendments were made to the Code of Criminal Procedure. These amendments were based on the three Anti-Organized Crime Acts of 1999.Restrictions have been placed on questioning of victims in court as witnesses, where the victim's safety is taken into account and the victim's usual location was identified.

2.5. Phase 4 — Legal Development

In the 2000s, specific legal developments took place in light of the above developments. First, in May 2000, two laws that sought to offer more protection to crime victims were enacted. This law created a victim protection system by amending the Code of Criminal Procedure. Specifically, they are as follows.

- Accompanying the witnesses during their examination
- Cloaking and video link method
- Elimination of the time limit for prosecution of sex crimes.
- Opinion polling system

In addition, in a special law, the following rights were given
- Right to file a petition for review with the board of public prosecutors
- The right to preferential court hearing
- The right to access the trial record
- Criminal reconciliation system

Next, in December 2004, the Basic Law for Crime Victims was enacted. This law establishes policies for the protection of basic rights of crime victims.

Article 1 of this law stipulates the purpose of the law.

> Article 1 This Act provides the Basic Principles of the measures for Crime Victims, clarifies the responsibilities of the State, Local governments, and citizens, and provides the basic matters of the measures for Crime Victims so that the measures for Crime Victims can be implemented comprehensively and systematically. The purpose of this Act is to promote and protect the rights and interests of Crime Victims.

And Article 3 presents the basic principles of the law.

> Article 3 (1) All Crime Victims shall have the right to be respected for their individual dignity and to be guaranteed treatment befitting their dignity.
> (2) Measures for Crime Victims shall be taken appropriately according to the situation and causes of the harm, the situation of Crime Victims, and other circumstances.
> (3) Measures for Crime Victims shall be taken so that Crime Victims may receive necessary support without interruption from the time they are harmed until they are able to lead a peaceful life again.

Articles 11 to 23 also enumerate the basic measures that the State should take for victims of crime by this law.
- Provision of consultation and information
- Assistance with claims for damages
- Provision of welfare services
- Preventing re-injury and ensuring safety
- Stability of residence
- Guaranteeing jobs

- Development of a system for participation in criminal proceedings
- Protection of victims during the investigation and trial process
- Enhancing public understanding
- Promotion of research
- Assistance to private organizations
- Ensuring victims' opinions and transparency of information

With this, it can be said that the framework for crime victim protection in Japan has been established. Now, it is time to further expand the victim protection based on the above-mentioned legal system. Next, I will look at (1) the development of victim protection in the Code of Criminal Procedure and (2) the development of the protection of the fundamental rights of crime victims.

III. The development of victim protection in criminal proceedings

3.1. General Remarks

As mentioned above, a system of protection was created for victims who participate in criminal trials as witnesses, and in 2007, a system was created to further develop this system through a partial amendment to the Code of Criminal Procedure. This is known as the victim participation system in criminal trials (Sakamaki 2020; p.441). In this system, victims of crimes (including, for example, their legal representatives and attorneys commissioned by victims) participate in criminal trials as "victims' intervenors". In this case, the victim participating in the proceedings is not a party to the proceedings. It is a way of fulfilling the victim's request through the cooperation of the prosecutor. It is provided for under Article 316-33 of the Code of Criminal Procedure.

3.2. Victims who can participate in criminal proceedings

This system only allows certain victims of crime to participate in criminal trials. Those who can participate are victims of certain serious crimes, such as crimes causing death or injury to a person through an intentional criminal act; victims of certain sex crimes, negligent driving manslaughter victims, etc.

3.3. Rights afforded to victims

The key rights afforded to victims are as follows
- Attendance at the trial date
- Opinions on the exercise of the prosecutor's powers
- Examination of Witnesses
- Questions for the defendant
- Statements of opinion on the facts and application of the law

3.4. Theoretical Analysis

I would like to provide some theoretical analysis of this system. Essentially, it is a system that, by recognizing the rights of victims, demonstrates that they are not outsiders in criminal cases, and confirms that the criminal and criminal systems therein have a message function to send to victims that they have not been forgotten and that they will not be forgotten. In this regard, what is particularly important in practice is the statement of opinion to the court . This could have an impact on sentencing.

There are no standards for sentencing in Japan in the Penal Code. Therefore, judges have formed that standard through case law. Basically, it is determined on the basis of the illegality and responsibility of the defendant's actions, taking into account the circumstances (Matsuzawa 2018: p.1). In that case, in Japan, sentencing by judges has been somewhat consistent, and the considering factors are fairly well-consolidated, even though the facts of the cases are quite different .

However, depending on the type of crime or special circumstances, the list of considering factors are not exhaustive. Therefore, it has been pointed out that the victim participation system may have a new impact on sentencing as these considering factors varies from case to case (Saeki 2020; p.222).

When it comes to victims' influence on sentencing, some have suggested that harsher penalties tend to be taken. On this basis, there is often a negative view of the victim participation system. However, given the importance of victims in criminal cases as a whole, this point does not hold true. Victims may benefit from being given the opportunity to participate in the criminal trial and to ensure that the criminal trial is conducted in a proper manner. In other words, it could be said that the victim participation system in criminal trials provides much consideration to victims and conveys the message that they are not forgotten and that the state cares about them (Hörnle 2006; s.950).

Many of the victims in Japan expect the criminal courts to reveal how the perpetrators are treated. It is more important to them that they are treated fairly in the Code of Criminal Procedure than that they are punished severely. Therefore, I believe that in Japan, the measurement of victim protection from procedural law is theoretically the right direction to take.

IV. The development of basic rights protection for victims of crime

4.1. General Remarks

As mentioned above, the protection of the basic rights of crime victims is governed by the Basic Law for Crime Victims, which was enacted in 2004. This law requires the State to promote basic measures for the protection of crime victims in a systematic manner. Therefore, the Basic Plan for Crime Victims was formulated.

The Basic Plan for Victims of Crime was developed by the Cabinet in

2005, and since then, a new Basic Plan has been developed approximately every five years. The most recent Third National Plan for Crime Victims was formulated in April 2016.

4.2. Structure of the Basic Plan

The Third Basic Plan for Crime Victims consists of the following four basic policies, which have been followed in the previous plans, and five key issues, which must be solved with special emphasis in the Third Plan. This is a task that must be done, and it can be considered a more specific implementation goal.

Four Basic Principles;
- Guarantee the right of crime victims, etc. to be treated accordingly to their dignity
- Take each measure properly, mindful of individual victim's circumstance
- Provide a seamless and continuous support
- Progress while building the national consensus

Five Key Issues;
- Efforts to recover the victims' damages and to provide them with economic support
- Efforts for the Victims to Recover from or to Prevent Mental and/or Physical Damage
- Efforts to broaden the opportunity for victims to participate in criminal procedures
- Efforts to improve the systems to support crime victims, etc.
- Efforts to foster the understanding among citizens and to earn their consideration and cooperation

The Basic Plan for Victims of Crime is reviewed every five years. Therefore, the next plan (the Fourth Plan) is currently being formulated. The Fourth Plan is scheduled to be released in April 2021.

4.3. The Crime Victims' Benefit Scheme

Since the third plan was formulated, the crime victims' benefit system was expanded, and I will mention it here.

The victim benefit system is a system that provides direct financial relief to victims, and its expansion has been long awaited. This amendment expands, to a certain extent, what was previously deemed inadequate. However, even with these amendments, there are many opinions that the system is still inadequate. It is hoped that the fourth plan will further enhance the system.

There are four main amendments to the criminal damage benefit system.

- The amount of survivor's benefits was increased for cases where an orphan is still under 18 years of age after 10 years from the time the criminal act was committed.
- Prior to the amendment, the period of benefit for serious injuries and illnesses, which before the amendment was set at one year from the date of injury or illness caused by the criminal act, was extended to three years.
- The amount of provisional benefits (a system for provisionally granting a portion of the benefits in cases where an award cannot be made because some of the facts necessary for the award cannot be found) was capped at one-third of the amount of the benefit equivalent, but now the amount equivalent to the benefit can be paid.
- The grounds for reduction or disallowance of payments in relation to inter-family crimes were reviewed. Specifically, firstly, it was decided that if the kinship relationship is broken, no limitation of benefits will be imposed on the grounds of such kinship. Second, a special exception to the benefits for persons under 18 years of age was established. This includes the fact that

when a person under 18 years of age is in a position to receive the Crime Victims' Benefit at the time of the criminal act, the payment shall not be restricted on the basis of the kinship between the person and the perpetrator.

V. Conclusion

5.1. Last remarks

Long "forgotten", victims seem to be beginning to see the light of day in Japan. Of course, there are still many issues that remain to be addressed. For example, in some special crimes, the state may be the victim, but there is no discussion in Japan about victim protection in such cases (For example, see, Colojoară & Rakitovan 2018; p.469). Special considerations also need to be taken into account in criminal proceedings when children are victims (as is the case in Hungary, see, BÉKÉS 2019; p.317). Although Japan's victim protection system is still inadequate, we hope that this paper will inform readers that such a system is now in operation in Japan and awaits further development.

5.2. Theoretical issues

In this paper - which I have been unable to fully discuss - due to my own lack of research -I have found that the rationale for the system of victim protection in criminal proceedings is actually not very well understood. A policy that says victims should be protected in criminal proceedings must be justified by a rationale, even if it has public support.

The basic idea on this issue, as discussed in3.4, is based on the function of the criminal justice system. It is that victim protection in criminal proceedings is guided by the ability of the criminal justice system to send a message to victims that you are not forgotten and that the state has not forgotten you.

The most detailed description of the message function of criminal law is the argument of the expressive function of punishment. The state's practice of imposing punishment functions as means to send a message of censure and disapproval to the accused, as well as a message to the victim that "the state has not forgotten you," in addition to preventing crimes or imposing appropriate punishments. It seems to me that this may be something that should be extended to criminal justice as a whole, and not just in penal theory.

5.3. Punishment as victim protection?

However, a distinction must be made between protecting victims and imposing severe punishments on behalf of victims for the perpetrators. Even if a victim says what I wrote in section 1.2 of this paper, promoting victim protection and abolishing the death penalty are logically separate issues. Certainly, I understand the desire of victims to put their perpetrators to death. It is natural that the families of those whose family members have been killed in a brutal manner would feel this way. But criminal law is not a device for revenge. It is a penal system in which the state humanely refines the reactive attitude of resentment and imposes a punishment deserved to the crime. There is theoretically no room in it for punishments that deprive people of life and bodily integrity.

The hope is that the system of victim protection will move in the direction of protecting victims in the original sense of the word, and that all the public will move away from the erroneous notion that heavier punishments are more protective of victims.

References:
- Hörnle, T., (2006). Die Rolle des Opfers in der Straftheorie und im materiellen Strafrecht. *Juristenzeitung 19/2006*, p. 950.
- Matsuzawa, S., (2018). Using Equity Reasons to evaluate Mitigating Circumstances - An Explanation of Sentencing Principles. *Waseda Bulletin of Comparative Law*,

36, p.1.
- Mitsui, M. et al. (eds.) (2020). Keijihou Nyuumon (Introduction to Criminal Law)
- Saeki, M., (2020). Hanzaihigaisha no Shihousanka to Ryoukei (Crime Victims' Judicial Participation and Sentencing)
- Sakamaki, M., (2020). Keijisohouhou 2nd ed. (Criminal Procedure Law)
The Third Basic Plan for Crime Victims (available in English on the website; https://www.npa.go.jp/hanzaihigai/kuwashiku/keikaku/pdf/dai3_basic_plan_english.pdf.)

Chapter 15
New Lay Judge System in Japan[1]

Presentation of the topic

The lay judge system was adopted by Japan's Parliament in 2004 and came into force in 2009. The Japanese system of lay judges has several distinct features: it is used for more serious crimes such as homicide, arson and the like. It is used only at first instance, i.e. the district court.[2] The court is usually composed of 3 legal judges and 6 lay judges who discuss and deliberate together. The lay judges take part in assessing the guilt or innocence of the defendant and in determining the sentence. In cases involving guilty pleas, a court with only one legal judge and four lay judges may be established by agreement between the defense and the prosecution. The vast majority of the provisions concerning the lay judge system are found in the "Law on the Implementation of the Lay Judge System in Criminal Procedure" (Law No.63, 28 May 2004) popularly called the "Lay Judge Law", *Saiban-in Ho*. Hereinafter abbreviated as "LL"). The introduction of the lay judge system has led to significant changes in Japanese Criminal Procedure.

In this article I will address the topics in the following order:
1. The history and general principles of the Japanese criminal justice system
2. The background to the introduction of a lay judge system in Japan
3. Participation of lay judges at first instance
4. Appointment of lay judges and their rights and duties

---

(1) This paper was originally written in Danish for anthology celebrating the 70th birthday of Professor Emeritus Vagn Greve of the University of Copenhagen (thus the primary audience was intended to be Scandinavians). A dedication to the professor is included at the end of this paper. Although it is not necessary to translate it into English, I have decided to append it for the sake of remembrance.

(2) Japan has three instances, 45 district courts, 8 courts of appeal and 1 supreme court.

5. New rules concerning the preparatory mode of the court
6. Form and content of the judgment
7. Assessment and analysis of the new system

I. History and general principles of Japanese criminal procedure

Japan has both a Civil Procedure Code and a Criminal Procedure Code. The current Japanese Criminal Procedure Code, which came into force in 1949, is the third since 1882. When the Meiji regime came to power in 1868, Japan drafted its national legislation under the strong influence of European jurisprudence. The first Japanese Code of Criminal Procedure was clearly influenced by the French Code of Criminal Procedure, but it chose not to adopt the rules of the jury system. In 1890, a new Criminal Procedure Law came into force, but without significant changes from the 1882 law. These were mainly structural changes. In 1924, a Prussian-inspired Criminal Procedure Code was introduced. Japanese criminal procedure legislation was thus based on a Civil Law legal tradition. There was also a jury system in Japan from 1923, but this was interrupted by World War II, and the participation of lay people was not resumed until the reforms that came into force in 2009.

The 1924 law was in force until immediately after World War II when, under the guidance of the occupying power, the United States, Japan was given a completely new constitution. The Constitution focuses on human rights, democracy, and peace (Preamble, Articles 11, 41, and 9). Reforms were necessary in all areas at the time of its introduction. The present Japanese Code of Criminal Procedure retained features of continental law, but also incorporated important elements of Anglo-American law. The Japanese legal system respects the guarantees of due process of law known from American law, the so-called "due process of law", and basically follows the adversarial proceedings system. At

Chapter 15 New Lay Judge System in Japan 199

the same time, the Japanese legal system adheres to the concept of substantive truth, which is familiar from continental law, and is also based on German law. These two approaches may be in conflict - for example, the question of the use of evidence obtained through illegal investigations. Harmonizing the two legal traditions still poses problems in Japan.

The evidentiary principle and the oral principle are also important principles in the Japanese Code of Criminal Procedure, yet they were difficult to apply in criminal proceedings. The number of documents in a case, the length of the proceedings and the fact that the judge was often changed during the course of the proceedings made the two principles lose some of their importance. With the introduction of the lay judge system, the oral and evidentiary principles are more easily respected.

II. The background to the introduction of a lay judge system in Japan

Prior to World War II, Japan's criminal justice system operated a jury system for serious cases. It was abolished during the war for various reasons. The Japanese were, and perhaps especially under World War II, an authoritarian people. They did not like to be judged by those of equal social status, such as their neighbors. The system was voluntary for the defendant, who could choose to have his case heard by a jury or by a court of legal judges alone. Most people opted for the latter, and the system fell increasingly out of use. For many years, legal professionals, defense lawyers in particular, had been calling for a return of the jury, but for a long time this remained an unrealistic idea.

In the late 1990s, however, the discussion began to take off. In July 1999, the Japanese government set up a commission to make proposals on how the judiciary could undergo the first comprehensive reform [3] since World

War II (The Judicial System Reform Council; Shiho Seido Kaikaku Shingikai). The Reform Council submitted its last report in June 2001, after which it was disbanded. Subsequently, in November 2001, the government established the Committee for Judicial Reform (Shiho Seido Kaikaku Suishin Honbu) within the Cabinet, based on the draft released by the council. The committee worked until its disbandment in 2004 for the adoption of the reforms. These reforms have since been gradually adopted by Parliament.

In connection with the revision of the criminal justice system, serious consideration was given to reintroducing lay judges into the judicial process. It is not entirely clear why the idea suddenly became popular, but at the same time there was widespread public dissatisfaction with long procedural delays, for example in the case of the poison gas attacks in the Tokyo underground. Here it took 9 years to reach a verdict. There was also widespread dissatisfaction with the severity of sentencing, which many consider too low, and the discussion turned to other countries for inspiration, including the United States, the United Kingdom, Germany, France and the Nordic countries. [4]

The Supreme Court proposed a system that was effectively a replica of the old pre-war system, in which legal judges retained absolute power. This proposal was met with strong protest and outrage in the media, among the public and among professionals. The Reform Committee set up a subcommittee with the sole purpose of discussing the establishment of a lay judge system in

---

(3) The reform covers several areas and, apart from the introduction of the lay judge system, the most notable is the educational reform. Inspired by the United States, so-called "Law-Schools" are being introduced as a kind of bridge course to various undergraduate programs, allowing students from a wide range of educational backgrounds who hold a bachelor's degree to complete their legal education in three years. At the end, they must pass the so-called "bar examination" before they are allowed to practice as lawyers.

(4) During the same period, I was doing post-doctoral work researching different lay judging systems, and together with Lawyer Hiroshi Sato, who also works in this area, we traveled around the Nordic countries to see what the traditions were there. The Nordic countries have adopted a lay judge system under adversarial proceedings system, which has been helpful in Japan's reforms.

Japan.

III. Participation of lay judges at first instance

The lay judge system was to be applicable only at first instance. This was decided without much discussion. There were several reasons, but primarily for reasons of convenience for lay judges and for reasons of procedural economy. As regards the cases in which lay judges should participate, it was decided that, as a general rule, they should only be involved in serious cases such as murder, arson, etc. Section 2(1) of the LL provides that trials in which lay judges participate are limited to cases involving the death penalty or life imprisonment or the intentional killing of a person. According to 2003 figures, such cases represent 3.9% of all first instance cases.

3.1. The discussion on the size of the panel

Following broad agreement on the introduction of the lay judge system, (Sometimes referred to as a *mixed panel system*, since lay and professional judges are on the panel together. In this paper, such a system will be referred to as just the lay *judge system*.) a central question in the preparations was how large a panel of lay judges was needed (whether a lay judge system or a jury system was desired). Here the Nordic countries were a good place to look, as Norway and Denmark had experience with both.

The Commission was divided on the issue. The Bar Association and American-inspired scholars argued strongly in favor of a jury system, considering it more democratic because of the sovereign power of jurors. They believed that in a lay judge system, there was a danger that lay judges would be dominated by professional judges. Those who wanted a lay judge system believed that the professional competence of the professional judges and the fact that the lay judges are rooted in the general public would lead to more nuanced and better reasoned judgments. They believed that the disadvantage of the jury system would be unreasoned verdicts and a high risk of miscarriages of justice.

The discussion ended with the realization that it was possible to create a *sui generis* system without being bound by existing systems, and that it would try to create a system that would combine the advantages of the judge and jury system. The Commission later decided that legal judges and lay judges would together discuss and decide on guilt or innocence and determine sentences.

Members of the committee who supported the jury system were disappointed with the decision. Their new goal was to maintain a large panel of lay judges, similar to the jury system, to counter the authoritative power of law judges. The committee therefore made two proposals. Plan A: One legal judge and 11 lay judges. Plan B: Three legal judges and 3-4 lay judges.

There was much discussion among members, as well as in the media and among experts. The result was a compromise of three legal judges and six lay judges (Article 2(2) of LL). For limited types of cases, a resource and time-saving process was established where the case is heard by one legal judge and four lay judges (Article 2(3) of LL). This process can be used in confession cases where the court considers it appropriate and where agreement can be reached between the prosecutor and the defense counsel on the use of this fast-track process. The lay judges enter into discussion with the legal judges and participate in the assessment of the evidence, the legal subsumption and the sentencing (Article 6(1) of LL). Only the legal judges can make decisions on the interpretation of the text of the law as well as decisions on the administration of justice (Article 6(2) of LL). Our system contains a security guarantee which largely corresponds to the (old) Danish system, double guarantee. That is, no one can be found guilty solely by the votes of the lay judges (Article 67 (2) of LL).

IV. Appointment of lay judges and their rights and duties

Lay judges are appointed by the Minister of Justice (Section 21 of the Act) from the "basic list of lay judge candidates" published annually by the Parliamentary Electoral Commission (Article 23 of LL). This list is based on a random drawing of lots among nationals who have reached the age of 20 (Article 13 of LL). The fact that the selection is purely arbitrary and not based on membership of citizens' associations, etc. as in the Nordic countries, means that it can be seen as quite democratic in Japan. However, some would argue that without any checks on the background of the judges, it is unlikely that everyone will be able to understand and discuss the issues and the written material presented to the court. In due course and on request, the courts select and allocate by lot a fixed number of lay judges to serve in forthcoming cases (Article 27 of LL). They will be summoned to a selection day immediately afterwards. Before convening on this day, the court may choose to send a questionnaire to the candidates. The purpose of this questionnaire is to identify in advance persons who are excluded or exempted for specified reasons.

Three types of exclusion and exemption grounds are distinguished.

a. Grounds for exclusion by Article 14 of LL. The excluded person does not possess knowledge corresponding to the level of primary school, has previously been sentenced to a minimum custodial sentence or has a mental or physical disability that renders him/her incapable of acting as a lay judge.

b. Grounds for exclusion by Article 15 of LL. The person disqualified held a profession or office of trust which renders him/her incapable of acting as a court judge, e.g. Member of Parliament or lawyer.

c. Grounds for disqualification by Article 16 of LL. The person concerned may choose to declare himself/herself unemployed if he/she is over 70 years of age, is obliged to care for sick or elderly family members or is engaged in important managerial work which cannot be performed by others.

All the arbitrarily selected lay judges are summoned to the selection day process, with the exception of those who may have been excluded on the basis of the questionnaire (Section 34(1)-(3) of LL). Should there be persons among those summoned who are covered by the rules on exclusion and exemption, they may also be excluded on the day itself (Article 34 (4) of LL). Both parties may, without further reason being given, exclude a maximum of 4 candidates (Article 36(1) of LL). This system is introduced from Anglo-American law, i.e. "peremptory challenge". Finally, a panel of lay judges is selected by drawing lots from among the remaining candidates who have not been excluded (Article 37(1) of LL).The lay judges are of course under a duty to act loyally and honestly and are subject to an obligation of confidentiality (Article 9(1), (3) and (4) of LL). If the duty of secrecy is violated, the judge may be punished with a fine of up to JPY 500,000 or imprisonment of up to 6 months.

V. New rules on the preparatory meeting of the court

In connection with the introduction of the lay judge system, the new rules governing the preparatory phase of the trial (Article 316-2 et seq. of the Code of Criminal Procedure) were laid down. In Japan, there had previously been rules governing the preparation of trials, but they led to what was considered an unacceptably time-consuming procedure, as was seen in the 1995 poison gas case. They call the change "from precis justice to core justice."

VI. Form and content of the judgment

The professional judges formulate the judgment. The detailed rules follow from the "Circular on the Rules of Criminal Procedure, Article 54", which was adopted by the Code of Criminal Procedure, and the judgment contains a statement of reasons for the conviction. As part of the reasoning, the judge's considerations are set out, although it can often be difficult to formulate them in legal terms. It is a great advantage of the Japanese system that reasons for the verdict are recorded, unlike the jury system where reasons for the verdict are not recorded.

6.1. Appeal to the Court of Appeal

The Judicial Practice Reform did not bring about any changes in the rules governing appeals. In the Court of Appeal, only legal judges are appointed.

VII. Assessment and analysis of the new system

In my view, the application of the new lay judge system to only a limited number of cases is problematic.. I believe that, as in the Nordic systems, panels should, in principle, hear both serious and minor criminal cases. From a procedural point of view, it may be difficult to assemble a large panel in every case. However, I do not find that there is sufficient justification for a panel as large as the one currently in place. A small panel ensures that everybody is heard and that there is a better discussion. The smaller panels that are seen in cases where the accused has confessed to the crime were an appropriate size (1-4) and my hope is that it will prove to work so well that such panels will be introduced in all criminal cases at a future stage. I think it is important that small cases are also heard by lay judges. Otherwise, there is a risk that Japanese criminal justice reform may become superficial.

In the Japanese system I also see problems with the limited powers of lay judges. As mentioned above, they are not required to participate in the interpretation of the law, but if the word "lay judge" is to have any meaning, I agree that, in principle, they should participate on an equal footing with the professional judges. There is probably no other system of judges in the world which provides for such separation. The rigid Japanese system stems from the strong influence of those who wanted a jury system. In the jury system, jurors and professional judges are sharply separated (they are not even allowed to have lunch in the same room). The basic idea of the jury system is that laymen alone can evaluate the evidence but they should not interfere with the law. The Japanese system has inherited these characteristics of the jury system, but they do not make sense in the context of the lay judge system. The reason why the jury system did not leave the interpretation of the law to the jury is because the jury alone cannot interpret the law. There is no necessity for such a limitation in the Japanese system, in which professional judges join the panel. I believe that the Japanese rules should be amended as soon as possible so that lay judges and professional judges participate on an equal footing in principle. There should not be any part of the judicial process where lay judges are excluded from participation.

I also believe that provision should be made for the participation of lay judges in the Court of Appeal, as is the case in Denmark and Norway.

It is a very new system that we have to introduce, and it is not without reason that a lot of time has been set aside for its implementation. The Japanese are still a people obedient to authority, and the general attitude is not to interfere in either politics or the affairs of one's neighbors. Coupled with a very inflexible labor market, it can be difficult to get popular support for the system. Even supporters of a lay judiciary system do not want to participate themselves. They don't want to take time off, they don't want to judge an equal, and they generally believe that professionals know best. I believe that a general change of attitude is needed to make it work. Surveys show that 70% of the population do not want to serve as a lay judge. I can also understand that Japanese people are concerned about the system because they have no idea that ordinary functioning people are being selected. As I said, they are chosen very arbitrarily among the population. I think that a class judge should be chosen among people with ordinary social interests, just as the Nordic countries choose among, for example, members of associations or other organizations.

Some argue that the Lay Judge System is contrary to the Constitution of Japan. It is true that the Constitution of Japan states that "judges may not rely on others" (Article 73, Paragraph 3 of the Constitution). At the same time, the preamble of the Constitution and subsequent Article 40 of the law clearly state that "the people have sovereignty". We find this claim of unconstitutionality to be entirely unpersuasive and baseless.

Conclusion

There are major cultural differences between Japan and the Nordic countries, but the legal system is absolutely comparable. This collection of countries that rely both on the adversarial proceedings system and the lay judge system can derive great benefit from cooperation. Japan is far more distant geographically, but "legally" still closer than one might think in Denmark and perhaps even closer than several of the European countries with which Denmark usually compares itself.

Finally, I would like to congratulate you, Vagn, on your 70th birthday, and thank you for the kind reception you have given me at the university and in your home. From 1996 to 2002 I worked at the University of Copenhagen as a visiting researcher, which meant a lot to me both professionally and personally. Since then I have had the opportunity to visit the university and research conferences in the Nordic countries, and I very much appreciate this opportunity. It is an honor to be allowed to write a small article for your festschrift.

Chapter 16
An analysis of the seven Mutual Legal Assistance (MLA) agreements concluded by Japan and the uniqueness of the EU-Japan MLA Agreement

I. Introduction

This paper examines the so-called international 'mutual legal assistance treaties/agreements' [1] in criminal matters that Japan has concluded. In Japan, the issue of international criminal mutual assistance has been examined from an international law perspective, including in recent years. [2] However, although major studies [3] from a criminal law perspective have been published, they are somewhat outdated and date back to before the conclusion of the international criminal assistance treaties and agreements that this paper deals with. This chapter looks at Japan's MLA Agreement from a positive law point of view and adds some considerations relating to criminal law theory. In doing so, it will highlight the uniqueness of the EU-Japan Agreement on Mutual Legal Assistance (MLA) in Criminal Matters, [4] which is, historically speaking, one of the most recent

---
(1) For the current status of international criminal assistance treaties and agreements that Japan has signed, see Yuichiro Tachi, *Kokusaikeijihou (Contemporary International Criminal Law)*, (Seibundo 2018) p.66-. Also, on criminal assistance treaties and agreements in general, see Neil Boister, *An Introduction to Transnational Criminal Law*, (2nd edn, OUP 2018).

(2) For example, Yurika Ishii, *Ekkyohanzai no Kokusaiteki Kisei (International Regulation of Transboundary Crime)* (Yuhikaku 2017).

(3) See Tadashi Morishita, *Kokusai Keiji Shihou Kyojo no Kenkyu (Studies on International Mutual Legal Assistance in Criminal Matters)* (Seibundo 1981) and the same work, *Kokusai juju kyosei no riron (Theories of International Mutual Legal Assistance in Criminal Matters)* (Seibundo 1983).

(4) The official and full name of the agreement is the Agreement between Japan and the European Union on Mutual Legal Assistance on Criminal Matters [2010] OJ L 39/20, hereinafter referred to as the EU-Japan MLA Agreement. As for the literature on the EU-Japan MLA Agreement, see (in Japanese) e.g., Nakauchi, Y., (The Expansion of the Criminal Assistance Network to 27

MLA agreements concluded by Japan. While Weyembergh and Wieczorek have already examined the negotiation process for the EU MLA Agreement looking at EU sources, [5] it is extremely difficult to investigate the negotiation process from the Japanese perspective as there are neither publicly available primary sources nor research papers in Japan that would help clarify such a process. [6] Therefore, this article opts for a legal theoretical perspective, and notably a comparative perspective, by analysing the agreements and treaties that Japan concluded prior to the EU-Japan MLA Agreement to highlight the 'uniqueness' and 'novelty' of the EU-Japan MLA Agreement. Before the conclusion of the latter, Japan had concluded six bilateral MLA treaties, [7] namely (1) the Japan-US MLA Treaty (July 2006), [8] (2) the Japan-Korea MLA Treaty (January 2007), [9] (3) the Japan-China MLA Treaty (November 2008), [10] (4) the Japan-

European Countries: The EU-Japan Criminal Assistance Agreement), *Rippou to Chousa*, No. 303 (2010), p.18 ff,; Nakano, T., Nichi-EU Keijikyoujo Kyoutei oyobi Nichiro Keijikhyoujo Jouyaku noHakkou (The EU-Japan MLA Agreement and the Russia-Japan MLA Treaty Entry into Force), *Keisatu Kouron*, Vol. 66, No. 3 (2011), p. 38 ff.

(5) See, Anne Weyembergh & Irene Wieczorek, Norm diffusion as a tool to uphold and promote EU values and interests: A case study on the EU Japan Mutual Legal Assistance Agreement, *New Journal of European Criminal Law*, 2020, Vol. 11 (4) 439-466.

(6) In writing this paper, I conducted two interviews with relevant officers of the Japanese National Police Agency (June and September 2019). I was able to obtain useful information about the practice of conducting investigations. I would like to express my sincere gratitude to the people concerned for this. However, I was only able to obtain general answers on the operation of the EU-Japan MLA Agreement in practice. Many of the interesting provisions of the EU-Japan MLA Agreement, which seem to have arisen from political and diplomatic dynamics, were not necessarily clarified, including their background, operation and reality. In view of this, the investigation of the EU-Japan MLA agreement from a Japanese perspective is inevitably fraught with difficulties.

(7) The text and full reference of each agreement can be viewed in both Japanese and English on the website of the Ministry of Foreign Affairs of Japan (www.mofa.go.jp).

(8) The official name of the agreement is the Treaty between Japan and the United States of America on Mutual Legal Assistance on Criminal Matters, hereinafter referred to as the US-Japan MLA Treaty.

(9) The official name of the agreement is the Treaty between Japan and the Republic of Korea on Mutual Legal Assistance in Criminal Matters, hereinafter referred to as the Korea-Japan MLA

Hong Kong MLA Agreement (September 2009), [11] (5) the Japan-EU MLA Agreement (January 2011) and (6) the Japan-Russia MLA Treaty (February 2011). [12] They will be discussed in this chapter.

II. Concept and history of international MLA in criminal matters: The case of Japan

2.1. Concept of international MLA in criminal matters

First, let us clarify the definition of MLA, which is the subject of this paper. MLA refers to "cooperation between nations in the criminal justice field, such as obtaining and providing evidence (e.g., testimony, statements, objects, etc.) necessary for the investigation or prosecution of a foreign criminal case when such evidence is available in the home country, at the request of the foreign country, on behalf of the investigative authorities of the foreign country". [13] There are usually two possible scenarios or stages in which cooperation can take place. The first is pre-trial cooperation during the investigative phase [14] and the second one takes place during the trial phase. [15]

In practice, MLA cooperation arises more often during the investigative phase, in cases in which the investigated crime has a transnational dimension,

---

Treaty.
(10) The official name of the agreement is the Treaty between Japan and the People's Republic of China on Mutual Legal Assistance in Criminal Matters, hereinafter referred to as the China-Japan MLA Treaty.
(11) The official name of the agreement is the Agreement between Japan and the Hong Kong Special Administrative Region of the People's Republic of China on Mutual Legal Assistance in Criminal Matters, hereinafter referred to as the Hong Kong-Japan MLA Treaty.
(12) The official name of the agreement is the Treaty between Japan and the Russian Federation on Mutual Legal Assistance on Criminal Matters, hereinafter referred to as the Russia-Japan MLA Treaty.
(13) Ishii, supra fn. 2 p.11. The quote has been translated from Japanese to English by the author.
(14) Tachi, supra fn. 1 p.66.
(15) Ishii, supra fn. 2 also mentions "international administrative mutual assistance".

for instance when criminal activities are spread over several countries. [16] Once the evidence has been collected, the trial activities are carried out in each country domestically.

The United States, which had already concluded a large number of treaties in the past, was the first country to conclude a bilateral MLA treaty with Japan. This was followed by Japan's conclusion of bilateral MLA treaties and agreements with the above-mentioned countries, namely Korea, China, Hong Kong, Russia and the EU.

2.2. History of Japan's progressive engagement with international MLA
2.2.1. From the Meiji Restoration to World War II [17]

It was after the Meiji Restoration in 1868 that Japan joined the international community in earnest. After the Meiji Restoration, Japan began to modernise and build international relations with other countries, which began with the conclusion of basic treaties. It was against this background that treaties on cooperation in criminal matters started to be concluded.

The first treaty that Japan signed with the United States for international

---

[16] Cooperation in investigative activities may be carried out via the International Criminal Police Organisation (ICPO; Interpol) or through MLA procedures (as a precondition, the ICPO exchanges information with the NCB (National Central Bureau, the National Police Agency in the case of Japan), which is the contact point for each member country, using a communication network).
The former route is used to obtain basic investigative information; for example, immigration records are a typical example. Anything other than compulsory measures is done through this route. The latter route is used when the information is to be used as evidence. For example, information related to communication services provided by foreign companies (subscriber information, communication records etc.) is often used. Based on the interviews mentioned in supra fn. 6.

[17] The following descriptions, from 2.2.1 to 2.2.4, are based on Yuki Furuta, *'Kokusai Sousa Kyojohou no Seitei ni tsuite'* (Enactment on the International Assistance in Investigation Act), *Keisatsu Kenkyuu*, Vol. 51, No. 7 (1980), p. 31-.

cooperation was the Extradition Treaty of 1886 (the current treaty, replacing the 1886 one, was signed in 1980). The following year, in 1887, the Extradition Ordinance (*Toubouhanzainin Hikiwatashi Jourei*), a Japanese domestic law to enforce the treaty, was enacted. This was followed, in 1905, by the enactment of a domestic law on international judicial cooperation called the Foreign Court Commissioned Assistance Law (*Gaikoku Saibansho no Shokutaku niyoru Kyoujohou*). This law regulated judicial cooperation not only for criminal cases, but also for civil cases. In other words, it provided for procedures such as the examination of evidence by Japanese courts in response to requests from foreign courts.

Extradition with the US was thus regulated in Japan in the late 19th and early 20th centuries, followed by the enactment of domestic laws. However, Japan would only conclude MLA agreements after World War II (WWII). Up until the conclusion of these agreements, mutual assistance had been requested through diplomatic channels. This delay can be attributed to the fact that Japan is an island nation, which meant that it was isolated and having fewer contacts with the mainland in the early 20th century. The fact that it is located across the sea from mainland China, a considerable distance from Europe, and in the Far East, may have had an impact in terms of the delay.

2.2.2. After World War II

After World War II, there was an increase in transnational crime and Japan was forced to develop its international investigative cooperation capacities. Thus, in 1980, Japan enacted the International Assistance in Investigation Act (*Kokusai Sousa Kyoujohou*) (Law No. 69 of 1980). The immediate reason for the enactment of this law was arguably the bribery scandal pitting the US airline Lockheed against the Japanese government and the bribery scandal pitting the US airline Douglas Grumman against the Japanese government. In the investigation of these cases, Japan's Ministry of Justice and the US Department of Justice entered into a plea bargain to mutually cooperate in the investigation.

The importance of this cooperation was also recognised in Japan, leading to the enactment of the above mentioned International Assistance in Investigation Act.

2.2.3. Contents of the International Assistance in Investigation Act

The enactment of the International Assistance in Investigation Act, which is still in force, establishes the basic framework for international investigative assistance in Japan. [18] The main elements of this Act are the following: (i) At the request of a foreign country, Japan will provide the evidence necessary for the State to investigate a criminal case. (ii) Upon request for assistance, the Minister of Foreign Affairs will provide evidence through diplomatic channels. (iii) The collection of evidence necessary for assistance may be investigated by prosecutors or police officers. (iv) The National Public Safety Commission may cooperate with the International Criminal Police Organisation (Interpol).

However, when following these internal rules, actual international investigative assistance takes time, especially when it is pursued through diplomatic channels. It usually takes about a month and sometimes several months or even more depending on the situation. This makes it difficult to conduct an effective investigation. That is why neighbouring countries have become aware of the fact that bilateral treaties on mutual cooperation in investigations are necessary.

2.2.4. Conclusion of the US-Japan MLA Treaty

The US-Japan MLA Treaty (2006) was the first bilateral MLA treaty concluded by Japan. At the time, Japan's most important partner for criminal

---

(18) Note that the name *Kokusai Sousa Kyoujohou* was later changed to, *Kokusai Sousa Kyoujo tou ni kansuru Houritu*, which is the current name. The reason for this change is that, in preparation for the conclusion of the US-Japan MLA Treaty, provisions were made for cases in which assistance is requested under the treaty.

assistance was (and presumably still is) the United States due to the high volume of cases between the two countries. At the time, the US had already concluded a number of MLA treaties. One of the first treaties was signed by the US with Switzerland in 1977. Since then, the US has concluded bilateral MLA treaties with more than 60 countries and territories. Before Japan, the first Asian country to conclude an MLA treaty with the US was Thailand (1986), followed by South Korea (1996), the Philippines (1996), Hong Kong (1998) and India (2005).[19]

Being the first, the US-Japan MLA Treaty is the basic template for bilateral MLA treaties that Japan has concluded since then. Treaties and agreements that Japan has concluded since then come in the form of adjustments made according to the actual conditions of the countries that have concluded the treaties and according to the diplomatic negotiations at the time that they were concluded.

III. The contents of the MLA treaties that Japan has concluded

3.1. General provisions
3.1.1. Introduction

This section summarises the contents of legal assistance in criminal matters, as stipulated in the MLA treaties and agreements that Japan has concluded. Japan has concluded seven MLA treaties and agreements, which have many points in common. This section (3.1) first outlines the general provisions which are common to all agreements, namely the duty to cooperate and the system of Central Authorities. As mentioned above, the 2006 US-Japan MLA Treaty is the basic model for the MLA treaties and agreements that Japan has

---

[19] The text of these agreements can be found at: https://www.state.gov/tias/ Last accessed 3 December 2021

subsequently concluded. There are thus considerable similarities in their form and contents.

3.1.2. The duty to cooperate

Assistance in criminal matters is an obligation under treaties and agreements. For example, Article 1.1 of the US-Japan MLA Treaty provides that "Each Contracting Party shall, upon request by the other Party, provide mutual assistance (hereinafter referred to as 'assistance') with investigations, prosecutions and other proceedings in criminal matters in accordance with the provisions of this Treaty".

A similar formula can be found in Article 1.1 of each MLA agreement that Japan has signed.

3.1.3. The system of Central Authorities

The MLA treaties and agreements adopt a system of Central Authorities. In other words, the MLA conventions and agreements allow for the prompt and appropriate implementation of MLA procedures by designating a Central Authority in charge of MLA, which was previously only possible through diplomatic channels and on a case-by-case basis. This system is common to all MLA treaties and agreements that Japan has concluded. The Central Authorities in Japan shall be the Minister of Justice or the National Public Safety Commission or persons designated by them. [20]

---

(20) See, for example, Article 2.1. of the US-Japan MLA Treaty. This is because investigative authority in Japan is divided between the prosecutors and the police, with communication with the prosecutors going through the Minister of Justice and communication with the police going through the National Public Safety Commission. See also Article 2 of the US-Japan MLA Treaty, Article 2 of the Korea-Japan MLA Treaty, Article 2 of the China-Japan MLA Treaty, Article 2 of the Hong Kong-Japan MLA Agreement, Article 4 of the EU-Japan MLA Agreement, Article 2 of the Russia-Japan MLA Treaty.

3.2. Type of assistance in each MLA treaty or agreement

3.2.1. Contents of mutual assistance

Article 1. 2. of the US-Japan MLA Treaty states that "The assistance shall include the following:, [21] (1) taking testimony, statements or items; (2) examining persons, items or places; (3) locating or identifying persons, items or places; (4) providing items in the possession of governmental departments or agencies; (5) presenting an invitation to a person whose appearance in the requesting Party is sought; (6) transfer of a person in custody for testimony or other purposes; (7) assisting in proceedings related to forfeiture and immobilisation of proceeds or instrumentalities of criminal offenders; and (8) any other assistance permitted under the laws of the requested Party and agreed upon between the central authorities of the Contracting Parties."

Almost all subsequent MLA treaties and agreements have included the above, albeit with some differences in wording. In order to obtain an accurate picture of the situation, it seems worthwhile to map the subtle differences in each MLA agreement. The EU-Japan MLA Agreement presents further specificities in comparison with the other agreements. These are more extensively presented in Section 5.

3.2.2. Mapping the contents of assistance

For mapping purposes, the provisions in the Japan-US MLA Treaty will be used as a basis for comparison. The following sub-sections (i) through (viii) discuss how the other MLA agreements refer to the type of assistance as listed in the aforementioned Article 1. 2. (1) to (8) of the US-Japan MLA Treaty.

(i) Taking testimony, statements or items

The first type of assistance is 'taking testimony, statement or items'.

---

[21] In addition to this, the following explanation is attached to the end of this article: "The term 'items', as used in this Treaty, means documents, records and articles of evidence."

The Hong Kong-Japan MLA Agreement (Art. 1) uses the same wording as the US-Japan MLA Treaty. The Korea-Japan MLA Treaty (Art. 1) and the Russia-Japan MLA Treaty (Art. 1) stipulate for the "taking testimony, statements or items, including through the execution of search and seizure". The EU-Japan MLA Agreement (Art. 3(a) and 3(c)) provides for the same content as the Korea-Japan MLA Treaty, but in two separate sections. Only the China-Japan MLA Treaty (Art. 1) mentions "taking evidence including testimony, statements, documents, records", while "executing search and seizure" is stipulated in a separate paragraph (Art. 2).

(ii) Examining persons, items or places

The Korea-Japan MLA Treaty (Art. 2), the Hong Kong-Japan MLA Agreement (Art. 2), the EU-Japan MLA Agreement (Art. 3(e)) and the Russia-Japan MLA Treaty (Art. 2) use the same wording as the US-Japan MLA Treaty, i.e. "examining persons, items or places". The China-Japanese MLA Treaty (Art. 3), on the other hand, speaks of "conducting expert evaluation of persons, places or documents, records or articles".

(iii) Locating or identifying persons, items or places

The Korea-Japan MLA Treaty (Art. 3), the Hong Kong-Japan MLA Agreement (Art. 3), the EU-Japan MLA Agreement (Art. 3(f)) and the Russia-Japan MLA Treaty (Art. 3) use the same wording as the US-Japan MLA Treaty: "Locating or identifying persons, items or places". The China-Japan MLA Treaty (Art. 4), on the other hand, stipulates "locating or identifying persons, places, documents, records or articles".

(iv) Providing items in the possession of governmental departments or agencies

On this, there is no MLA treaty or agreement that uses the same wording as the US-Japan MLA Treaty. The Korea-Japan MLA Treaty (Art. 4)

and the EU-Japan MLA Agreement (Art. 3(g)) stipulate "providing items in the possession of the legislative, administrative or judicial authorities of the requested Party as well as the local authorities thereof". The Russia-Japan MLA Treaty (Art. 4) stipulates that "providing items in the possession of the legislative, administrative judicial or other national authorities of the requested Party as well as the local authorities thereof". The China-Japan MLA Treaty (Art. 5) stipulates "providing documents, records or articles in the possession of the legislative, administrative or judicial authorities of the requested Party as well as the local authorities thereof". The Hong Kong-Japan MLA Treaty (Art. 4) stipulates "providing items in the possession of the authorities of the requested Party".

(v) Presenting an invitation to a person whose appearance in the requesting Party is sought

The Korea-Japan MLA Treaty (Art. 5) uses the same wording for the US-Japan MLA Treaty: "presenting an invitation to a person whose appearance in the requesting Party is sought". On the other hand, the Hong Kong-Japan MLA Treaty (Art. 5) stipulates "presenting an invitation to a person whose appearance before an appropriate authority in the requested Party is sought". The China-Japan MLA Agreement (Art. 6) stipulates "presenting an invitation to a person whose appearance in the requesting Party is sought for giving testimony or assisting in investigations, prosecutions or other proceedings". The EU-Japan MLA Agreement (Art. 3(h)) stipulates "serving documents and informing a person of an invitation to appear in the requested State". The Russia-Japan MLA Convention (Art. 5) stipulates "informing a person of an invitation to appear in the requesting Party or serving a document requesting a person to appear in the requesting Party".

(vi) Transfer of a person in custody for testimony or other purposes

　　The Korea-Japan MLA Treaty (Art. 6) uses the same wording as the US-Japan MLA Treaty: "transfer of a person in custody for testimony or other purposes". On the other hand, the Hong Kong-Japan MLA Agreement (Art. 6) and the China-Japan MLA Treaty (Art. 7) stipulates "transfer of a person in custody for giving testimony or otherwise assisting in investigations, prosecutions or other proceedings". The Japan-EU MLA Agreement (Art. 3(i)) stipulates "temporary transfer of a person in custody for testimony or other evidentiary purposes". The Russia-Japan MLA Treaty (Art. 3(vi)) stipulates "temporary transfer of a person who is being detained or is serving a sentence in the territory of the respondent Party for giving testimony or for other purposes indicated in the request".

(vii) Assisting in proceedings related to forfeiture and immobilisation of proceeds or instrumentalities of criminal offenders

　　The Korea-Japan MLA Treaty (Art. 8), the Hong Kong-Japan MLA Agreement (Art. 8), the China-Japan MLA Treaty (Art. 9) and the Russia-Japan MLA Treaty (Art. 8) use the same wording as the US-Japan MLA Treaty: "assisting in proceedings related to forfeiture and immobilisation of proceeds or instrumentalities of criminal offenders". The Japan-EU MLA Agreement (Art. 3(j)), on the other hand, stipulates "assisting in proceedings related to freezing or seizure and confiscation of proceeds or instruments".

(viii) Any other assistance permitted under the laws of the requested Party and agreed upon between the Central Authorities of the Contracting Parties

　　The Korea-Japan MLA Treaty (9), the Hong Kong-Japan MLA Agreement (9) and the China-Japan MLA Treaty (11) use the same wording for the US-Japan MLA Treaty: "Any other assistance permitted under the laws of the requested Party and agreed upon between the Central Authorities of the Contracting

Parties". The EU-Japan MLA Agreement (k), on the other hand, provides for "any other assistance permitted under the laws of the requested State and agreed upon between Japan and a Member State". The Russia-Japan MLA Treaty (9) provides for "any other assistance that is not contrary to the laws of the requested Party and agreed upon between the Central Authorities of the Parties".

(ix) Provisions not included in the US-Japan MLA Treaty but included in other treaties and agreements

A type of assistance which is not included in the US-Japan MLA Treaty but is included in other treaties and agreements is "serving judicial documents". The Japan-Korea MLA Treaty (Art. 7) and the Japan-Hong Kong MLA Agreement (Art. 7) provide for "service of judicial documents". The China-Japan MLA Treaty (Art. 8) and the Russia-Japan MLA Treaty (Art. 7) stipulate "serving documents related to criminal proceedings". The EU-Japan MLA Agreement stipulates "serving documents" under Art. 3(h) "serving documents and informing a person of an invitation to appear in the requested State". In addition to this, the Japan-China MLA treaty also stipulates "providing criminal records" (Art. 10) as a separate type of assistance.

3.2.3. Summary

From the detailed summary above which maps out the types of mutual assistance covered, it can be seen that there is not much difference in the type of assistance provided for by each treaty. Admittedly, a number of differences have been highlighted. However, these mainly concern linguistic aspects or the structure of the agreements. It is unlikely, in my view, that the differences as to how the agreements are framed will mark a significant difference as to how judicial cooperation is carried out. The differences in formulation might just be the result of specific negotiation requests on the side of Japan's partner, which preferred a particular formulation of the text possibly for translation reasons or even diplomatic reasons. Hong Kong and China might have wanted their treaties to be formulated differently so as to highlight a unique relationship with Japan. The one treaty that does stand out as different from the others is the EU-Japan Agreement. Indeed, in addition to the above points, it has some important specificities in terms of type of assistance provided and grounds for refusal. This is where the 'uniqueness' of the EU-Japan MLA Agreement can be seen and this is therefore discussed more extensively in the next section.

IV. The EU-Japan MLA Agreement: Background and its 'uniqueness' or 'novelty'

4.1. Background to the conclusion of the EU-Japan MLA Agreement [22]

The history of the EU-Japan MLA Agreement dates back to 2002, when Hans G. Nilsson, then Head of Unit at the Council's General Secretariat, proposed the idea of a Japan-EU MLA Agreement. It was favourably received by Germany and France. At that time, there was no MLA agreement between Japan and any of the EU member States (only France had attempted to conclude one).

Japan, on the other hand, did not seem to have much interest in concluding an MLA agreement with the EU. In terms of concrete figures, there were only 37 MLA requests from Japan to the EU in the ten years from 1999 to 2009. On the other hand, the number of MLA requests from EU member States to Japan came to 130. The fact that Japan was not so active in concluding an MLA agreement with the EU may be due to this practical background.

Before entering into negotiations for an agreement with the EU, Japan had concluded MLA treaties with the US and South Korea, as mentioned above. It had also been in discussions with Hong Kong and China regarding

---

(22) The following description is based on Weyembergh & Wieczorek, supra fn. 5, p. 443-.

the conclusion of MLA treaties and agreements. Basically, it can be said that Japan was interested in MLAs in the Asia-Pacific region, which was natural given the geographical proximity of that region.

However, in this context, informal talks between Japan and the EU began in 2007, according to Japanese literature,[23] so it can be said that Japan was not completely indifferent. Japan's increased willingness to negotiate the agreement might have been due to the fact that the government at the time was a Democratic Party government that was in favour of the abolition of the death penalty. Indeed, the presence of the death penalty represented a stumbling block during the negotiations with the EU.

Japan approved the launch of formal consultations in February 2009. After four rounds of formal negotiations, agreement on the text of the proposed agreement was reached in November 2009. The EU-Japan MLA Agreement entered into force in January 2010.

As described above, this agreement was more an EU-led initiative. It is considered a success for the EU considering that, at the outset, not all member States supported the agreement.[24]

4.2. The 'uniqueness' and 'novelty' of the EU-Japan MLA Agreement
4.2.1. Unique type of assistance in the EU-Japan MLA

First of all, there are two new additions to the type of assistance offered by the EU-Japan MLA. Article 3 of the Japan-EU MLA Agreement provides for two mutual assistance pieces of content that do not exist in other treaties and agreements. Article 3(b), "enabling the hearing by videoconference", and Article 3(d), "obtaining records, documents or report of bank accounts". Both of these were introduced at the request of the EU.

The EU already has experience with videoconferencing. In that sense,

---

[23] Nakauchi, supra fn. 4, p. 20.
[24] See, Weyembergh & Wieczorek, supra fn. 5, p. 455.

this provision is meant to export the EU's experience to Japan. For example, if a country in the EU needs to interview a person in Japan as a witness or an expert witness, the Japanese side will be able to obtain testimony or statements from that person via videoconference, according to the procedures regulated by Article 16 of the EU-Japan MLA Agreement.

Moreover, the EU-Japan MLA Agreement sets out the possibility for EU and Japanese authorities to acquire bank account records, which has not been clearly defined in previous treaties and agreements. The acquisition of bank account records was considered to be included under "taking items" under the previous treaties, but this has been made more explicit at the request of the EU in the EU-Japan MLA Treaty, which regulates it in Article 18. This provision was arguably put in place in order to prevent tax evasion and money laundering and it is believed that it will make the investigation of international illicit funds faster and more appropriate.

4.2.3. A unique ground for refusal of assistance: Offence punishable by death under the national laws

The above two provisions on type of assistance are distinctive but there are provisions in the EU-Japan MLA Agreement that are of even greater significance. Article 11(b) of the EU-Japan MLA Agreement stipulates that assistance can be refused in cases of "offence punishable by death under the laws". In other words, assistance in the case of "offence punishable by death under the laws" can be denied if it is found that there is a risk of harm to the "essential interest of the requested state". This was incorporated into the agreement at the strong request of the EU. [25]

These 'uniquenesses' and this 'novelty' are viewed positively by the EU side as successful examples of 'norm diffusion' from the EU. For example,

---

(25) Weyembergh & Wieczorek, Supra fn. 5.

Weyembergh and Wieczorek evaluate the significance of the EU's ability to insert a clause stating that assistance for crimes punishable by the death penalty constitutes an "essential interest of the state" as a ground for refusal of criminal assistance as a result of the negotiations, stating as follows: "The EU does not want to cooperate with third states' fundamental rights violations, and it ideally wants to obstruct capital executions in the specific case. Beyond that, given the broader abolitionist mission of the EU, the rationale for inserting this clause was arguably also to put pressure on Japan to change its policy on capital punishment, that is, for the EU to also promote its values". [26] This unique aspect of the EU-Japan MLA Agreement is discussed more in detail in the next section, which addresses the main rationales for the ground for refusal.

V. The role for values and legal culture in shaping the text of international agreements

5.1. Introduction

A last aspect which deserves discussion relates to the grounds for refusal included in the treaties and agreements. These are particularly interesting as they are more connected to the debate on the role played by values and legal culture in shaping the text of international agreements.

As mentioned above, the EU-Japan MLA Agreement contains unique new provisions on the content and grounds for denial of mutual assistance. This seems to be very much related to the relationship between international agreements and treaties and the legal culture of both the EU and Japan. The expansion of the EU's value system is a very important objective for the EU and it is understandable that the EU would develop the promotion of its own value system in these situations.

---

[26] Weyembergh & Wieczorek, Supra fn. 5, p. 453. On the other hand, the EU failed to have it incorporated in the MLA agreement that it signed with the United States.

On the surface, the conclusion of international agreements and the text agreed upon may seem to be simply the result of a diplomatic and political negotiation process between diplomatic authorities but, in fact, it seems to be the result of much more deeply rooted issues. In other words, if we delve deeper into this issue, we will find that it comes down to the position that the negotiating teams held during the negotiations and that the resulting text is a product of values and attitudes of the States that sign the treaty regarding their respective criminal justice systems, punishment and crimes.

In other words, in general, treaties often include an obligation to cooperate but, in exceptional cases, they may refuse to cooperate. The reasons and circumstances for refusal of assistance are basically derived from the values of the State. Diplomatic and political exchanges in the process of negotiating treaties and agreements can involve a clash of national values. At the root of this is the legal culture of the entire legal system of the State, and furthermore, this comes down to the legal consciousness of the people who constitute the State.

Normally, two grounds for the denial of mutual legal assistance can be found in MLA treaties : (1) cases related to political offences [27] and (2) cases where assistance would infringe on national security or vital interests. [28] The reasons for these grounds for refusal are linked to sensitive political decisions for each State.

On the other hand, when looking at the MLA treaties and agreements that Japan has concluded, there are differences as to whether or not the following two grounds for refusal are included: *the principle of double jeopardy and the requirement of double criminality.*

---

(27) See, by way of example, Article 11(1)a of the EU-Japan Agreement or Article 3(1)1 of the US-Japan Agreement.

(28) See, by way of example, Article 11(1)b of the EU-Japan Agreement and Article 3(1)2 of the US-Japan Agreement.

The principle of double jeopardy refers to the principle that a person cannot be found guilty of an act for which he or she was once acquitted (Article 39 of the Japanese Constitution also stipulates the same purpose). Article 3. 1. (7) of the Japan-Hong Kong Mutual Assistance Treaty stipulates this as a ground for denial of assistance. Since Hong Kong had concluded similar treaties with other countries, there was a strong request to incorporate the principle of double jeopardy as a ground for refusal of assistance in the treaty with Japan and the Japanese side accepted this request. Korea and China also requested the same provision, but as a result of negotiations, it was not adopted. Regarding this issue, Article 5 of the Japanese Penal Code stipulates that a person that has been convicted in a foreign country may be punished again. The idea is that, even if the act were to be tried and punished in a foreign country, it is permissible to punish it again because Japan also has jurisdiction. Japan may not have felt the necessity to define the grounds for denial of assistance. This issue may give rise to various theoretical issues to be considered but, in order to focus consistently on the differences in legal culture and awareness, this author has decided to leave such issues for a future study. Instead, this paper focuses on the principle of double criminality as an issue more closely related to legal culture and legal consciousness. [29] It then goes on to discuss the death penalty-based ground for refusal, which is a key example of a clash of values.

5.2. Grounds for refusal of assistance (Part 1) : Double criminality requirement

The double criminality requirement/principle is defined as follows: assistance in criminal matters can only be provided with respect to criminal procedures concerning facts that are a crime in both the requesting and the

---

[29] For more information on the principle of prohibition of double punishment in international law, see, Moe Ochi, *Kokusai Keijitetuzukihou no Taikei* (A system of International Criminal Procedural Law), (Shinzansha 2020).

requested country. This is stipulated in Japan's domestic law, the International Assistance in Investigation Act (Article 2, Paragraph 2). The EU-Japan MLA Agreement also contains this requirement (Article 11. 2).

However, in other agreements, double criminality requirements have become less stringent. This is the case, for example, of the US-Japan MLA Treaty [30] and of instruments which regulate MLA among EU member States. [31] It has been pointed out that "The application of double (or dual) criminality [⋯] to legal assistance has been criticised as 'an unnecessary and outmoded barrier to cooperation' and is becoming less common". [32] It has also been pointed out that "there is a tendency to relax the double criminality requirement for assistance that merely involves the exchange of evidence, especially assistance that does not require compulsory search". [33] Interviews with Japanese police officers reveal that, in practice, there is little awareness of the double criminality requirement in investigations. [34]

From a normative perspective, the need to respect the principle of double

---

(30) Article 1 (4) of the US-Japan MLA Treaty stipulates: "Except as otherwise provided for in this Treaty, assistance shall be provided without regard to whether the conduct that is the subject of the investigation, prosecution or other proceeding in the requesting Party would constitute a criminal offense under the laws of the requested party". As an exception, in the case of compulsory measures, it shall be left to the discretion of the respondent State. See, Article 3. 1. (4).

(31) See Art. 11 (c) of the Directive 2014/41/EU of the European Parliament and of the Council of 3 April 2014 regarding the European Investigation Order in criminal matters, *OJ L 130, 1.5.2014, p. 1–36*. See also, at a Council of Europe level, the European Convention on Mutual Assistance in Criminal Matters, (20.IV.1959, CETS 030), which, in Art. 5, gives the *option* and not the obligation to require respect for double criminality.

(32) Boister, supra fn. 1, p. 319. For related references, see note (42) on the same page of the book.

(33) Keisuke Chida, *Keiji ni kansuru Kokusaijouyaku o meguru shomondai* (Issues Related to International Treaties in Criminal Matters) Keijihou Journal, No. 27 (2011), p. 36.

(34) In the case of Japan, the Ministry of Justice or the National Public Safety Commission is the Central Authority for the MLA treaties and agreements. It was reported that, as long as an investigation is ordered in the field, Japanese investigators in the field are almost never aware of this issue of double criminality or verify it in practice. According to the interview mentioned in supra fn. 6.

criminality flows from the principle of legality, which prescribes that no-one can be punished for a fact which was not a crime at the time that it was committed. From this principle it follows that contributing via MLA to the investigations of an act that is not considered a crime in the executing country could be considered a violation of the principle of legality as per Japan's Constitution and legal doctrine. [35] It seems natural, then, that the dual criminality requirement is strictly observed in bilateral treaties. Why, then, is it allowed to be relaxed in treaties with the US?

The reasons for loosening the double criminality requirement can be of a practical nature, namely to speed up the MLA in practice so as to carry out effective investigative activities. From a theoretical perspective, such a relaxation of the principle is justified on the basis of a common understanding between the two countries that there is sufficient convergence in values such that they can both operate based on slightly different definitions of crimes.

Furthermore, the main point of MLA is that the requested countries collect evidence on behalf of the other country that has signed the treaty and to provide information obtained through such investigations. If an act is not punishable in the requested country but is punishable in the requesting country, it can be argued that investigating it on behalf of the requesting country is technically a violation of the principle of legality of crime. At least in Japanese constitutional law, the principle of double criminality is conceptualised as a safeguard to the principle of legality of crimes. However, according to an interview at the Japan National Police Agency, in the field of investigations, there are almost no cases in which there is a sense of discomfort in the investigations linked to the need to respect double criminality. In most of the cases, even if there is no specific provision providing punishment in the requested country for the behaviour under investigation, there is an overlapping understanding in both countries of

---

(35) In Japan, Article 31 (and Article 39) of the Constitution is interpreted to guarantee this and, in the United States, Article 4 of the Amendment is interpreted to guarantee this.

wrongdoing, culpability and responsibility. [36]

In other words, what is important is whether the two countries can have a 'common understanding'. This requires understanding and respect for each other's legal culture. This seem to be the case between Japan and the US. Whereas, even though Japan and the EU share some common values, there still seem to be some major differences. This may be one of the reasons why the EU-Japan MLA Agreement continues to require strict dual criminality requirements. The different position on the issue of the death penalty between Japan and the EU, for example, is a good illustration of a divergence of values between the EU and Japan. The next section turns to this.

5.3. Grounds for refusal of assistance (Part 2) : Offence punishable by death under the laws

As a starting point for a discussion on the death penalty-based ground for refusal, it is important to recognise the following. In the first place, the Treaty on European Union (TEU) gives the EU specific obligations regarding its external actions. Article 3(5) of the Treaty states that "the Union shall uphold and promote its values and interests and contribute to the protection of its citizens". Furthermore, Article 21(2) (a) of the Treaty states that the EU shall (a) safeguard its values, fundamental interests, security, independence and integrity" in its external actions. [37] From this perspective, the EU wants to propagate its values outside the EU and the inclusion of a clause in the EU-Japan MLA Agreement that allows the EU to refuse to assist with crimes punishable by the death penalty is a diplomatic and political success for the EU.

By contrast, some of the Japanese literature points out that there was an unwillingness on the side of Japan to accept such a clause. On this point, the Japanese literature says: "(1) In the current situation where EU member States

---

(36) See supra fn. 6.
(37) See, Weyembergh & Wieczorek, supra fn. 5, p.440.

have not adopted the death penalty, only EU member States can effectively refuse to provide assistance on the basis of the death penalty and this treaty is disadvantageous to Japan. (2) It has been pointed out that allowing EU member States not to provide assistance to Japan for crimes punishable by the death penalty in Japan may affect the nature of the death penalty system in Japan". [38] On the other hand, Japan's Ministry of Foreign Affairs has stressed the importance of concluding this agreement, pointing out that (1) the EU can refuse to provide assistance for the same reason even without this agreement and (2) this agreement establishes a framework for the collection of evidence and other matters and has nothing to do with the debate on the abolition or existence of the death penalty in Japan. [39]

　The issue of the death penalty is an extremely difficult one for Japan. As a criminal law scholar, this author naturally understands the norms presented by the EU. However, it is important to point out here that Europe's perspective different from Japan's perspective. The penal system is constructed by normatively refining the reactive attitude of resentment towards wrongdoing, which exists as a fact. [40] Although the author will not enter into the debate on the abolition of the death penalty here, it is his view that, at the time of writing this paper, all attempts to justify - from a normative point of view - the death penalty as a form of punishment in Japan have failed and almost all criminal jurists would agree. However, before normative refinement, we have to think about how to deal with what exists as a fact.

　In order to understand the attitude towards the death penalty in Japan as well as the debate on its abolition, it is essential to consider the following questions. These are questions that are often raised in public discussions

---

(38) Nakauchi, supra fn. 4, pp.24-25.
(39) See, Nakauchi, supra fn. 4, p.25.
(40) Shin Matsuzawa, *'Hinan, Gaiaku, Ouhou'* (Censure, Hard Treatment and Retribution), *Waseda Hougaku* Vol.95 No.4, 2020, p.1-.

about the death penalty in Japan. Can criminal justice, as a means of achieving justice, clearly answer the following questions?: (1) Who would not wish for the death of the perpetrator if they were the victims (or the bereaved family)? (2) Is this not a natural human emotion? (3) How can a victim of a homicide, and the family, be compensated? (4) Why would the State, which failed to protect the lives of the victims, protect the lives of the perpetrators who took the lives of the victims?

By comparison with the EU, it should also be noted that Japan's criminal justice system does not have measures similar to those present in Germany, which are known as *'Maßregeln der Besserung und Sicherung'*. These measures (including indefinite detention) can be imposed on individuals who are considered socially dangerous as something separate from criminal punishment and Japanese citizens might therefore feel reassured by the presence of death penalty. [41] Moreover, Japan has a different cultural background from the Christian culture of divine forgiveness.

VI. Conclusion

This paper has examined the international MLA treaties and agreements that Japan has concluded, including with a focus on the EU-Japan MLA Agreement. However, it was argued, in order to understand them more deeply, that it is necessary to pay attention to the legal culture and legal consciousness of each contracting country. Understanding such background information is fundamental if one is to capture the potential differences between the agreements concluded in the field. In concluding MLA treaties and agreements, it seems important to determine precisely whether the two countries have common

---

(41) *Maßregeln der Besserung und Sicherung* and punishment are naturally two completely different things. However, we cannot discuss the legal system while ignoring how the general public feels about it.

values regarding crime and punishment and, if so, to what extent they can cooperate on the basis of these common values.

For instance, given the existence of shared values between them, member States of the EU agreed to loosen the double criminality requirement. When considering the practical functioning of the EU-Japan MLA, it is therefore important to consider the importance of this dimension of values. In other words, it is essential to consider the following question: To what extent is a mutual understanding of criminal justice and human rights possible, and how far does it exist, between the EU and Japan?

This is naturally a difficult question to answer. For instance, even within the EU there are considerable differences in values between western and eastern Europe. Looking at the EU and Japan, one can appreciate how both sides advocate liberalism and respect for fundamental human rights as important values, but there are still considerable differences. Suami provides an interesting analysis of how the EU and Japan attach different levels of importance to the protection of human rights in vertical situations (i.e. enforcing rights against the State) or in horizontal situations (i.e. enforcing rights against private parties). [42] A more concrete example can be seen, in terms of the extent to which people value the right to self-determination, when dealing with the response to Covid-19, which saw much stricter restrictions being imposed in Japan and fewer protests by Japanese citizens.

Conversely. Japan might perceive that the US has a similar understanding in terms of values underpinning the protection of human rights. And Japan and the USA have had very strong links in a number of areas, particularly in the economic sphere, which naturally influences the development of a feeling of cultural proximity. One of the clearest examples of proximities in terms of

---

(42) T. Suami, 'Rule of law and human rights in the context of the EU-Japan relationship: are both the EU and Japan really sharing the same values?' in D. Vanoverbeke et al (eds), *The Changing Role of Law in Japan* (Cheltenham: Edward Elgar Publishing, 2014).

values is the presence of death penalties in Japan and in several of the states of the United States. This sets the US-Japan relationship apart from the EU-Japan relationship considering the EU's strong opposition to capital punishment.

In a further example, which emerged from the research for this paper, this author asked Japanese investigators[43] if there is any possibility that the Joint Investigation Team (JIT) system recently introduced in the EU will be introduced in Japan. They said that introducing it would be "unimaginable". JIT is a cooperation mechanism establishing and organising a team of foreign police and/or judicial authorities to be placed under the command of the home country's police/judicial authorities and to cooperate in a transnational investigation. As a precondition for this, it is necessary to entrust a part of a State's sovereignty, namely its investigative authority, to another country. Japan is very wary of doing this. Interestingly, this is true not only *vis à vis* the EU, but even *vis à vis* the US despite the fact that mutual trust is thought to be strong between the EU and Japan as well as between the US and Japan. The Japanese investigators interviewed by this author regarded it as highly unlikely that US police would allow Japanese police to operate on US territory. It seems to this author that a relationship of trust as well as a common understanding of crime and punishment is a prerequisite for creating any cooperation mechanism such as a JIT.

As a personal value judgment, this author agrees with the norms set out by the EU but, at the same time, it would be unfortunate if Japan could only change due to pressure exerted from outside. This author's hope is that these problems will be solved by the Japanese people themselves in the process of a normative refinement of the country's penal system.

(**43**) Based on interviews in supra fn. 6.

Last Chapter
The Methods of Legal Dogmatics of Criminal Law
——From a Realistic Perspective——

I. Foreword[1]

Can legal dogmatics [2] of criminal law be deemed a science? This question would most likely draw a response that it is naturally a science. And the word "science" is included in "Legal Science," which is the resaerch of law.

How about if I ask does legal dogmatics of criminal law have objectivity? This question would probably prompt divided answers. In one country, legal dogmatics of criminal law is understood to be presentation of systematic dogmatic deemed appropriate by individual scholars of criminal law. In such a country, it would hardly be objective, because the dogmatics of criminal law cannot be established without subjective value judgment by the scholars. Perhaps some people in the same country may argue that there is objectivity. Such argument will be based on understanding that criminal law scholars will select and present objectively correct dogmatic from the legal text. Is such an understanding appropriate?

In another country, legal dogmatics of criminal law is understood to be the description of present status of effective criminal law by the scholars. In

---

(1) I would like to express my deepest gratitude to Professor Thomas Elholm and Professor Petter Asp for their many discussions in the preparation of this paper.
In this paper, in light of the difficulties in accessing the Scandinavian and Japanese literature, where possible, English or German references have been cited.

(2) The "legal dogmatics" here means the German word "die Rechtsdogmatik", which means to interpret the Code in a systematic and consistent manner. In the countries of the continental legal system, the development of legal dogmatics is one of the most important challenges in criminal law.

such a country, the dogmatics would be considered objective, because the scholars of criminal law only describe the facts. However, can legal dogmatics that only describe facts stand? Moreover, can description of facts always be considered objective? How can we be certain that it does not become presentation of one's opinion disguised as description of facts?

May be some countries fall between the two, by taking a method such as stating the facts and making limited presentation of personal opinions. However, wouldn't such a method ultimately conclude in the first method, in that the dogmatics will evolve based on personal opinions? In addition, how can the difference between descriptions of facts and opinions be established?

Various questions like these may be presented on the characteristics of legal dogmatics of criminal law. In this paper, the author will review these issues by referencing information on the author's native country Japan, as well as Germany, Denmark and Sweden.

II. What is Legal Dogmatics of Criminal Law?

2.1. Characteristics of legal dogmatics of criminal law in Germany

The answers to the questions, "what is legal dogmatics of criminal law?" and "what is the academic nature of legal dogmatics of criminal law?" may seem self-evident, but in reality, it is not clear at all. To begin with, the word dogmatics came from dogmatic theology. The characteristics of legal dogmatics of criminal law imagined from this is, just as dogmatic theology seeks to interpret the bible without contradiction, to interpret the criminal code within the scope of its text without contradiction.

Perhaps this approach is most thoroughly pursued in Germany. Nothing can surpass the German criminal law studies in its effort to interpret the criminal code systematically, without contradiction, and normatively through establishment of the central dogma and use of logical deduction to reach conclusion on various dogmatics of criminal law.

For example, there was the doctrine of final conduct (finale Handlungslehre) which dominated the German criminal jurisprudence in the mid-twentieth century. According to its proponent Hans Welzel, when human action is captured ontologically, its feature is in its purposiveness (finalität), and he strongly objected to the conventional theory, calling it the causal theory (kausale Handlungslehre).[3] Various conceptual results introduced by his teleological theory of human action gave impact to judicial precedence and legislation. However, basically its development was based on the notion that the result produced from the central dogma using logical deduction is duly justified, rather than on the resolution of some problems that arose in society.

Perhaps the readers may question my reference to the teleological theory of human action which was a theory from the mid-twentieth century. I introduced this theory because it is most typical of the German approach and would be helpful for grasping the framework; however, this style of argument is still the controlling majority in German criminal jurisprudence. For example, more recent debate between the school seeking to construct a system of criminal law based on empirical science led by Claus Roxin[4] and the school advocating a model of functionalism based on the sociological systems theory developed by Niklas Luhmann led by Günter Jakobs[5] show that both sides are utilizing the same methodology whereby the theoretical system is constructed by establishing the central dogma and applying logical deduction. In particular, a student of Jakobs has gone so far as applying logical deduction to the systems theory to assert relativization or resolution of the distinction between illegality (Rechtswidrigkeit) and responsibility (Schuld).[6]

---

(3) Hans Welzel, *Das Deutsches Strafrecht* (11th edn. De Gruyter 1969) §8.
(4) Claus Roxin & Luís Greco, *Strafrecht Allgemeiner Teil, Band I* (5th edn. C.H.Beck 2020); Roxin, *Strafrecht Allgemeiner Teil, Band II* (C.H.Beck 2003).
(5) Günther Jakobs, *Strafrecht Allgemeiner Teil* (2nd edn, De Gruyter 1991).

Perhaps these forms of discussion typically witnessed in German criminal jurisprudence can be described as constructing theoretical system based on the proponent's individual value judgments, and advocating the same under the name of "science." This may be the antithesis to an approach that considers what criminal jurisprudence can do to resolve the practical issues.

2.2. Characteristics of legal dogmatics of criminal law in Japan

Above stated approach can be seen in the author's native country, Japan. Under the influence of German criminal theory, Japan has spent considerable energy on structuring the system of criminal theory (Verbrechenslehle; a theory discussing the factors constituting the act of crime). There were heated debates between the classic and modern scholars during the first half of the twentieth century. And later happened a bebate between the proponents of the "negative value inherent in acts" theory (Handlungsunwert-teorie; a theory that places emphasis on the breach of socio-ethical norms of the "act," and considers that level of illegality differs between willful and negligent acts, so subjective aspects will affect the determination of illegality) and the "negative value inherent in results" theory (Erfolgsunwert-theorie; a theory that places emphasis on the illegal "result," i.e., the occurrence or risk of violation of legal interest, and considers that illegality should be determined objectively) near the end of the century. [7]

However, these debates are also based on the views on human nature in criminal law; or the views of the proponent on the characteristics of criminal law, i.e., whether to emphasize the function of criminal law to maintain social

---

(6) Heiko H. Lesch, *Der Verbrechensbegriff. Grundlinie einer funktionalen Revision* (Carl Heymanns Verlag 1999) 2. Kapitel, I; Michael Pawlik, 'Der wichtigste dogmatische Fortschritt der Letzten Menschenalter?: Anmerkungen zur Unterscheidung von Unrecht und Schuld im Strafrecht' in *Festschrift für Harro Otto* (Carl Heymanns Verlag 2007).

(7) Ryuichi Hirano, 'Deutsche Strafrechtsdogmatik aus japanischer Sicht' in Hans Joachim Hirsch and Thomas Weigend (eds) *Strafrecht und Kriminalpolitik in Japan und Deutschland* (Duncker & Humblot 1989).

order, or its function to resolve disputes in court. Application of various logic and creative theories will ultimately conclude in determination of philosophical or political value judgment of the proponent.

2.3. Appropriateness of normative construction of legal dogmatics of criminal law

Such theory of legal dogmatics mainly evolved as part of discussion on determination of characteristics of norms, based on German criminal jurisprudence. For example, during the first half of the twentieth century, Edmund Mezger's theory argued that by having the evaluation standards (Bewertungsnorm: a standard for evaluating an act) precede the determination standards (Bestimmungsnorm: a standard for prohibiting or ordering certain acts by citizens), illegality shall be determined objectively, and responsibility should be determined subjectively. [8] In mid-twentieth century Germany, Armin Kaufmann thoroughly implemented the teleological theory of human action, to conclude that standards for determination of illegality and responsibility should be based on the actor. [9] In latter half of the twentieth century Japan, there was a debate on whether to capture illegality under monism or dualism, arising from the perspective of ex ante or ex post determination of the breach of norms.

These debates take the form of "clarification of characteristics of norms," and at first may seem objective and scientific. It leaves the impression that by accurately recognizing the characteristics of the norms that exist objectively, truly correct answers can be obtained for various questions presented with respect to dogmatic of criminal law. However, this is not correct. To begin with, anyone who has studied law at all would know that to assume there is a

---

(8) Edmund Mezger, *Strafrecht: Ein Lehrbuch* (3rd edn. Duncker & Humblot 1949) Zweiter Hauptteil, Zweiter Abschnitt.
(9) Armin Kaufmann, *Lebendiges und Totes in Bindings Normentheorie* (O. Schwartz 1954) Viertes Kapitel.

truly correct answer in legal studies is incorrect. A number of conclusions can be reached on one issue. The majority view may converge on one or the other, but this is not because one is "true" or "false"; rather, it is a matter of degree of appropriateness. The difference is purely relative, and the opposite conclusion may be reached at a different time or place. Structuring a theory based on normative logic which may seem objective at a first glance will ultimately have to involve value judgment, and its appropriateness cannot avoid coming under dispute.

2.4. Orientation towards a more scientific dogmatic of criminal law

Is it impossible to have a scientific dogmatic of criminal law? Can criminal jurisprudence not stand as a science? Construction of scientific dogmatic of criminal law has been an issue pursued in various countries, with some indication from jurisprudence on the difficult issue of the science of legal studies. Let us review this issue in the next chapter.

III. Methodologies for Scientific Dogmatic of Criminal Law

3.1. Pre-War: Positivism

In fact, there was a period when scientific dogmatic of criminal law dominated the academia in Germany. This was the modernist school of criminal theory. It developed the reformatory punishment theory which argued for punishment as a means of improvement and education for the offender, based on the understanding that a crime was a product of the nature of the offender and environment, against the classic criminal theory which argued for retributive punishment as a response to crime, based on the dogmatic that a crime was a product of free will of the offender. The dicta by Franz von Liszt that "Social policy is both the best and most effective crime policy" [10] is very well known, and is founded on positivism, i.e., criminal theory based on scientific research and studies.

Modernist school theory of criminal law was scientific to the extent that it was based on scientific knowledge, but in reality, it could not escape tendencies to consider punishment as "a good thing" for improving and educating the criminal, which resulted in subjective tendencies of criminal theory. Subjectivist criminal theory may become foundation for abuse of power by the State if used arbitrarily. In Japan and Germany where the abuse of power by the State was experienced during WWII, the modernist school declined rapidly after the war.

3.2. Post-War: Empirical studies of law

Then, was scientific dogmatic of criminal law totally lost after the war? In reality, orientation towards scientific dogmatic had continued uninterruptedly in Germany and Japan. "Alternativ-Entwurf eines Strafgesetzbuches, Allgemeiner Teil" (alternative proposal for the general part of the German criminal law) published in 1966 by a group of West German scholars is very well known. With the slogan "Farewell to Kant and Hegel,"[11] the proposal held "de-metaphisicalizing of criminal law" as one of its aims. It argued that based on the results of criminological research, the purpose of punishment should be focused not only on general prevention, for which the certainty of effect has not been enough proven, but also on special prevention, aimed at education and improvement of the offenders. The proposal argued that to realize the goal of prevention of crimes, criminal law founded on empirical science became necessary. This approach gave significant impact on the revision of criminal law in West Germany, and led to the preventive integration theory (präventive Vereinigungstheorie), which aims to integrate the reinforcement of people's trust in the law and the resocialization of offenders, and the comprehensive

---

(10) Franz v. Liszt, *Strafrechtliche Aufsätze und Vorträge, 2. Band* (I. Guttentag 1905) 246.

(11) Ulrich Klug, 'Abschied von Kant und Hegel' in Jürgen Baumann (ed), *Programm für ein neues Strafgesetzbuch: Der Alternativ-Entwurf der Strafrechtslehrer* (Fischer 1968).

criminal theory (gesamt Strafrechtwissenschaft), which considers criminal law, criminal procedure, and criminal policy in a comprehensive manner, led by scholars such as Claus Roxin.

In post-WWII Japan, influence from the US legal studies became more prominent, and the so-called empirical legal studies started to influence various areas of positive laws. The "debate on dogmatics" started among the civil code and legal philosophy scholars over the scientific nature of the dogmatics of civil code. Wide ranging topics were discussed in the debate on legal dogmatics, one of which was its objectivity. In legal dogmaticcs, constant blending of facts and values occur, and the issue was how to separate the two to secure objectivity. Legal philosopher Junichi Aomi separated "selection of ends and means," and citing Max Weber, argued that while there is significant room for the value judgments of the interpreter in selection of ends, selection of means can be discussed in a completely scientific and objective manner. [12] He sought the bases of objectivity in selection of means in the recognition of empirical facts. In criminal law studies, Ryuichi Hirano asserted the need for dogmatics of criminal law that emphasize the function of criminal law, in response to the empirical jurisprudence and the debate on legal dogmatics. Hirano, who thoroughly studied Anglo-American jurisprudence, criticized the traditional theory of the functions of criminal law. His reasoning is, in short, that metaphysical concepts should be removed from criminal theory, and that functions of criminal law should be reconstructed from pragmatic aspects. He argues that these functions could be confirmed by empirical facts. The normalizing function and the maintaining function cannot be confirmed by empirical facts. Therefore, he finds that the function of protecting interest and the function of guaranteeing freedom of action are the most important functions of criminal law.

---

(12) Jun'ichi Aomi, 'Gendai Hokaishakugaku niokeru Kyakkansei no Mondai' in Gendaihogaku no Hoho (Iwanami 1966) 3-24.

The views of the alternative proposal group in Germany and Hirano in Japan are scientific in that they discuss "what effects arise from which dogmatics," based on knowledge of empirical science. These approaches realized dramatic progress from how the conventional debates in Germany and Japan involved "logical deduction from the central philosophical concept or dogma" or "commingling of personal values under the banner of objectively capturing the structure of the norm." However, how can one ensure that the "end" to which this knowledge of empirical science applied is objectively correct? This is where these theories appear incomplete. Of course, ends such as reducing crimes or securing freedom of citizens are clear and objectively correct. However, determination on what will be considered a crime, or how much of the freedom should be secured in relation to other national and social interests (conflict of interests between citizens is also a possibility), ultimately cannot stay free from various values and politics. Rather, it can be deemed to be political. That the West Germany's alternative proposal group and Hirano sought to separate criminal law from ethics was a coincidence, and there is no self-evident relation with having their foundation on empirical science.

This is also evident from the rivalry within the German school of functionalism which emphasize functionality of criminal law caused by the difference in definition of its function, and resulted in the opposing views explained above. That is, Roxin and Jakobs both profess "functionalism," but where the former perceives the purpose of criminal law as protection of legal interests, the latter aims to stabilize the norm through criminal law, resulting in completely different theories.

The situation is the same in Japan. At present, the majority of criminal law scholars agree that the purpose of criminal law is to protect the legal interests that can be recognized with empirical science. That is to say, previously seen proponents of social / national ethics and protection of the spirit of the people as the purpose of criminal law do not exist for most part, and the "infringement of legal interests" doctrine is the overwhelming majority. If this is the case, the doctrine should converge to the negative value theory. However, the debate on whether to choose negative value inherent in acts or results still remains. This is because there are various opinions on when the optimal timing of determination of occurrence and risk of infringement of legal interest is, and intervention with criminal laws is, to achieve the goal. Although they all follow the "infringement of legal interests" doctrine, their theories on criminal law are completely different.

3.3. Orientation towards science in legal philosophy (science of legal studies) : Scandinavian case

3.3.1. Introduction

The scientific approach continues to be pursued in dogmatic of criminal law, but science in legal studies had been debated longer in areas of jurisprudence and legal philosophy. Representative texts include "Pure Theory of Law" by Hans Kelsen [13] in continental Europe, and "legal pragmatism" promoted by Oliver W. Holms, Benjamin N. Cardozo, and Roscoe Pound in the US. [14]

However, strictly in relation to dogmatic of criminal law, these theories do not seem to have had significant direct impact. For example, in Germany, while the pure theory may have had some influence, dogmatic of criminal law that fully implemented the pure theory is almost non-existent, except for some efforts made by Kelsen himself in later years. And in the US, although theories of criminology and criminal procedures that were influenced by legal pragmatism followed by legal realism do exist, they do not appear to have fully developed within the context of theory of dogmatic of criminal law.

---

(13) Hans Kelsen, *Pure theory of law* (Max Knight tr, 2nd edn. University of California Press 1967).
(14) Oliver W. Holmes, *The Common Law* (Little Brown 1881); Benjamin N. Cardozo, *The Nature of the Judicial Process* (Yale University Press 1921); Roscoe Pound, *Social Control Through Law* (Yale University Press 1942).

In contrast, science in legal studies pursued in jurisprudence had broad impact on regular positive law in Denmark. The methodological theory of Alf Ross [15] is an example. Before we review his theory and how it developed in dogmatic of criminal law, let us take a look at its origin, the Scandinavian legal realism.

3.3.2. Scandinavian legal realism
(i) Uppsala school

Scandinavian legal realism was founded by Axel Hägerström, [16] a Swedish philosopher. As Hägerström was a professor at Uppsala University and the theory was mainly constructed in this university, it is also referred to as the Uppsala school.

According to Hägerström, all concepts must correspond with reality, because concepts that do not have corresponding reality are metaphysical concepts that do not have objective substance. From this perspective, rights and obligations are metaphysical concepts that do not have corresponding reality in the real world. This leads to the argument that "rights and obligations do not exist. They are merely superstitious beliefs." However, the concepts of rights and obligations have psychological power in the real world, and produce certain effects. Hägerström argued that this situation is logically contradictory, and is just "magic." [17]

This argument, along with his use of rampant language, brought strong opposition. The theory was developed further by his student, Karl Olivecrona. [18] Olivecrona inherited Hägerström's theory, and constructed a grand theory by

---

(15) Alf Ross, Professor, Univerisity of Copenhagen. 1899-1979.
(16) Axel Hägerström, Professor of Philosophy, Uppsala University, 1868-1939.
(17) Axel Hägerström, *Inquiries into the nature of law and morals* (Karl Olivecrona ed; C.D. Broad tr, Almqvist & Wiksell 1932).
(18) Karl Olivecrona, Profesor of Law, Lund University, 1897-1980.

incorporating, rather than expelling, the concept of rights and obligations into legal studies. With respect to the situation referred to as "magic" by Hägerström, Olivecrona believes that while rights and obligations certainly do not have semantic reference, the word "right" serves an important function by influencing the human mind and behavior to direct them; therefore, using it as a sign has considerable significance. In general, Scandinavian legal realism is characterized by its analysis on psychological aspects of the binding forces of the law. This is clearly apparent in the way Olivecrona focused on the psychological power that rights and obligations bring to the real society, treated this as a fact, denied the aspects of law that required corresponding reality, and introduced the concept of "law as fact." [19]

Olivecrona's denial of the "ought to be" aspect of the law is crucial. Traditionally, and perhaps still today, most people would have thought the following; the law is to be obeyed because it has legitimacy, and the law is binding because it is legitimized. But, in fact, it's not. The law is binding simply because the vast majority of people feel bound by it (legal discourse or legal something) and follow it. In other words, law is not something to be considered from norms, but from facts. Such a turn in perception is what should be called an "Olivecronic turn", and this paper is based on such a "turn".

(ii) **Alf Ross**

Danish legal philosopher Alf Ross was influenced by Scandinavian legal realism, and developed a unique theory based on traditional issues at the center of Danish legal studies. The traditional issues refer to the theory on sources of law. This is a theory on what constitutes source of law, which is supported by interest in where the source of "law with binding force" lies.

The theory presented by Ross [20] starts by attempting to answer this ques-

---

(**19**) Karl Olivecrona, *Law as Fact* (1st edn, OUP 1939).

tion along the lines of Scandinavian legal realism. The Scandinavian legal realists rejected concepts that did not have corresponding reality in the real world, and structured legal studies purely based on facts. Following this, Ross argued that legal studies must describe objective facts that have corresponding reality in a factual manner. He attempts to distinguish statements on law (legal statements) based on whether it is a statement of facts, or on value judgment and opinions. Ross was interested in a "law with binding force." This means that legal statements are distinguished between statements on law with binding force and statements on value judgments and opinions concerning the law with binding force. Ross classifies the former as dogmatic assertions and the latter as assertions of legal politics, and further divides the latter to proposals to legislators and proposal to judges. He states that only the former is objective and factual, and is befitting to be called science, therefore, its description should be the mission of legal studies. Legal politics which makes proposal to legislators and judges is not denied as activities for legal scholars, but it is deemed to be a supplementary.

In this way, Ross positions the theory of legal dogmatics as a study that provides descriptions of "law with binding force" in an objective and factual manner. The next question would be, what is a "law with binding force"?

3.4. Ross theory as applied by Waaben

3.4.1. Ross theory: The concept of valid law and prediction theory

Ross refers to the "law with binding force" as valid law. This concept is the key to modern Danish legal studies (and broader Scandinavian legal studies). Valid law is referred to as "Gældenderet" in Danish, which corresponds to "Geltendes Recht" in German. German and Japanese scholars would probably assume that it refers to the legal texts themselves. Criminal law scholars in

---

(20) Alf Ross, *On Law and Justice* (Jakob v. H. Holtermann ed, Uta Bindreitered tr, OUP 2019).

Germany and Japan refer to statements on current criminal laws (Geltendes Strafrecht) as dogmatic of criminal law. This means that in Germany and Japan, statements on current criminal codes will be part of legal dogmatics on criminal law, whether it be statements of fact or value judgment. As stated above, this is why arguments based on personal opinions and philosophical views are made under the name of legal dogmatic in Germany and Japan.

Ross does not take this approach. He captures valid law from a thoroughly realistic point of view. In sum, valid law is the thought process (ideology) of judges. That is to say, judges make decisions by referring to laws, precedents, practical customs, and opinions of attorneys and prosecutors, but the thought process of the judge that forms the foundation for all of this is the valid law.

The reason why Ross took this approach is self-evident when one considers his position as a realist. Decisions made by the judges have the ultimate authority in real society. Even if certain provisions existed in a legal text, it would not have real authority unless the judges agree so. Ideologies of the judges present themselves to the real society in forms of decisions, and control the real society. Ideologies of judges that are not presented in specific decisions will have controlling functions by predictions of their decisions on hypothetical cases. Describing the thought process of judges is the duty of legal dogmatics.

According to his theory, description of the judges' thought process will enable prediction of future decisions. And if the description made in legal dogmatic is consistent with the future decision, it is proven to be true, and if inconsistent, it is proven to be false. In this way, legal dogmatic can be proven to be true or false in an objective manner, according to Ross. This theory is called the "prediction theory" in Denmark.

3.4.2. Method of conceptual structure by Waaben: Criticism of German methodology

Ross' theory is the product of his study of jurisprudence, and the conclusion that the thought process of the judges is the valid law was reached as a result of pursuit of science of legal studies and binding authority of laws. As such, it was not created with presumption to apply the theory to dogmatic of actual laws. Therefore, utilization of his theory for dogmatic of actual laws (criminal law in this paper) requires certain adjustments, and the peculiarity of criminal laws must also be taken into consideration. Knud Waaben [21] tackled this difficult problem, and applied his theory to dogmatic of criminal law.

According to Waaben, "it is wrong to consider the decisions themselves as valid law." [22] And to describe valid law, the reference must be much wider than and include the hidden foundation of, what appears in the decisions. Valid law is the aggregate of thoughts and ideology of judges. The decisions themselves, a judge's thoughts particular to a case, and motivation for the decision, etc., are just part of the aggregate. [23]

Therefore, in describing valid law, studying the judicial precedents becomes important. Studies of judicial precedents in Japan (and perhaps in Germany) would probably emphasize extraction of the basic theory that the decision is founded on from the numerous precedents. Japanese scholars refer to this as the judicial precedents theory.

Judicial precedents theory is based on the general approach of judges, so one might assert it may be referring to the same thing as valid law. Studies of judicial precedents theory are conducted in Germany as well as Japan. What is so new about the approach taken by Ross?

---

(21) Knud Waaben, Professor in Law, University of Copenhagen, 1921-2008.
(22) Knud Waaben, *Det kriminelle forsæt* (Gyldendal 1957) 44.
(23) Ross's theory is often referred to as a sub-genre of American behavioristic legal realism, but it will be seen from what I have written here that it is false.

Certainly, they share a lot in common. One key characteristic in common is that they both require objectivity. However, significant differences also exist. The judicial precedents theory is derived from finding shared features among the numerous decisions themselves, and is based on ex post facto inductive reasoning. On the other hand, valid law is not derived from finding shared features among the decisions. It is extracted from analyzing the psyche of the judges, and is determined not based on the decisions themselves, but from the analysis of the motivation behind the decision.

Furthermore, the structure of judicial precedents theory varies according to the theoretical structure adopted by the person performing the analysis. In other words, decisions are categorized based on the personal and philosophical positions of the author, and the objectivity is lost. The situation is probably the same in Japan.

Either way, in Germany and Japan, judicial precedents are grouped into abstract legal propositions. Waaben is also critical of this. He says "German criminal law scholars try to summarize the basic definition in short words to cover all cases presented in positive trial, and often depart from reality." [24] In short, according to Waaben, valid law is not something that can be explained completely and uniformly using abstract norm.

Then, can valid law only be described as an accumulation of cases? Should we abandon establishment of abstract normative propositions like the American fact-skeptic Jerome Frank and abandon prediction of decisions? [25] The answer is no. Although Waaben doubts abstract norms, he does not abandon them. His approach is to utilize abstract norms, without considering it to be complete. Valid law is open to future revaluation. As a principle, it expects the abstract norm presented as valid law to be incomplete. Waaben states that "the contents of concept of intent can only get close to full description," [26]

---

(24) Waaben (n 22) 363.
(25) Jerome Frank, *Law and the modern mind* (Brentano's Inc 1930).

referring to the particular concept he studied.

3.4.3. Application by the author

I basically agree with Waaben's application of Ross' theory, but with some adjustments, which can be summarized as follows: In sum, valid law is structured by verbalizing, theorizing, and systemizing the thought process of the judges who have the role of creating actual law, including their assumptions. Therefore, it is necessary to apprehend the facts inherent in the judge's thought process by contemplating the depth of the judge's psyche. Valid law can be apprehended from the judge's thought process, so to the extent it can be predicted to exist for real, it is not bound by the wordings in the decision that does not seem to directly reflect the judge's thought process; furthermore, it is not necessarily fully bound by the conclusion of the decision. Accordingly, an dogmatic of criminal law that describes valid law is not an accumulation of analysis of judicial precedents, and highly abstract theoretical structure that cannot be produced by merely analyzing judicial precedents is plausible. Of course, the judges themselves are not processing individual cases based on a perfect theoretical system, so the extracted theoretical system can also be incomplete. There may be cases where consolidation of theories is difficult, but basically, I shall continue to aim to clarify the definition of concepts to enable consistent application (furthermore, to enable the public to act freely with understanding of these concepts). Legal dogmatics of criminal law not only indicates the standard for decision making by judges; it is also a standard that sets forth the scope for the public to act freely. In this respect, I will not adopt the method of "listing significant items," such as listing the points for legal determination, or motivation of judges that form the grounds for legal determination.

---

(26) Waaben (n 22) 345.

I have organized a joint research groups based on these methodologies. [27] More specifically, the joint research was conducted among judges and scholars. Scholars presented (what was deemed to be) valid law and sought comments from judges, and also sought critical comments from peers. Through these exercises, we tried to establish a more objective valid law. However, the comments from participating judges were not deemed to be absolute. One may think the judges are best positioned to apprehend the thought process of judges; but in reality, there may be deep psyche or subconscious attitudes that the judge is not aware of, which the scholars can reveal with external observation.

IV. Criticism of the Methodology/Issues and Review

4.1. Introduction

Against the methodology presented above, various criticisms have been made, against Ross mainly by Danish legal philosophers, and against my opinions that applied Ross' theory, by Japanese criminal law scholars. In addition, there were issues I noticed or got pointed out in discussion with other scholars. Let me summarize and review these issues.

4.2. Is valid law only applicable to thought process of judges?

Frequent criticism of the methodology is that valid law is not only applicable to thought process of the judges. In particular, in countries that adopt principle of discretionary prosecution (such as the UK and US, of course, and Japan, Denmark, Sweden, etc.), thought process of prosecutors who have the authority to determine whether or not to prosecute actually has significant impact on distinction of acts that will or won't be penalized.

Furthermore, Henrik Zahle, [28] who criticizes Ross' theory from a post-

---

(27) The Research Group for Defining Valid Law in Japanese Criminal Justice. http://www.waseda.jp/prj-genkeiken/

modernist legal perspective, is critical of the one-sidedness of the theory. He argues that the laws that function to regulate real society are not limited to decisions by the court. There are many laws that are effectively functioning outside the courts, such as decisions and orders determined by the administration, and practical decisions made by government offices. They are valid without going through judge's ideologies. Therefore, it should be understood that the source of law has multiple centers, and there are different methods to determine the appropriateness for each. [29]

Certainly, there is some truth in this criticism. In particular, in a country with high conviction rates (Japan), the decision by the prosecutor to prosecute or not has a significant impact. If we are to simply consider what regulates the society, it would be important to consider those points to determine whether the accused is guilty or innocent. However, if we are reviewing whether or not it has the level of substance to be considered a law, decisions by judges and decisions to prosecute by prosecutors do not appear to have the same legal level of substance. In addition, study of the psyche behind the decisions of prosecutors on whether or not to prosecute would have to be conducted with virtually no precedents or evidence available, and would be extremely difficult in practice. If the psyche of the prosecutors cannot be studied, I believe it is beneficial to construct functional dogmatic of criminal law by application to thought process of judges to the extent they can be clarified.

4.3. Can predictions be proven true or false?

Ross argues that by reconciling the predictions and facts, dogmatic can be proven to be true or false. This is one approach, as the theory is modeled on conventional natural science. However, it is difficult to reconcile the predictions

---

(28) Henrik Zahle, Professor in Law, University of Copenhagen, 1943-2006.
(29) Henrik Zahle, 'Retsdogmatik og retskritik' in E.M.Basse og Vibeke Jensen (eds), *Regulering og Styring I*, (Djøf 1989) 45-52.

and facts. Is it sufficient for a prediction to be deemed true if it is consistent with one decision? Is a prediction never deemed to be true unless there is a decision? Many issues remain. These are issues of objectivity in science including natural sciences, and are more of an issue for philosophy of science. If we turn to debates in philosophy of science, presently the debate over distinction between science and pseudoscience is at a stalemate.

In the 1970s Denmark, Preben Stuer Lauridsen, [30] professor of legal philosophy, a successor of Ross, criticized him starting from the point that a solitary statement consistent with the truth does not exist (multiple statements may exist), and ultimately sought to have whether or not debates and criticism among scholars can arrive at an agreement/consistency as the standard for verification. This argument appears to have certain appropriateness. It cannot be denied that whether or not there is an agreement among the peers is one of important indications in evaluation of a theory (so-called coherence theory). [31] With such adjustment, Ross' theory is considered to have appropriateness at present.

However, it would be insufficient if the agreement and consistency referred to only meant that there is a majority agreement, or that it is consistent with the greater majority view of the public. It must be performed as a review by a soundly and reasonably organized group of experts. Then, the next issue would shift to the procedural and methodological point of how to examine whether or not the group of jurists including present scholars (in various countries) is qualified as the expert group. On this issue, we can only assume that the group of jurists in each country is such a group at the moment.

---

(30) Preben Stuer Lauridsen, Professor in Law, University of Copenhagen, 1940-2013.
(31) Preben Stuer Lauridsen, 'On a Fundamental Problem in the Legal Theory of Prediction', in *Scandinavian Studies in Law, vol.20* (Stockholm Inst for Scandinavian Law 1976) 203-204.

4.4. Judges subjected to prediction react to the situation: Can there be science in such a relationship?

This is a frequently presented criticism not just as a question for the science of methodology above, but for social sciences as a whole. On this question, I believe that there is science, at least in the methodology. Judges are most likely to refer to the results of the studies based on dogmatic of criminal law as proposed by this paper; however, they are unlikely to try to outwit the prediction, or intentionally refrain from the predicted opinion due to having read such studies. This is because the results of such studies are not produced for the practical purpose of controlling the judges; rather, they derive from a purely academic interest in clarifying the valid law. For a judge to try to outwit such result to avoid being controlled is meaningless in reality. If a judge who came across the result of the studies thought "if the present operation is continued, such a decision can be expected in the future; this is not desirable," and changes the present operation, it is a value judgment of the judge rather than influence from the dogmatic, and the judge is controlling his/her own conduct.

Japanese scholar of sociology of law, Takeyoshi Kawashima, [32] promoted predictive legal studies which predict future decisions by courts, based on legal realism's views on trials. [33] He stated that such prediction "is nothing more than a prediction mediated through our practical behavior of controlling future decisions through judicial precedents," and saw it as an issue of "how best to control future decisions with past judicial precedents, and how they should be controlled." This indicates an approach where the judges, who are the subject of observation, try to control decisions by observing the scholars who are conducting the observation. However, considering prediction as such

---

[32] Takeyoshi Kawashima, Professor in Law, Tokyo Univerity, 1901-1992.
[33] Takeyoshi Kawashima, *Horitsugaku no gendaiteki Mondaiten: Kawashima Takeyoshi Chosakushu vol.5* (Iwanami 1982) 290-291.

practical activity would bring issues of assessment and value judgment into dogmatic which should be objective. On this point, the view taken by Ross (and this paper) does not aim at such control, and thus would not create such problems.

4.5. Distinction between legal dogmatics and legal politics

Legal dogmatics and legal politics handle facts and evaluation, and it is often thought that distinction between the two can be made for certain. However, in the area of legal studies where facts and values intersect, these borders may become vague. For example: (i) a judge who read a document shown as a text on legal dogmatics wrote a decision influenced by the text. Should this be considered legal politics?; (ii) or, the author meant the text to be legal politics, but a judge who had not read the piece wrote a similar decision, and it became established as an objective practice. Should this be considered legal dogmatics?

In my view, the answers to both (i) and (ii) are "no." Then, how can legal dogmatics and legal politics be separated? The difficulty is presented due to the fact that the subject of the observation is the thought process of judges, who most certainly will be observing the results from the other side.

I personally have some remaining questions on how to structure the standard for determination, though the conclusion is clear. I would like to present the following provisional statement: Legal dogmatics and legal politics can be distinguished through methodology, i.e., the material that the decision was based on, and the analytical methods that lead to the conclusion. If the materials that the decision was based on were facts of empirical science, and the method used to reach the conclusion was the analysis of empirical facts, it would be legal dogmatics; all others are legal politics. That is to say, legal dogmatics and legal politics may be distinguished by methodology. That is why the methodology for legal dogmatics of criminal law becomes significant.

4.6. Would it not be an obstacle to nurturing students and jurists capable of external criticism?

Some point to this, from the perspective of legal education. However, to limit legal dogmatics to description of facts is not to prohibit criticism of the present status. Ross believed that proposals to judges and legislators should be made separately as part of legal politics, as a matter of judgment. The above criticism is out of place. [34]

4.7. What are the features of judges' thought process?

Some ask that if legal dogmatics practiced by scholars is description of facts, what is it that the judges do. Judges can be seen as creating laws to resolve specific cases. In other words, application of laws to specific cases is itself a process of creation of law based on certain values. However, individual judges are not free from general thought process of judges. They are not arbitrarily creating laws based on individual values. [35] The decisions are made by paying attention to the shared value judgments accumulated among the judges, and to that extent, they are objective.

4.8. Conclusion

As stated above, although some issues remain to be resolved, certain answers have been obtained to the criticism and inherent problems with respect to the methodology for legal dogmatics of criminal law presented in this paper.

---

(34) Those who ask these questions miss the point.
(35) The distinction between the two is crucial to understanding the methodology of this paper.

V. Method for Dogmatic of Criminal Law: Methodology for extraction and structuring of theories

5.1. Methodology for extraction of theory

Dogmatic of criminal law extracts ideologies of the judges to create a theory. Let me summarize the discussions thus far, and clarify the methodology:

The first point of reference in trying to understand the ideologies of judges is judicial precedents. However, they should not be treated as the golden rule. Because judicial precedents are court decisions on a certain case at the time, and although it will be binding on future decisions, it will not have absolute authority in a country under statutory law system. In particular, the reasoning proposition is likely to be documentation of the judges' thought process, but it does not necessarily reflect all of the judges' thought process, and could be an afterthought in some cases. The reasoning proposition is not deemed to be judicial precedent itself in the study of judicial precedents. Only the conclusive proposition constitutes the judicial precedent. If the judicial precedents are mishandled, it will become case law positivism, which analyses judicial precedents as law. This is inconsistent with the methodology adopted in this paper.

The next point of reference would be literature authored by the judges. They are valuable basic materials that outline the ideologies of judges prepared by the judges themselves. However, they too, do not reflect all of the judges' ideologies. Aside from the fact they are written by the individual, it does not necessarily reflect subconscious thoughts of the writer. Valid law is the entire ideology of judges, so the deep subconscious must be extracted to determine the criteria for the decisions.

The third point of reference is the study of literature that affected the judges. As judges are jurists, they will refer to books and scholarly articles.

Books and articles commonly cited can be deemed to have significant influence on the thought process of the judges. By examining such literature, we can infer the theoretical systems and concepts in the thought process of the judges.

The fourth point of reference would be communication with the judges. Communication is essential to seek candid opinion of the judges that do not appear in judicial precedence and literature. For this purpose, as already mentioned, I have organized a research group called "the Research Group for Defining Valid Law in Japanese Criminal Justice" with like-minded scholars, and hold periodic meetings with judges. A judge's positioning varies by country. [36] For example, in Germany, Scandinavia and Japan, Supreme Court justices are neutral and independent of political ideology, but in the US, political agendas are often involved in the appointment process. We must allow for some variables for each country on this point.

5.2. Method of theoretical structuring

Creation of theoretical system on judges' ideologies extracted through methods described above will require certain contrivance. That is, to structure a system of criminal theory, the conventional method used in Japan is to follow a system starting from considering the relevance of the general elements of offencees (Tatbestandmässigkeit), illegality (Rechtswidrigkeit), and responsibility (Schuld), similar to Germany. However, it appears that a criminal theory system that focuses more on criminal procedure and identification theory needs to be created. The reason being that the criminal theory system created in the judges' ideology would always focus on the resolution of the case, i.e., the procedural law. In Japan, facts that the prosecutors must prove shall be positioned general elements of offences. And in an exceptional case where an issue of law arises, the lack of justifiable cause for noncompliance with law or

---

(36) See, n27.

non-imputability that the prosecutors are liable for proving should be deemed to be justifiable noncompliance or non-imputability. In Anglo-American law, you can call them defence. Thus, as a starting point for dogmatic of criminal law, a system comprising of relevance of general enements of offences, justifiable noncompliance (defence of justification) and non-imputability (defence of excuse) seems to be the most appropriate.

Next, let us turn to the methodology for structure of concepts. I have already explained how abstract concepts may be included as part of valid law. In particular, the basic approach would be to examine materials centering on judicial precedents without reserve, capture the thought process the judges are applying to resolve the issues, and reflect this on the concept as faithfully as possible. Use of such abstract concept will contribute to mutual understanding and legal discussions among jurists. That is to say, legal concepts are shared codes available for discussion among jurists. To ignore this in dogmatic of criminal law would be unproductive. Note that a perfect concept does not exist, as Waaben has pointed out, and it is unlikely to exist in the thought process of the judges who are the subject of fact finding. However, we shall not give up on creating concepts. It is important to specify and document the concept presented as the terminus of the judges' thought process, using empirical facts as well as conventional normative analysis methods used by the judges in their thought process.

In relation to the above two points, we must consider how best to capture the intricacies of fact finding and legal issues. For example, suppose several seemingly unrelated facts emerge in the process of identification of legal requisites (e.g., in Japanese practice, a party that claimed the largest share of criminal proceeds after the crime is frequently penalized as the principal offender. However, whether or not a person is the principal offender or accomplice should be determined based on their role in the criminal conduct, and should not be related to the situation after the crime.) In addition, not all of the facts need to be revealed, and there are instances when the legal requisites are identified by comprehensive consideration of the facts (e.g., using the above example, if claiming the largest share of criminal proceeds is only one of the reasons the person may be penalized as the principal offender, and such fact is not a legal requisite, but has a significance in the identification process). Such an example is likely to exist in many countries, not only in Japan. Perhaps the common procedure is to create an abstract norm in the study of jurisprudence, and leave the rest to the customary practice in fact finding. However, this does not capture the thought process of the judges. Further, mere existence of abstract norms would not serve much purpose in practice. On the other hand, mere listing of facts would not enable discussions among jurists. Abstract norms are important shared code for the jurists to have discussions and to understand each other.

The question is how to link the facts to be identified and the requisite norms, when they stand separated. I do not have a good answer to resolve this problem. Developing this method will be the key issue.

VI. Methods of Criminal Law Policies: Preliminary Observation

6.1. Foundation of legal politics of criminal law

According to Ross and Waaben, legal politics of criminal law, i.e., proposal to judges and legislators is a secondary duty for criminal law scholars, unlike legal dogmatics. In Denmark where Ross' theory had a strong influence, this seems to have been the conventional wisdom for a long time. Certainly, when criminal law studies are pursued as science, proposals based on personal value judgments and philosophy would not be considered scientific. But at the same time, it may be necessary to make certain proposals as an expert on valid law, on condition the value judgments are clearly stated as such.

In particular, in recent Denmark, Sweden and Japan, it has been pointed out that there are tendencies to impose unnecessarily strict penalties against the background of a type of populism, and to make legislation that only clarify the value judgments of the government and doesn't have real effects. The latter is referred to as symbolic legislation, and there is a wide debate in Germany about its problems.

Under these circumstances, it seems significant that the criminal law scholars as experts logically develop legal politics of criminal law, and examine the justification for criminalization.

For example, the Danish criminal law scholar Vagn Greve [37] asserted the propriety of practical criminal theory and criminal legislation from the viewpoint of human rights. His book related to criminal legislation regulating freedom of expression [38] are an example of this assertion. In the midst of a myriad of perspectives, Greve says that it is a necessity as a professional to explain how these can be evaluated and analyzed from the viewpoint of criminal theory.

Of course, when there is a situation where basic principles are neglected, such as nulla poena sine lege, the culpability principle, and legal benefit protectionism, it is necessary to object that there are certain questions regarding these topics from a professional viewpoint. When there is also a situation where basic values such as freedom, democracy, basic human rights, and peace are trampled on by the power of the state, it could be said that us scholars are obligated to fight against such power.

However, most legislators who are deserving of criticism craft new laws based on advice from legal professionals including jurists. In the case of judges, they are regarded as professionals in the sense that they are practitioners of the law, through amending jurisprudence, specializing in its use, and accumulating experience.

---

(37) Vagn Greve, Professor in Law, University of Copenhagen, 1938-2014.
(38) Vagn Greve, *Bånd på hånd og mund: strafforfølgelse eller ytringsfrihed?* (Djøf 2008).

It is very important to voice your opinion, as a specialist of criminal jurisprudence, against those legislators. However, we need to prove and establish on what grounds our opinions are "professional." Are those opinions based on the scholars' self-righteousness? Are they based on political and ideological biases that largely deviate from societal values, norms, and justice? Are they just scholars' own, subjective opinions? Scholars must constantly practice rigid self-discipline and be subject to criticism set upon by the concept of freedom of speech.

Personally, I find nothing wrong with Greve's humane words; I most certainly agree with him. However, that does not mean I can assert with my utmost confidence that his opinion and method of thinking are "objectively correct" as a "professional." A situation where "all" scholars are unanimously in agreement with Greve's dogmatic will and should never exist.

In my opinion I believe that the first responsibility of a criminologist is to utilize Valid Law, and subsequently I believe that Greve's statement is more political than scholarly. If it were so, Greve's statement is not really a study of jurisprudence but an analysis of his own dogmatics from a legal point of view. This is not necessarily said to be aimed to undermine Greve's accomplishments. If anything, the author was deeply impressed by Greve's works. However, the author seems reluctant to label his work as jurisprudence or legal dogmatic studies; mainly because it is almost inevitable to separate objective theory from subjective value judgements, which will render the theory "un-scientific." Rather, it should called something along the lines of "theoretical legal analyses" or "theoretical legal consideration." It is necessary to consider such studies as something independent and completely different from legal dogmatic studies. Such differentiation enables one to clearly see where they stand within the realm of legal studies, and also assert that one's value judgement is derived from which field of study.

6.2. Function of creation of law by judges and legal politics of criminal law

In this methodology, proposals to judges are considered to be legal politics of criminal law, and part of political activity involving value judgment. The activity by judges to process cases and prepare decisions is considered to be a function of creation of law, i.e., a type of legislative function. This is where the relationship with the principle of legality becomes an issue. Legalism is a significant corollary of principle of legality. It argues that criminal law must be established in the form of legislation by the parliament. If a judge is involved in the function of creation of law, would that violate the principle of legality?

Karl Larenz of Germany referred to selection of semantics within the scope of statutes as interpretation (Auslegung); and where it is outside the scope of statutes, the act becomes creation of law. Under this theory, principle of legality prohibits analogical interpretation in criminal law, requiring interpretation within the scope of statutes, so the judges do not engage in creation of law, and their activities would not violate the principle of legality. Many scholars in Germany and Japan seem to agree. However, if this approach is taken, interpretation within the scope of statutes would mean the act of identifying the objectively correct interpretation among the various possibilities. And notwithstanding that this act is actually based on subjective value judgment. If this is the case, subjective value judgment is being made under the disguise of objectivity, and there will be no means to control this. This is the dark side of legal positivism which assumes that a correct interpretation exists in statues. It is more realistic to think that selecting one semantic from various possibilities in the statutes involves value judgment, and that determination of the meaning of the law, i.e., creation of a law that did not exist, is being conducted.

Against these approaches, one may suggest that it may be less complicated to refer to such acts within the scope of statutes as interpretation rather than creation of law, and this would also avoid violating the principle of legality.

However, hiding the activity of creation of law under the name of interpretation would lead to a bigger problem. To clarify that the act involves subjective value judgment, legal interpretation by the judges should be referred to as creation of law. According to this line of thought, principle of legality becomes a standard that indicates the limits of creation of laws in criminal trials, rather than a principle that prohibits creation of laws by judges.

6.3. On the definition of logic

There are many people who insist that it is acceptable to label legal analyses as a science, since they are based on meticulous theoretical construction are further based on logic. However, as long as this is based on the speaker's own value judgement, it remains as another criminal policy.

For example, the sentencing theory proposed by Andreas von Hirsch is a theoretical framework that is shared by many scholars. Along with Andrew Ashworth and Andrew Simester, von Hirsch has published collaborative works that do not clearly indicate which portion was done by whom. [39] This is also another theory that is based upon a certain value judgement, and von Hirsch mentions so in various publications. If the pros and cons of a theory analysis are considered by people who shared the same value judgements, the theory does indeed achieve a level of objectivity with the limits of the points in common. However, it is obvious that this type of objectivity is limited to those who share the same value judgements, and consequently the said theory does not resonate to those who do not agree with those judgements.

Additionally if a theory is proven through experimental sciences, it is possible to claim that theory is scientific. However, it is impossible to establish a standard with just facts. It is inevitable to have a certain level of subjectivity to

---

(39) Andrew von Hirsch & Andrew Ashworth, *Proportionate Sentencing: Exploring the Principles* (OUP 2005); Andrew P Simester and Andreas von Hirsch, *Crimes, Harms and Wrongs: On the principle of criminalization* (Hart Publishing, 2011).

accompany such standards. For these reasons, citing experimental science is simply not enough to call a theory as something totally scientific.

Von Hirsch's sentencing theory [40] happens to cite experimental science. In other words, von Hirsch, through references from criminology, asserts that it is unnecessary to consider preventative effects in sentencing since there are no preventative measures in penalties. There is a certain level of science in this assertion.

However, those who believe that it is important to send a message to regulators of society through announcing to consider positive general prevention (i.e. Jakobs, a supporter of positive general prevention), whether or not there actually are preventative effects, do not think there is any substance in citing experimental science as von Hirsch does. On the other hand, the Luhmann's sociological system theory used by Jakobs has been established as a scientific theory in sociology, but von Hirsch barely holds any interest in it.

There are certain differences in how one normatively evaluates facts, and they are caused by the difference in which value judgement is chosen to be emphasized. These value judgements are about which facts are to be chosen to be evaluated, and the theorists' true intentions can be inferred from them. Facts and standards can be separated.

Some theorists say that facts and standards are interactive and are impossible to separate by principle, and therefore dogmatic theories based solely on facts is impossible. Indeed, it is possible for the line drawn between facts and standards to become unclear, and the statement that the definition of a fact can change according to standards. However, those who claim that separating the two are impossible tend to divide de lege lata and de lege feranda. They also do not deny the existence of policy-building activities. The line between facts and standards are indeed ambiguous, but there are clear

---

(**40**) Andreas von Hirsch, *Deserved Criminal Sentences* (Hart Publishing 2017).

differences. The same could be said for criminal jurisprudence. The border between subjectivity and objectivity is ambiguous; objectivity is influenced by subjectivity. The gravity of firing a pistol with criminal intent is objectively different from simply firing a pistol by accident, but this does not mean that subjectivity and objectivity should be discussed as a combined, single concept. Concepts that can be separated should be separated where possible. A more objective dogmatic theory should be sought after in order to avoid a Weber-like "war of the gods" situation in the field of criminal dogmatic studies.

VII. Conclusion

I have examined the features of legal dogmatics of criminal law to present answers to the various issues identified at the beginning of this paper.

I believe the most appropriate methodology is one following Ross' methodology, to separate fact finding and value judgment, and limit the duty of legal dogmatics of criminal law to the former, making the presentation of systematic and verbalized thought process of judges as primary duty of criminal law scholars. However, for determination of objectivity of legal dogmatism, rather than the simple reconciliation of theory and facts promoted by Ross, I would adopt the view taken by Stuer Lauridsen that it should be done through coordination and agreement among the peers. I also believe that limiting the subject of fact finding to the thought process of judges is a functional option at the moment.

As to the specific methods, this paper has referred to the methodology of Knud Waaben who specifically applied the view presented by Alf Ross to dogmatic of criminal law, and made certain adjustments. In sum, the code for communication among jurists involves abstract concepts and norms, and this is important to enable legal discussions. Also, as criminal law has the function to secure freedom of activity by the public, it is important to construct and present a theoretical system using abstract norms on condition it is clarified to the point consistent judgment is possible, basically using conventional conceptual structure rather than methods such as "list of important judgment items" which tend to make the determination process vague.

Legal dogmatic studies can be said to be exceedingly academic, in the sense that it involves normative theoretical analysis unique to jurisprudence while keeping experimental science in the picture. I believe there are many legal scholars who will remain skeptical when legal dogmatic studies is deemed unscientific, and my own wish to pursue legal dogmatic studies as a science will remain unchanged. For these reasons, it is vital to remove the unscientific elements and reconstruct legal dogmatic studies that will live up to the name of science.

If, for instance, it is claimed that normative analyses are a science, the inner value judgements will achieve the name of "science" and will consequently become a very powerful influence. Of course, if those value judgements are significant and meaningful for everybody, there should not be a problem; however, needless to say, such common ideas do not exist. Some may refute that value judgements such as democracy, peace, and human rights are meaningful for anybody. Additionally, principles in criminal jurisprudence such as nulla poena sine lege, the culpability principle, and legal benefit protectionism may also be regarded as something of universal significance. However, value judgements of this caliber are too general and vague to become a worthy foundation for normative analyses because the value judgements themselves are open to dogmatic and there could be an infinite amount of perspectives. What if one of those perspectives were said to be the one scientific truth? The other existing perspectives will potentially be deemed unscientific and completely obliterated. Establishing just one view as the truth or the correct answer and denying all others should not be allowed in any instance.

Alternatively, what if all perspectives were considered a scientific truth?

It seems plausible, but in reality there are many underlying problems. Each theory will assert its correctness and closure will be very hard to achieve. In Japan and Germany, scholars sought after their own criminal jurisprudence theory cased on their own value judgements, and because of this, legal dogmatics studies became more subjective, opposition between theories became unstoppable, and discussions stalled. In countries without this sort of history, the repercussions of this stance is less visible. (In Sweden, for example, a textbook on the basic studies of criminal jurisprudence has been successfully published as an allotment-less, complete joint authorship between Jareborg, Asp, and Ulväng, and that publication keeps a solid framework and an undeviating discussion on the system of criminal jurisprudence. [41] This is not possible to achieve in Japan and Germany, because there is always some disagreement between the authors.)

Rather, these problems should be solved by separating legal dogmatic studies from value judgements. Namely, it should be said that the theories of Sweden and Denmark (Scandinavian Legal Realism) are still large influences and retain its significance, even today.

Above attempt is literally just an attempt. I believe it is essential to conduct further examination on the issue through discussion with peers around the world. In this sense, this attempt aims to give objectivity to the dogmatic of criminal law, but it is based on the value judgment I believe to be appropriate. I would like to present these methods of study as a paradigm, but will not say that such approach is objectively and academically justifiable. My main emphasis is that it is important to plainly identify value judgment as such.

---

(41) Petter Asp, Magnus Ulväng & Nils Jareborg, *Kriminalrättens Grunder* (2nd ed, Iustus 2018).

About the Author

Shin Matsuzawa   Professor of Law, Waseda University

早稲田大学比較法研究所
叢書52号

Essays on Criminal Law in Japan

| 2024年10月15日 | 初版第1刷発行 | 本体価格2,760円＋税 |

著 者　　松　澤　　　伸

発 行 者　　早稲田大学比較法研究所
　　　　　　所長　岡　田　正　則

発 行 所　　早稲田大学比較法研究所
　　　　　　〒169-8050　東京都新宿区西早稲田1-6-1
　　　　　　　　　　電　話　03（3208）8610

印刷所
発売所　　株式会社　成　文　堂
　　　　　〒169-0051　新宿区西早稲田1-9-38
　　　　　電話 03-3203-9201（代表）　Fax 03-3203-9206

©2024

ISBN978-4-7923-5428-2 C3032

早稲田大学比較法研究所叢書　既刊ご案内

巻数	書名	著者・訳者	発行年
1	比較法	ガッタリッジ著　水田義雄 監訳	1964年
2	イギリス船舶保険契約論	葛城照三 著	1962年 *
3	二条陣屋の研究・公事宿の研究	滝川政次郎 著	1962年 *
4	法治国における統治行為	ルンプ著　有倉・竹内 共訳	1964年
5	イギリス行政訴訟法の研究	佐藤立夫 著	1968年
6	小野梓稿『國憲論網　羅瑪律要』	福島正夫他 編	1974年 *
7	LEX XII TABULARUM 12表法原文・邦訳および解説	佐藤篤士 著	1969年 *
8	開発途上国における国有化	入江啓四郎 著	1974年
9	社会主義比較法学	チッレ著　直川誠蔵 訳	1979年
10	西ドイツ現代刑事訴訟・刑法・行刑論文集	ペーテルス著　内田一郎 編訳	1980年
11	現代ドイツ公法学を築いた碩学たち	佐藤立夫 著	1982年
12	中国における法の継承性論争	西村幸次郎 編訳	1983年
13	比較法社会学研究	黒木三郎 著	1984年
14	刑法審査修正関係諸案	杉山晴康他 著	1984年
15	西ドイツの新用益賃貸借法制	田山輝明 編・監訳	1986年
16	アメリカ合衆国の連邦最高裁判所 DUE PROCESS OF LAW の保障	ウィルバー 著　内田一郎 編訳	1986年
17	英米不法行為判例研究	矢頭敏也 著	1988年
18	刑法改正審査委員会決議録刑法草案	杉山晴康他 編	1989年
19	Intellectual Property Protection and Management	土井輝生 著	1992年
20	イギリス法と欧州共同体法	矢頭敏也 訳編	1992年
21	改訂 LEX XII TABULARUM 12表法原文・邦訳および解説	佐藤篤士 著	1993年
22	ドイツ憲法	エクハルト・シュタイン 著　浦田賢治他 訳	1993年 *
23	知的・精神的障害者とその権利―研修と実務の手引―	フォルカー・ヤコビ 著　田山輝明 監訳	1996年
24	International Business Transactions : Contract and Dispute Resolution	土井輝生 著	1996年
25	中国の経済発展と法	小口彦太 編	1998年 *
26	ヨーロッパにおける民事訴訟法理論の諸相	早稲田大学外国民事訴訟法研究会 編	1999年
27	核兵器使用の違法性―国際司法裁判所の勧告的意見―	バロース 著　浦田賢治 監訳	2001年
28	国家の法的関与と自由―アジア・オセアニア法制の比較研究― State Legal Intervention and Freedom : Comparative Studies on Asian-Oceanic Legal Systems	大須賀明 編	2001年

29	注解 中華人民共和国新刑法	野村稔・張 凌 共著	2002年
30	比較法研究の新段階——法の継受と移植の理論		2003年
		早稲田大学比較法研究所 編	
31	Reflections on Global Constitutionalism	浦田賢治 著	2005年
32	日本法の国際的文脈——西欧・アジアとの連鎖		2005年
		早稲田大学比較法研究所 編	
33	日本法のアイデンティティに関する総合的・比較法的研究——源流の法とグローバル化の法		2006年
		早稲田大学比較法研究所 編	
34	比較と歴史のなかの日本法学——比較法学への日本からの発信		2008年
		早稲田大学比較法研究所 編	
35	デンマーク司法運営法——刑事訴訟関連規定——	松澤伸 訳著	2008年
36	アメリカ最高裁とレーンキスト・コート	宮川成雄 編	2009年
37	比較法と法律学——新世紀を展望して		2010年
		早稲田大学比較法研究所 編	
38	ドイツ環境法	岡田正則 監訳	2012年
39	21世紀刑法学への挑戦——グローバル化情報社会とリスク社会の中で——	甲斐克則 監訳 田口守一	2012年
40	知的財産の国際私法原則研究——東アジアからの日韓共同提案——	木棚照一 編著	2012年
41	日本法の中の外国法——基本法の比較法的考察——		2014年
		早稲田大学比較法研究所 編	
42	環境と契約——日仏の視線の交錯	吉田克己=マチルド・ブトネ 編	2014年
43	持続可能社会への転換と法・法律学——Law and Sustainability	楜澤能生 編	2016年
44	プロボノ活動の原則と実務——公共奉仕と専門職——	石田京子 訳	2018年
45	民事法の解釈適用と憲法原則——中国民法典編纂に向けた日中比較——	中村民雄 編	2018年
46	近代法の形成と実践——19世紀日本における在野法曹の世界——	D. E. フラハティ 著 浅古 弘 監訳	2019年 *
47	法の支配と法治主義	J. R. シルケナート他 編 岡田正則他 編訳	2020年
48	持続可能な世界への法——Law and Sustainability の推進——	中村民雄 編	2020年 *
49	スイス民事訴訟法概論	松村和德・吉田純平 共著	2022年
50	持続可能な農地利用のための農地法制の比較研究——ドイツ、中国、日本——	楜澤能生・文元春 編	2023年
51	アメリカ最高裁とロバーツ・コート——先例拘束原理の展開—	宮川成雄 編	2024年
52	Essays on Criminal Law in Japan	松澤伸 著	2024年

＊は絶版です